ROUTLEDGE LIBRARY EDITIONS: COLONIALISM AND IMPERIALISM

Volume 20

COLONIALISM AND UNDERDEVELOPMENT IN GHANA

COLONIALISM AND UNDERDEVELOPMENT IN GHANA

RHODA HOWARD

LONDON AND NEW YORK

First published in 1978 by Croom Helm Ltd

This edition first published in 2023
by Routledge
4 Park Square, Milton Park, Abingdon, Oxon OX14 4RN

and by Routledge
605 Third Avenue, New York, NY 10158

Routledge is an imprint of the Taylor & Francis Group, an informa business

© 1978 Rhoda Howard

All rights reserved. No part of this book may be reprinted or reproduced or utilised in any form or by any electronic, mechanical, or other means, now known or hereafter invented, including photocopying and recording, or in any information storage or retrieval system, without permission in writing from the publishers.

Trademark notice: Product or corporate names may be trademarks or registered trademarks, and are used only for identification and explanation without intent to infringe.

British Library Cataloguing in Publication Data
A catalogue record for this book is available from the British Library

ISBN: 978-1-032-41054-8 (Set)
ISBN: 978-1-032-43809-2 (Volume 20) (hbk)
ISBN: 978-1-032-43813-9 (Volume 20) (pbk)
ISBN: 978-1-003-36894-6 (Volume 20) (ebk)

DOI: 10.4324/9781003368946

Publisher's Note
The publisher has gone to great lengths to ensure the quality of this reprint but points out that some imperfections in the original copies may be apparent.

Disclaimer
The publisher has made every effort to trace copyright holders and would welcome correspondence from those they have been unable to trace.

COLONIALISM AND UNDERDEVELOPMENT IN GHANA

Rhoda Howard

CROOM HELM   LONDON

© 1978 Rhoda Howard
Croom Helm Ltd, 2–10 St John's Road, London SW11

British Library Cataloguing in Publication Data

Howard, Rhoda
   Colonialism and underdevelopment in Ghana.
   1. Ghana – Economic conditions
   I. Title
   330.9'667'03   HC517.G6

ISBN 0-85664-551-6

Printed in Great Britain by offset lithography by
Billing & Sons Ltd, Guildford, London and Worcester

CONTENTS

List of Tables

Acknowledgements

Abbreviations

Preface

1.	Colonialism and Underdevelopment in Ghana	15
2.	The Institution of Colonial Rule in Ghana	27
3.	The Creation of Ghana's Peripheral Capitalist Economy	59
4.	Oligopolisation of the Ghanaian Economy	94
5.	The State and Peripheral Capitalism: the Role of the Colonial Government in Underdeveloping Ghana	146
6.	The Peripheral Economy and Class Formation	181

Postscript: The Colonial Heritage of Contempory Ghana	223
Bibliography	232
Index	238

LIST OF TABLES

3.1	Gold, Diamonds and Manganese as Percentages of Total Ghana Exports by Value, by Five-Year Averages, 1885–1939	61
3.2	Major Agricultural Products as Percentages of Total Ghana Exports by Value, by Five-Year Averages, 1885–1939	70
3.3	Consumer and Investment Imported Goods, Per Cent of the Total by Value, by Five-Year Averages, 1900–39	80
3.4	Ghana: Total Imports and Exports by Value, by Five-Year Totals, 1885–1939	86
3.5	World Net Imports of Raw Cocoa as Percentages of the Total, by Five-Year Averages, 1900–1939	88
3.6	Ghana: Direction of Trade in Percentages, by Five-Year Averages, 1885–1939	89
4.1	Trade Agreements in the Gold Coast	107
4.2	Ordinary Dividend Rates for Selected Companies, by Five-Year Averages, 1886–1939	110
5.1	Import and Export Dues as Per Cent of Government Revenue, by Five-Year Averages, 1885–1939	161
5.2	Government Revenue from Railways by Five-Year Averages, 1900–39	169
5.3	Uses of the Railway by Different Sectors of the Economy, Percentages by Five-Year Averages (Main Products Only) 1900–39	172
5.4	Cocoa Exported by Road and Rail, Percentages by Five-Year Averages, 1900–39	174

ACKNOWLEDGEMENTS

I owe thanks to numerous individuals in England and Ghana for the assistance they gave me in obtaining access to documents which I sought, as well as to all those who kindly allowed me to interview them about their experiences in colonial Ghana.

Many colleagues and friends have offered me advice and criticism during the preparation of this book and of the doctoral dissertation on which it was based. I am indebted especially to Immanuel Wallerstein, E.R. Brett, Peter Gutkind and Donald Von Eschen. Any errors or omissions are, of course, my own.

Lois Shelton ably assisted me in my research during June and July of 1977. Bonita Lowinske patiently typed two drafts of this book, while Joyce Moore Bailey most conscientiously prepared the index. I am most grateful to all of them for their unflagging efforts.

The research for this book was made possible through the generous financial assistance of the Canada Council, which both supported me in the preparation of my doctoral dissertation and granted additional support for extra research and preparation of the manuscript in 1977.

Quotations from the Manchester Chamber of Commerce are published with the permission of the City of Manchester Cultural Services.

Rhoda Howard

ABBREVIATIONS

A&ETC	African and Eastern Trade Corporation
ARPS	Aborigines' Rights Protection Society
Cad	Cadbury Archives
GCCMines	Gold Coast Chamber of Mines
GCLegCo	Gold Coast Legislative Council
GNA	National Archives of Ghana (unless otherwise indicated, all GNA documents are from Accra files)
JH	John Holt Archives
JWAC	Joint West Africa Committee
LivCC	Liverpool Chamber of Commerce
LonCC	London Chamber of Commerce
ManCC	Manchester Chamber of Commerce
RCSR	Royal Commission on Shipping Rings
UAC	United Africa Company (and United Africa Company Archives)
UAC Rankin File	File including document 1/5066, 'Draft of History of the company by Mr J.J. Rankin', and document 1/5550, 'The history of the company to 1938', UAC Archives
WACB	West African Currency Board

N.B. Place name spellings are contemporary except inside quotations.

PREFACE

This book is primarily concerned with Ghana's integration into the world economic system, and the effects which such integration had on its development. The time period covered is meant to coincide both with the institution of formal political control in Ghana, and with the use of that control to promote Ghana's development as a peripheral capitalist nation, specifically as a supplier of primary agricultural and mineral products and as a buyer of manufactured goods. The assumption of formal political control in Ghana was a gradual process extending from 1874 to 1901; however, by 1885 the colonial government was relatively firmly established in the Gold Coast Colony and the outlines of the import-export economy were beginning to take shape; 1939 is taken as the cut-off point for this book as it ends the classic colonial period; wartime economic re-organisation was followed rapidly by preparations of decolonisation.

Because the major purpose of this book is to examine Ghana's role in the world economy, it concentrates on the Gold Coast Colony and Ashanti, which had the strongest external links. The Northern Territories, except as a labour reserve, remained peripheral to the export-import economy, while Togoland did not become part of Ghana until 1918 when a League of Nations Mandate was created over the former German territories of Africa.

The reader will note that throughout the book the term Ghana is used interchangeably with the term Gold Coast, despite the fact that the colonial name for the country was Gold Coast and that the name Ghana was instituted only with independence in 1957. In adopting this practice the author is following Kwabina Dickson in his *Historical Geography of Ghana*.[1] The reasons for this practice are threefold. First, the terms are used interchangeably for stylistic reasons, especially to avoid the use of the term 'Gold Coasters' when referring to the colony's inhabitants. Second, the intent is to emphasise the continuity between colonial and post-colonial economies even at the risk of using anachronistic terms. Finally, neither Ghana nor Gold Coast is the correct name for the colony during the period under discussion; Gold Coast referred only to the Gold Coast Colony, which was administered separately from Ashanti and the Northern Territories until 1936. Given that neither term is precisely accurate, it seems that there would be no serious objection to using both.

Note

1. Kwabina B. Dickson, *A Historical Geography of Ghana* (Cambridge University Press, Cambridge, 1971).

for my parents
Michael Howard and Mary Byrne Howard
with gratitude

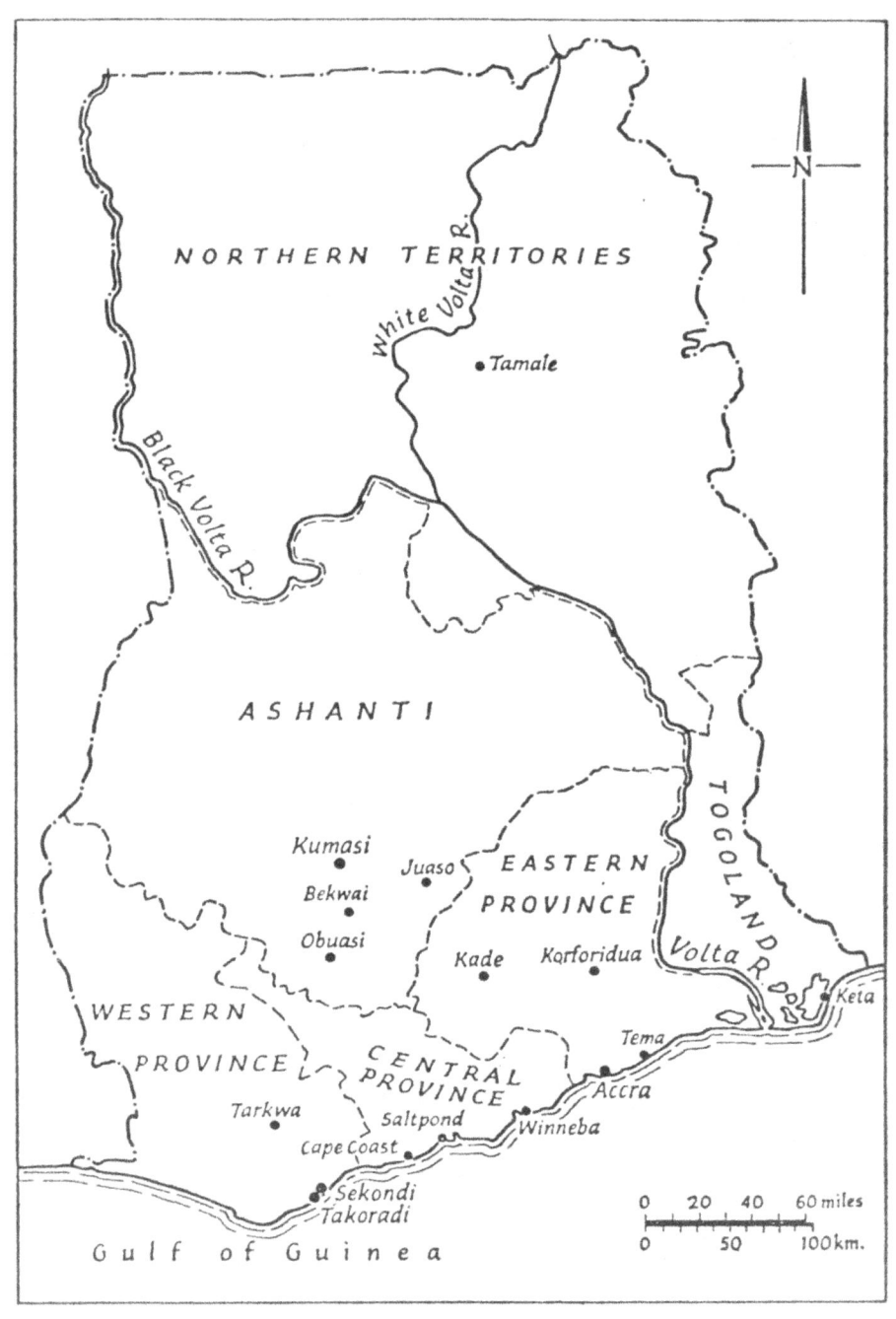

The Gold Coast with Togoland under British mandate, 1945 (from Gold Coast Survey Department, Accra 1945).

1 COLONIALISM AND UNDERDEVELOPMENT IN GHANA

This book is essentially an attempt to provide documentation of the thesis that the integration of the colonial economy of Ghana into the world capitalist system in the late nineteenth and early twentieth centuries had two contradictory effects. Ghana's economic integration into the world system resulted in its development as a peripheral capitalist economy, but, concomitant with this, in the underdevelopment of its capitalist potential.

Theoretical debates about the formation of the world economic system centre, among other issues, on the question of whether the world system, having been created by the geographical extension of capitalist activities out of Western Europe, is therefore itself capitalist. One school argues that if capitalist trade relations dominate the world system, then the mode of production in all its component parts must also be capitalist.[1] The other school argues that although the dominant mode of production is capitalism, subordinate modes of production in the world economic system need not necessarily be capitalist; in fact, they can remain in a pre-capitalist stage, or they can be transitional.[2] The latter school argues that it is the internal developments in a specific social formation, especially the changes in relations of production (i.e. class relations) which determine the mode of production.

In adopting the view that Ghana's integration into the world capitalist system during the colonial era witnessed its emergence as a 'peripheral' capitalist economy, I am essentially opting for the latter approach. During the colonial period, Ghana's economy underwent a transition from its various pre-capitalist social formations to a quasi-capitalist organisation of production. Clearly, as this book will document, such a transition to capitalism was incomplete (indeed, one can argue that the transition to capitalism is still incomplete in contemporary Ghana). The incompleteness of the transition, however, was not a result of strictly chronological features (i.e. Ghana had not yet had enough 'time' to become capitalist); it was a result of the very structures of the world capitalist system, which prevented the formation of a developed capitalist mode of production in 'peripheral' areas.

It is thus apposite to adopt Samir Amin's term 'peripheral capitalism';[3] not simply in the sense that 'Third World' or former colonial areas are geographically peripheral to the core capitalist states of Western Europe and North America; but more precisely in the analytic sense that the underdevelopment of capitalism in these economies is a structural imperative; it is a direct result of the integration of their originally pre-capitalist societies into a world economic system dominated (in the colonial period, politically and ideologically as well as economically) by developed capitalist powers.

It is not, however, the assumption of this thesis that, without contact with Europe and without the institution of colonial rule, Ghana would necessarily have eventually developed into a full-fledged, independent capitalist economy. One can speculate only to a limited degree as to what the nature of economic development in Ghana would have been had there been no integration or contact at all between Ghana and the emerging capitalist European nations. To engage in such speculation would require construction of models of pre-contact Ghanaian societies, followed by construction of models of internal structural changes which would have been generated in each society, ignoring external factors such as war, conquest or trade. Such an approach can have only limited value. When, therefore, the concept of underdevelopment is used, it is not necessarily meant to imply that Ghana was following a pre-ordained path of changes in her modes of production,[4] similar to the stages which had been followed by Western Europe. Nor is it meant to imply that without contact with the world economy, Ghana would necessarily have become capitalist.

The concept of underdevelopment used in this book is that which implies that the productive forces of Ghana suffered constraints imposed both by an external market and by an external bourgeoisie bolstered by the powers of a foreign state. Peripheral capitalist societies are underdeveloped because the forces for change unleashed by their contacts with core capitalist countries, especially the development of new social groupings with the potential to become indigenous, productive capitalists, are constrained by their externally-oriented economies. They cannot imitate the model of capitalist development in the Western world. The structure of the international market system, reinforced by production organised primarily for export, restricts them. When peripheral capitalist countries also undergo periods of formal colonial rule, then they are also constrained by a foreign state structure which regulates their internal economic development in its own interests, or at least, in the interests of its own bourgeoisie. In the case of Ghana, the imposition of foreign political rule was a necessary factor in providing the infrastructure of the peripheral capitalist economy; specifically, in monetising the economy and in organising and constructing a transport system. But political rule *per se* was simply an adjunct of economic policy; actual political domination was an exacerbatory, but not a determining, factor in Ghana's underdevelopment. Ghana's peripheral economic status should not be attributed to the fact that it underwent formal colonial rule.

Prior to its encounter with representatives of the rising merchant classes of Europe in the late fifteenth and early sixteenth centuries, Ghana was composed of a number of pre-capitalist economic formations. These varied from Marx's 'primitive communal'[5] societies in which there was at most a sexual or age-graded division of labour, little surplus, and very little exchange to (in later years) the development of a quasi-feudal state in Ashanti.[6] The period of Ghana's integration into the world capitalist system prior to the beginning of its formal colonisation in 1874 coincides with the period of development and consolidation of capitalism and capitalist production in Western Europe. Ghana played two roles in the early development of this Western European capitalism. Originally, it provided gold, which was necessary for Europe's long-distance trade with Arab and Asian countries. Later, it provided slaves to work on the plantations of the West Indies and America. After the slave trade was abolished, a new role emerged as a supplier of raw materials for the developing industrial production of Great Britain.

It can be safely stated that by the late nineteenth century, when Ghana was colonised, the world economic system was capitalist, or rather, it was dominated by capitalism. Ghana's international economic relations, therefore, were with a dominant capitalist power. Ghana was subjected to the demands of capitalist profit both in international trade and in internal trade, but its sale of cheap bulk commodities in the international market-place did not result in the emergence of internal capitalism; rather it resulted in an almost monocultural system of agricultural production dependent for profits upon the European-controlled external market, and organised internally on the basis of pre-capitalist land tenure relationships. The cheap bulk commodities which Ghana produced were exchanged for more expensive manufactured consumer goods, further reinforcing Ghana's external dependence and reducing the opportunities for development of a diversified internal system of production and exchange.

Ghana's agricultural sector developed both before and during colonial rule, as producers changed from cultivating the soil purely for their own use needs to cultivating cash-crops for profit. The search for profit resulted in rural social differentiation as some farmers made larger profits than others, were able to consolidate large areas of land for their own use, and began to engage in money-lending and the hiring of labour. But land remained communally owned and, without private ownership in land, capitalist productive developments could not be consolidated.

Of interest in this regard is the fact that it was Africans, as well as Europeans, who prevented the consolidation of cash-crop farming into private land ownership. This was an anomalous situation inasmuch as it was largely the Ghanaian petty bourgeoisie, which, one could argue, might well have benefited from private property in land, which prevented such a conversion from taking place. In 1895, the British government proposed declaring all the unoccupied land in Ghana as Crown Land, which would be leased to entrepreneurs (in principle either British or Ghanaian, but in practice primarily Europeans who had larger supplies of cash) for purposes of mining or cash-crop cultivation. Such a measure might have benefited those few Ghanaians who had acquired enough profits through trade to compete with Europeans for land. But it would also threaten the interests of all Ghanaian peasants who had access to land usufruct through the pre-capitalist tribal structure; and, as well, it would threaten the interest of that large number of Ghanaian professionals, bureaucrats, and petty traders who could look forward to investing in cash-crop production through usufruct of land to which they had free access by traditional law, but who would not be able to afford to buy or rent land. Given the constraints of being a colony run by a foreign state structure and given the fact that the Ghanaian petty bourgeoisie had to compete against the international capitalist bourgeoisie in Britain, preservation of a pre-capitalist mode of production seemed to be the only way in which the Ghanaians could ensure that they did not hand over all positions of power, both political and economic, to Europeans.

Again, the contradiction is that even before formal European control was established in Ghana in 1874, capitalism was both developing and underdeveloped. An indigenous community trading for a profit on the world market had already established itself. At the same time a new professional elite, literate in English, had emerged. Both of these classes had an interest in the continuation of the process of stratification along capitalist lines, which was developing in Ghana, as both of them might have been able to establish themselves as members of a new capitalist elite as against the 'traditional' pre-capitalist leaders of the past. Nevertheless, because not only were they obliged to trade in an international market, in which the terms of exchange became increasingly unequal,[7] but also because they were subjected, as of 1874, to a state system which permitted Europeans to move into Ghana and take over positions both in the professions and in trade which had formerly been held by Ghanaians, their only recourse was to return to the pre-capitalist modes of ownership, that is, to prevent the development of pure capitalism in their colony. It could be argued that even at this early stage Ghanaian intellectuals understood the meaning of peripheral capitalism in an imperial context.

One of the seminal theories of the interrelationship between capitalism and imperialism was formulated by V.I. Lenin in his *Imperialism, the Highest Stage of Capitalism*.[8] Lenin posited several reasons for the acquisition of colonies by capitalist nations, some of which apply to Ghana.

One of the most important of these reasons was that colonies would provide raw materials which could be used for production in the imperialist economy. Ghana provided such raw materials in the form of cocoa, palm oil, palm kernels, timber and other crops, and also in the form of minerals. A characteristic of this use of colonies for raw materials, Lenin reasoned, was the cartelisation of raw materials buyers in the late nineteenth century. These buyers tried to capture raw materials sources so that they could obtain a dominant position both over the actual producers and over the manufacturers of capitalist Europe.[9] Such cartelisation emerged in Ghana's cocoa export trade, as well as in other of Ghana's exports, during the late nineteenth and early twentieth centuries. Extreme cartelisation of the buying of cocoa, and attempts by these organised buyers to obtain power over distribution by controlling the commodity markets in London and New York, were combined with attempts to take over or bring into their cartelised system companies which had previously been solely concerned with manufacture. Ghana's major function during the colonial period was to be a source of raw materials for this type of international cartelised trading group.

A second function of colonies, Lenin postulated, was to provide new markets for the capitalist powers. He argued that the export of manufactured goods was typical of capitalism,[10] which needed a constantly expanding market for these manufactured goods because of the fact that there were not enough buyers within the capitalist nations themselves to support capitalist production. Over-production of manufactured goods had as its counterpart the under-consumption of those same goods as fewer workers were employed in the machine-dominated factories.[11]

By encouraging Ghanaians to produce crops such as cocoa, the Europeans also ensured that Ghana would become more dependent on the exchange economy and that Ghanaians would have the cash and the desire to buy new goods. Also, because they no longer produced all of the goods which they used, they would be obliged to buy from the capitalist producers. For example, as they diverted their attention to the production of cocoa and other crops for the European market, Ghanaians started to import cloth, pots and containers, salt and sugar, all of which they had previously produced on their own. Production for use gave way to production for exchange, but Ghanaians were dependent for this exchange on the core capitalist countries. Both Africans and Europeans were discouraged from producing anything within the colony which might compete with imported consumer goods.

A third function which Lenin maintained the colonies fulfilled was that of providing super-profits for the capitalist world. Basing his argument on the labour theory of value, Lenin contended that in the colonial countries, where less capital per unit of labour-power was used, the rate of profit from production would be higher.[12] This argument, however, was of little relevance to Ghana where Europeans were not engaged in the actual organisation of production, except in the mines, which employed only a miniscule percentage of Ghana's population. The profits for Europeans came primarily from trade, not from industry.

Precisely because European profits came from trade, not from industry, it was essential that Ghana, as a peripheral capitalist economy, should not be fully developed. The productive forces of a peripheral capitalist economy must be kept in check, obliging it to rely for its supply of manufactured goods, either consumer or producer, on imports from core capitalist states. It is also important that a peripheral capitalist economy has means of supporting its producer classes other than by the purely capitalist means of wages. In a peripheral economy, producers are only partially integrated into the world trading network. They still maintain some contact with pre-capitalist subsistence forms of agriculture, hence, it is possible to underpay peripheral peasants for the goods they produce because it can be assumed that part of their support comes from their traditional communities. Furthermore, rent is not a cost to be calculated into the final prices paid for raw materials, as access to land is determined not by the producer's ability to make profits from the land, but rather by his 'traditional' pre-capitalist rights. This underpayment of producers for their goods constitutes one of the principal sources of trade profits for the core capitalists.

In theoretical terms, the basis of the profit extracted from the trade relationship between Europe and Ghana was unequal exchange.[13] Unequal exchange is fundamentally a non-capitalistic way to make profits. Profits within pure capitalism are made by the creation of surplus-value, that is, by the establishment of a system in which the labourer sells his use-value to a capitalist in return for payment of exchange-value. The amount of exchange-value which a capitalist pays a labourer for his use-value corresponds to his historically determined subsistence needs and is much less than the amount of exchange-value which the labourer produces. The difference between the two exchange-values constitutes surplus-value, which is appropriated by the capitalist as profit. Goods using the same amount of labour-power are then exchanged at equal rates; each of the two exchanging capitalists making his profit from the difference between the price of the exchange and the price of the labour-power.

However, while this type of profit is made within capitalist nations, such as Britain or America, profit can also be made between nations, one of which is capitalist while the other is not, through unequal exchange. When unequal exchange takes place, goods which are of equal value in terms of the labour-power which enters into them are not exchanged for equal prices. Rather, one costs far less on the market than the other; the labour-power, which is of equal use-value in both situations, is renumerated unequally. Where both sides of the trade are controlled by the same capitalist class, as in Ghana's export-import trade, extra profits are made through this unequal remuneration of the producers (in the case of Ghana, of the peasant producer class). The real cost, in terms of labour-power, might be far more for one of the goods exchanged than for the other, yet the price offered could be less.

For example, during the colonial period, a Ghanaian might have sold one hundred loads of cocoa in return for twelve bolts of cloth. The amount of labour-power which went into the production of the hundred loads of cocoa might have been far more than the amount of labour-power, including the labour-power necessary for the manufacture of the machinery involved, which went into the production of the twelve bolts of cloth. However, because of monopoly control of trade, pricing agreements, and the foreign domination of Ghana, the price offered for the hundred loads of cocoa would have equalled the price which the Ghanaian paid for the twelve bolts of cloth.

Thus, in analysing peripheral capitalism one must also concern oneself with the actual mechanisms by which, through underdevelopment of the mode of production, unequal exchange can be maintained. One of the secondary means by which in a capitalist system unequal exchange can be maintained and a peripheral capitalist society can remain underdeveloped is through the institution of monopolistic or oligopolistic controls on capitalist competition. That is to say, that the monopoly stage of developed capitalism in the core, imposed on underdeveloped capitalism in the periphery, further exacerbates unequal relationships. In the case of Ghana the issue is not monopoly industrial production, but rather the highly oligopolistic organisation within the trading, banking and shipping sectors. It is clear that throughout the period during which Ghana was a colony, the economy became more and more monopolised. Not only were there fewer and fewer European traders competing for the same goods, but also, those European traders developed closer and closer contacts with expatriate banks and shipping companies. Much of the opposition to British rule emanating from the Ghanaian petty bourgeoisie, as well as from the ordinary Ghanaian producer and consumer, during the period of colonial rule, centered around this oligopolistic structure.

To the Ghanaian petty bourgeoisie, monopoly by a few Europeans meant Africans' exclusion from trade. Between the late nineteenth century and the mid-twentieth century, the position of the Ghanaian petty bourgeoisie relative to the metropolitan bourgeoisie, far from improving, worsened. Although more and more opportunities arose for Ghanaians to participate as brokers, traders, and even occasionally as importers or exporters in the expanding commercial economy, they were subject to ever-greater constraints by the formation of buyers' and sellers' cartels, international cocoa exchanges and preferential practices by the European-owned shipping lines and banks. Similarly, as buyers' and sellers' agreements were established, Ghanaian cocoa farmers found that they had little bargaining power and that, even when they could obtain a good price for their products, much of it was eaten up by the rises in prices of consumer goods which always seemed to accompany higher cocoa prices.

Had Ghana been an independent nation-state, rather than a colony, the expansion of European monopoly control over its economy might not have been so rapid or so complete. Instead, one might have seen a situation in which the state structure acted as a moderator between the indigenous and the metropolitan bourgeoisies. But such speculation is historically anachronistic, since no state structure had developed in Ghana prior to its colonisation. Indeed, even under colonial rule Ghana was comprised of three separate territorial units, the Gold Coast, Ashanti and the Northern Territories. All three units were administered from Accra, however, by a colonial state which while occasionally attempting to act as a mediator in situations of conflict between the indigenous petty bourgeoisie and the metropolitan bourgeoisie, clearly perceived its primary mandate to be to fulfil the economic needs of the British Empire.

The state acted as a mechanism to maintain law and order in Ghana, preventing any rebellion against the Europeans; as the agent of the metropolitan bourgeoisie; and as a moderator in conflicts between different sections of the metropolitan bourgeoisie.[14] Such conflicts in Ghana, while subdued, sometimes took place between mine owners, those engaged in shipping and finance, and those engaged purely in trade. While the state permitted minimal participation by the indigenous petty bourgeoisie in the running of Ghana's affairs, this was clearly token, whereas the participation of the expatriate bourgeoisie in matters of state in Ghana was of prime importance.

During the first forty years of colonial rule, the state was engaged in creating an infrastructure, primarily in transport, to accommodate the needs of the import-export economy. Cash-crop production was guaranteed by the enterprise of African farmers, hence, it was not necessary for the state to play an active role in recruitment of labour-power for the rural agricultural sector, although it was obliged to assist in recruiting 'volunteers' for underground mining, porterage and public works projects. In the later colonial period, the role of the state was to ensure that the mode of production remained peripheral. Thus, the state did not permit developments in industrial production, did not encourage diversification of Ghanaian agriculture, and did not even encourage the development of higher quality crops. As long as the dominant trading and mining sectors, along with the banks and shippers, could obtain reasonable profits from the maintenance of Ghanaian society in its peripheral capitalist mode of production, the state was willing to guarantee the continuation of this level of underdevelopment.

The underdevelopment of the productive forces and the thwarting of Ghana's possible transition to capitalist production were paralleled on the political and social levels by the underdevelopment of social classes in Ghana. Such a statement is not meant to imply, however, that there was no development in social stratification along capitalist lines. Such, indeed, was not the case. Rather, while intermediate social classes did develop, the two social classes most typical of capitalism, the bourgeoisie and the proletariat, did not. Ghana had a substantial petty-bourgeois sector; there were many professionals, bureaucrats and, above all, traders. But because of monopoly control in international trade, combined with Ghana's role as a consumer of light industrial products, it was not possible for the petty bourgeoisie to develop into an indigenous capitalist class. Similarly, in production, the colonial period witnessed the stratification of the rural areas into a class of rich farmers, a middle peasantry, and an indebted peasantry, as well as a migrant agricultural labour force.[15] Although private ownership in land was never formally instituted, there was private property in the crops grown on the land. Those who were successful in marketing their privately grown crops could acquire more land for cultivation by paying extra tribute to the tribal authorities, or by leasing land from other tribes. They could also acquire extra land by lending money to the less successful peasant producers, and taking over usufruct in lieu of payments of debts. But while the society thus separated into richer and poorer producers, class formation was not consolidated into the creation of a landless rural proletariat available for use as a labour pool by a developing urban bourgeoisie.

The classes which developed in Ghana during the period of colonial rule are reflected in the social composition of those who took part in the Ghana cocoa boycott in 1937–38. The boycott was led by petty-bourgeois elements, but with the support both of rich and poor farmers, of some of the migrant labourers from Northern Ghana, of petty traders in the cities, and even with the support of the few people employed as wage earners, such as truck drivers and surf-boat loaders. The cocoa boycott compressed into a nutshell the basic social outlines of Ghana's peripheral capitalist society.

Thus, Ghana in both its economic and its social formations was typical of the peripheral capitalist societies which were created in what is now known as the 'Third World' during the period of European colonial rule. This book will provide basic historical data documenting the description of Ghana's peripheral economy which has been outlined above. Ghana's underdevelopment is documented at the same time as its changing role in the world economic system, that is, its very development, is also documented. Certainly, there was change in Ghana's economy during the period of colonial rule; certainly, new methods of production and new social classes developed. But inherent in this development was the contradiction that Ghana's economy was subsumed by the needs of the core capitalist economies; and that it was not in the interests of the core capitalist nations to allow capitalism to develop completely in Ghana. Rather, its role was to be secondary to the needs of capitalism in the core, and therefore, not only its productive forces but its people would find their overall evolution thwarted. This development of a peripheral economy, under both the economic and the political rule of Great Britain, continues to be reflected in the economy of contemporary Ghana.

Notes

1. A leading exponent of this approach is Andre Gunder Frank. See, for example, his 'Destroy Capitalism, not Feudalism', in his collected essays, *Latin America: Underdevelopment or Revolution* (Monthly Review Press, New York, 1969). Immanuel Wallerstein also adopts this approach, in explicitly referring to the world economic system as a capitalist world economy. 'We have insisted that the modern world-economy is, and only can be, a capitalist world-economy. It is for this reason that we have rejected the appellation of "feudalism" for the various forms of capitalist agriculture based on coerced labour which grew up in a world-economy.' See Wallerstein, *The Modern-World-System* (Academic Press, New York, 1974), p. 350.
2. See, for example, Ernesto Laclau, who in his 'Feudalism and Capitalism in Latin America', *New Left Review*, No. 67 (May—June 1971) criticises Frank, arguing that 'the world capitalist system . . . includes . . . various modes of production', p. 37.
3. Samir Amin, *Accumulation on a World Scale* (Monthly Review Press, New York, 1974), Vol. 1, Ch. 2.
4. The concept of 'mode of production' used in this chapter follows the definition proposed by Hindess and Hirst. 'A mode of production is an articulated combination of relations and forces of production structured by the dominance of the relations of production.' Barry Hindess and Paul Q. Hirst, *Pre-Capitalist Modes of Production* (Routledge and Kegan Paul, London, 1975), p. 9.
5. Karl Marx, *Pre-Capitalist Economic Formations* (International Publishers, New York, 1965), p. 69.
6. G.N. Brown, 'Asante and Fante in the Nineteenth Century', in Joseph C. Anene and Godfrey N. Brown (eds.), *Africa in the Nineteenth and Twentieth Centuries* (Thomas Nelson and Sons, London, 1966), p. 246.
7. The concept of unequal exchange used in this discussion is based on Arghiri Emmanuel, *Unequal Exchange: A Study of the Imperialism of Trade* (Monthly Review Press, New York, 1972), especially chapter 3.
8. V.I. Lenin, *Imperialism, the Highest Stage of Capitalism* (Foreign Languages Press, Peking, 1969).
9. Ibid., p. 27.
10. Ibid., p. 72.
11. 'The growing extent of the means of production . . . is an expression of the growing productiveness of labour. The increase of the latter appears, therefore, in the diminution of the mass of labour in proportion to the mass of means of production moved by it . . . ', Karl Marx, *Capital* (3 vols., International Publishers,

New York, 1967), Vol. 1, p. 622.
12. Lenin, *Imperialism*, p. 9.
13. See Emmanuel, *Unequal Exchange*.
14. Nicos Poulantzas argues that the 'state can only truly serve the ruling class in so far as it is relatively autonomous from the diverse fractions of this class, precisely in order to be able to organize the hegemony of the whole of this class.' This seems to have been the role of the colonial state in Ghana, and was reflected in the occasional conflict between the administrative bureaucracy and a section of the expatriate bourgeoisie, but never between the bureaucracy and the whole of the bourgeoisie. See Nicos Poulantzas, 'The Problem of the Capitalist State', in Robin Blackburn (ed.), *Ideology in Social Science* (Fontana/Collins, Glasgow, 1972), p. 247.
15. The terminology of social class development in Ghana is adopted from Rodolfo Stavenhagen, *Social Classes in Agrarian Societies* (Anchor Press/Doubleday, Garden City, NY, 1975).

2 THE INSTITUTION OF COLONIAL RULE IN GHANA

The exact character of the takeover of Ghana as a colony in the late nineteenth and early twentieth centuries was a result of the role which it had begun to play in the world economic system from the late fifteenth century. Peripheral capitalism is distinguished by its reliance on the import-export sector, to the detriment of the development of the internal economy. Ghana's transition from self-sufficiency in pre-capitalist modes of production to dependent peripheral capitalism was effected through changes from its role as an equal partner in the exchange of gold for European goods, to its role as an exporter of slaves, to its new role, in the colonial period, as an importer of light consumer goods in exchange for the export of raw materials. At each stage, more Africans were drawn into the import-export economy and Ghana's existence became more and more dependent on its ties to the world economy.

Battles over land use and land rights in the early colonial period were to be crucial for Ghana's eventual development, as well as for social and political changes in the later period. Once Ghana was integrated into the world economy, and that integration was ensured by the establishment of colonial rule, a number of attempts were made by the colonial state to remove control of land from Ghanaians. These attempts did not reach fruition, partly because of highly organised African opposition, but also because it became increasingly evident that enough agricultural and arboricultural goods to fulfil world demand could be produced in Ghana without resorting to the institution of a plantation economy, as in the West Indies, or a settler economy, as in Kenya. Control of the essential means of production, land and labour power, remained in African hands. Only in mining did Europeans control production; otherwise they were confined to distribution.

1. Ghana's Integration into the World Economy

The beginnings of European contact with the West African coast came with the Portuguese,[1] who first set foot on what soon became known as the Gold Coast in 1471, and established the fort of Elmina there in 1482. The Portuguese were searching for African sources of gold, which was especially needed in the fifteenth century to pay for the goods which

Europe imported from East Asia and the Levant.[2] West Africa had long been one of the major sources of Europe's gold, but Europeans had hitherto been dependent for their supply on Arab traders who obtained their gold through overland savannah routes. The Spanish and Portuguese had tried to conquer the Maghreb area, partly to obtain control of this gold trade, but without success. Hence it was a major breakthrough for the Europeans when the Portuguese reached the Gold Coast by sea. The gold which the Europeans received was obtained primarily as dust from alluvial washings and small pits. According to J.D. Fage, by the beginning of the sixteenth century £100,000 worth of gold was travelling every year to Portugal from Ghana; this constituted about one-tenth of the world's supply.[3] Sylvia Harrop gives the figure as £350,000 per annum.[4]

There was little European demand for slaves in the fifteenth century. By the sixteenth century, however, the Portuguese had begun to trade in slaves to work in their Brazilian colony. With the discovery of huge deposits of precious metals in the Americas, the demand for African gold had declined while the demand for African slaves to work the American mines had grown. This need for slaves multiplied rapidly after the establishment of plantation agriculture, producing coffee, cotton, sugar and tobacco, in the West Indies and North America.

The slave trade emerged as a very important aspect of the commercial integration of the Gold Coast into the world economy from the early seventeenth to the early nineteenth century, both in terms of volume and in terms of the effect it had on indigenous African society. Unfortunately for the European traders, it was difficult for Africans to provide both gold and slaves simultaneously. European traders frequently bemoaned the fact that while wars between the African states stimulated the supply of slaves, they cut off the supply of gold, while times of peace had the opposite effect. The slave trade meant war, kidnappings, and violation of peaceful trade in a situation in which one's very home was unsafe from attack. One Dutch record reported: '[A]s one fortunate marauding makes a native rich in a day, they therefore exert themselves rather in war, robbery and plunder than in the old business of digging and collecting gold.'[5] The loss of able-bodied workers on the Gold Coast to slavery also had tremendous repercussions. There were fewer people to engage in the labour intensive process of digging and sifting for gold. There were also fewer people to act as porters to transport inland the goods with which Europeans paid for gold. And finally, there were fewer people to engage in indigenous domestic agriculture and production.

Eric Williams's book, *Capitalism and Slavery*,[6] provides an excellent introductory exposition of the role which the slave trade played in the world economy. The slave trade in West Africa was part of the Triangular Trade between England, West Africa, and the West Indies and Americas. The heart of the Triangular Trade was the West Indies; it was the function of West Africa to act as a labour reserve for this productive core. The sugar, cotton, coffee, tobacco and other goods produced in the West Indies were transported to Britain to be processed and manufactured. The Europeans used West Africa as an area of free plunder; they ransacked it for gold and slaves and were not concerned with the effects of their plunder on the people or the economy of the area itself.[7] West Africa, in other words, was a secondary adjunct to the West Indian and American economies during the slave-trading era.

However, by the eighteenth century West Africa had also become a market for the textiles and light consumer goods produced in the British Isles. The supply of slaves had always been dependent on the ability of the Europeans to provide African traders with consumer goods. But in the early years of the trade the British had bought cloths for the trade in India, as well as in parts of West Africa itself such as Morocco, Mauritania, the Senegambia, Ivory Coast, Benin and Yorubaland.[8] It was not until the late eighteenth century that the African trade became an essential market for British production. 'British exports to Africa, valued at £130,000 in 1720, had risen to £866,000 in 1775.'[9] As Britain changed from a mercantile to an industrial capitalist nation, so also West Africa changed from being a simple supplier of slaves for the merchant traders to being a market for the industrialists.

British preponderance in Ghana coincided with the introduction of the slave trade. It must be noted, however, that it was not a foregone conclusion that the British would become the predominant European power on the Gold Coast. Indeed, until the point arrived in the seventeenth century when England's naval power enabled her to outstrip her rivals, this was far from clear. On the entire West African coast, the Gold Coast was the area most densely settled with European forts and factories. At one period or another there were forts from Portugal, Britain, the United Provinces, France, Sweden and Denmark, indeed even from Brandenburg and Prussia.[10] Conflicts between the emerging nation-states in Europe determined Britain's ultimate preponderance in Ghana. Portugal had declined as a power in West Africa by the early seventeenth century, while Denmark and Holland did not cede control of their Gold Coast forts to Britain until 1850 and 1872 respectively.[11]

The slave trade was officially abolished by Britain in 1807, partly as a result of humanitarian protests but partly as a result of economic factors, namely over-production of sugar in the West Indies, which were 'saturated' with slaves.[12] As a result, Ghana no longer had a role in the world economy as a supplier of labour-power. There was no immediate economic replacement for the production of slaves, and British interest in Ghana consequently declined. British disinterest at the time is reflected in its ambiguous political policy. The period from 1807 to the 1860s can be described as one of 'informal empire' in Ghana, to use a term coined by Gallagher and Robinson.[13] That is, the control of Britain, which already by this time was the dominant power on the Coast, was tightening, but it was still based on informal, not formal, means. British administrators were sent out to the Gold Coast forts but the territory itself did not yet have formal status as a colony. The British government wavered throughout this period in the degree of control which it wished to maintain. In 1821 the Colonial Office took over the Gold Coast forts, but by 1828 it had put the forts under the control of a Committee of Merchants. In 1843 the government again took over responsibility, and the Gold Coast forts were ruled jointly with the colony of Sierra Leone from 1844 to 1850. The period from 1850 to 1865 was the only period during which the Gold Coast had its own separate, resident governor until the assumption of formal control of the Colony in 1874. In 1865, a Parliamentary Committee of Investigation recommended complete withdrawal from Ghana; instead of implementing this, however, the Colonial Office simply put the area under the jurisdiction of the Sierra Leone governor once again.

The eventual decision to take over complete political control in Ghana reflected Britain's deepening economic interests. Although the coastal areas of Ghana were now thoroughly integrated into the world economy and as such were a market for British-produced manufactured goods, the hinterland was coming under the increasing control of the Ashanti nation. The nineteenth century witnessed the expansion of the Ashanti kingdom as the only block to the incursion of the British into the hinterland. 'Ashanti in this period can best be regarded as a separate economy, having important relations not only with the Gold Coast but also with other parts [of Africa], such as the territories to the north and the Ivory Coast.'[14] The Ashanti were still very much involved in the now technically illegitimate slave trade. The kingdom was, moreover, a thriving commercial centre. In the early half of the century, the savannah trade was still flourishing, and Kumasi, Ashanti's capital, was one of its centres. In 1812 Kumasi was 'not only the meeting point for the routes from Timbuktu and Hausaland, but was

The Institution of Colonial Rule in Ghana

also the nerve centre for four important routes to the coast.'[15] It was not until the middle of the century, when steam transport up the rivers from the coast became cheaper than the camel trade, that the Europeans began to put a stop to this 2,000-year-old commerce.[16]

Several wars took place during the nineteenth century between the Ashanti and the Fanti people of the coast. The principal reason for the Ashanti expansionary movement to the south was to eliminate the Fanti middlemen from the coastal trade; the Ashanti wanted direct access to the coast. The British, wavering between involvement and non-involvement in these 'internal' matters, finally decided to take the Fanti side. It was evident to the British that the slave trade could not be eliminated completely until the powerful and well-organised Ashanti were prevented from trading with other European nations; moreover, it was difficult to establish trade routes for Europeans when such a large proportion of the territory through which such routes were to go was controlled by Ashanti.

> European merchants were naturally reluctant to venture their capital, and Africans were discouraged from developing new lines of trade to replace the traffic in slaves, in a country in which there were no settled relations between the coast and the hinterland.[17]

Although Ashanti was first 'conquered', and Kumasi burned, in 1874, the final subjugation of the Ashanti did not occur until 1896. The last breath of the Ashanti nation was spent on a 1900 uprising in protest against a demand by the British governor that the Golden Stool, the religious symbol of Ashanti nationhood, be turned over to him.

The British decision to take over the hinterland areas reflected Ghana's new role in the world economy. Ghana had originally become an outlet for British manufactured goods when these were exported to the coast in payment for slaves; but when the slave trade was abolished Ghana remained a consumer. In payment for consumer goods, Ghanaians began to turn to cash-crop production. The supersession of the slave trade by such production ensured a continuing and expanding market; whereas the slave trade, by its constant removal of labour-power, had effectively limited the market. At the same time, the cash-crop economy responded to the industrial core's growing need for raw materials. The European economy had changed from one of mercantile capitalism to one of industrial capitalism, and the Gold Coast was now a full-fledged peripheral area. No longer could the Europeans simply raid for slaves, disregarding the effect on the Gold Coast of such raids.

Capitalism in the centre . . . took on its complete form; the function of mercantilism — the primitive accumulation of wealth — lost its importance . . . The old periphery — America of the plantations — and its periphery — Africa of the slave trade — had to give way to a new periphery. The function of the new periphery was to provide *products* . . . raw materials and agricultural produce.[18]

Ghana's function at this time, then, was to act as a supplier of raw materials and agricultural produce. Originally, production of these goods was still of an *extractive* nature; organised production and cultivation for the capitalist world market did not as yet exist. '[O] ne cannot call the primitive process of oil extraction from palm nuts, the extraction of kernels and washing and crushing of auriferous ores, technical transformations.'[19] Robert Szereszewski argues that the level and character of the economy remained static for centuries until the introduction of cocoa in the 1890s. Products for export changed, but the mode of production did not, as the raiding of human communities for slaves was replaced by the simple extraction of the natural resources of Ghana.

However, Szereszewski's argument belies the formation of new social groups, which took place in nineteenth-century Ghana, consequent upon the evolution of production for trade. In this connection, it is useful to distinguish between tribal cultivators and peasants. According to Rodolfo Stavenhagen

Tribal cultivators live in relatively closed, self-contained societies, and while they may engage in trade or barter with other groups, they are not economically integrated into wider social units . . . peasant societies do form part of wider economic, social and political units . . . [20]

The original production of cash-crops for the European market in Ghana might have been casual sale by tribal cultivators (still members of pre-capitalist economic formations) of easily extracted agricultural goods such as palm nuts. But by the late 1870s, a peasantry was emerging which was specifically engaged in cash-crop production for the market and which formed part of the wider social unit of the entire world economy.

This emergence of a peasantry had been partially a consequence of the abolition, not only of the slave trade, but also of all internal slavery in British possessions, including the protectorate of the Gold Coast, in

1833. Domestic slavery was included in the prohibition, causing social dislocation in production. There were many complaints from African slave-owners to the British when domestic slavery was abolished. The Africans argued that agricultural production was failing without the labour of domestic slaves. Several chiefs presented a statement to the British.

> First that they are as it were deprived of the power of holding domestic slavery, which has greatly reduced their power and dignity as kings and chiefs ... They agree to follow agricultural pursuits if they will be permitted to hold domestic slavery for reason assigned by them ... They observed also that the country in sixty or seventy years past was in a thriving condition when domestic slavery was prevalent, but now since the great alteration that has taken place with reference to the slave holding, the country is totally deprived of its wealth.[21]

Formerly, the coastal Fanti had used slaves to produce foodstuffs which were then sold to passing European ships. The abolition of domestic slavery had the effect of cutting back on this particular type of enterprise.[22] Reports from various British settlements shortly after the abolition of the trade indicated economic decline. One observer, stationed at Komenda, wrote that: 'The progress of agriculture has decreased since the abolition of the slave trade, there not being that vent for their commodities which there was when shipping had frequent recourse here.'[23]

The ban on domestic slavery was extended to the entire Gold Coast colony in 1874, and to Ashanti and the Northern Territories in 1900. Domestic slaves were then free to become independent cash-crop cultivators for the world market; liberated from pre-capitalist constraints on production, they were free to respond to the demand for new products from Ghana.

While gold remained an important product in the nineteenth century, the economy of Ghana during the period of informal empire was based upon the export of palm oil and palm kernels. In the period from 1881 to 1885, for instance, 73 per cent of the total exports were palm products, oil accounting for 47 per cent and kernels for 26 per cent.[24] In the same years, gold accounted for 10 per cent of exports.[25] Apart from these two products, there was a brief boom in rubber in the latter part of the century. But the export of both palm products and rubber declined with the introduction of cocoa as a cash-crop in the early twentieth century.

The new cash-crop economy, concentrating first on palm products and rubber and later on cocoa, resulted in the further incursion of the British into Ghana in order to regulate trade and production in the interests of those buyer nations which constituted the core of the world capitalist system. Thus, the period of informal empire in Ghana came to an end in 1874, when the territory along the coast on which British forts and trading factories were established became the Gold Coast Colony. Ashanti, however, remained independent until 1896 and the Northern Territories until they were added as a protectorate in 1900.

While the assumption of formal political control by Europeans in Africa is often attributed to the Berlin Conference and the 'scramble for Africa' of 1884, it is clear that the scramble cannot explain the takeover of the Gold Coast Colony which occurred ten years prior to the Conference. The Proclamation announcing the takeover clearly indicated that law and order and the protection of trade were important purposes of the establishment of a colonial state. The Proclamation listed, among other purposes,

> The protection and encouragement of trade and traders, including the construction, maintenance and improvement of roads, paths, bridges, harbour works, waterways, telegraphs, and other public works which benefit trade and promote civilization . . . [and] the maintenance of an armed police force for the preservation of internal order and the prevention of foreign aggression.[26]

The takeovers of Ashanti and the Northern Territories were more direct results of political, as well as economic, pressures. The scramble for Africa was inciting a fear in certain British circles that if it did not obtain tighter control on all its spheres of influence, it might lose them altogether to its French and German rivals. At the same time, because they needed better transportation and better systems of protection for their trade inland from the Colony, British commercial houses were pressuring the Colonial Office for military takeovers of Ashanti and the Northern Territories. Moreover, in Ghana, the situation was ripe for direct political takeover precisely because the social and political organisations of indigenous Ghanaian society were not conducive to the type of trade in which Europeans were beginning to engage. Intertribal wars had facilitated the export of slaves; they did not, however, facilitate the free export of palm oil, rubber, and later cocoa. Nor did intertribal boundaries and tolls facilitate the free import of cheap European goods for the African consumer. The foremost need of the European traders in the colony was for fast, efficient, cheap and orderly transport both of exports and imports. Hence, the first priority was railroads, and later motor roads. In order to be able to build these roads, the Europeans needed peace and good government. Later, they pressed for the abolition of tolls into Ashanti and the North, so that their goods could have free access.

Gallagher and Robinson argue that there was 'no strong political or commercial movement in Britain in favour of African acquisitions.'[27] Such a statement does not seem to have been applicable for Ghana. Rather, from the 1870s on, the powerful Chambers of Commerce of London, Liverpool, and Manchester were actively pressing the Colonial Office for additional takeovers. In 1894, for example, the Manchester and London Chambers of Commerce urged London to bring Ashanti within the British sphere of influence,[28] in order to make trade routes more secure from intertribal conflict, as well as from conflict between Ashanti and the Europeans. From 1894 until the final complete 'pacification' (to use contemporary terminology) of Ashanti in 1900, petitions and letters from British Chambers of Commerce interested in Africa made a steady stream to the Colonial Office. Nor was the pressure only to take over Ashanti. In 1894 the Manchester and Glasgow Chambers of Commerce also urged the government to take over the Northern Territories, in order to curb 'disturbances' which were affecting trade.[29]

From the point of view of British businessmen, the affirmation of British law in the colonies was also imperative. In dealings between African and European traders, it was necessary to make sure that both were operating under the same set of rules; the introduction of British commercial law would ensure this. Similarly, a legal structure was needed to regulate access to land. African laws had evolved in pre-capitalist conditions, but since Ghana was now integrated into the capitalist world economy, it needed developed capitalist law.

Much of this pressure, aside from demanding law and order to facilitate trade inland, was also geared towards the takeover of the gold mines of Ashanti. Europeans were no longer content simply to buy gold from Africans as they had done in the past; they were now anxious to construct their own mines. As one contemporary observer commented about the 1896 campaign against Ashanti,

> One of the main motives for the expedition . . . not admitted till

after its conclusion, was, of course, command of the mineral wealth in which the interior of the Gold Coast is supposed to abound. Before the troops had returned from Kumasi, in fact, several speculators had begun arrangements with local chiefs and others, with the object of obtaining valuable concessions [of land] at low prices.[30]

When King Prempeh of Ashanti was interrogated after the conquest, he made it quite clear that he had not permitted Europeans access to gold land.

No land has been given to any white man. A long time ago . . . some white men came, but they went away and they were not given any land. No white man has ever been allowed to dig for gold; neither English, French, or Dutch, nor German.

They have been digging for gold all this time; we ourselves dig, not any white man.[31]

It was because of such intransigent opposition to the European incursion that the expedition against Ashanti took place. As soon as the kingdom was conquered, the Colonial Office began negotiations to take over the mines.[32]

Thus, it can be seen that a primary aim of the British in taking over Ashanti and the Northern Territories was precisely to attain the economic objectives which Gallagher and Robinson deny were crucial to British policy in the late nineteenth century. How important the scramble for Africa was in comparison to these economic aims cannot be decided here,[33] but the economic motive has been established. Nevertheless, the motive for the British takeover was not specifically to protect foreign investment or to engage in land-grabbing. While trade with Ghana was extensive and profitable, and was expected to expand as Ghana became a major exporter of agricultural and arboricultural produce, actual foreign investment in the country was miniscule. While there were many who would have liked to take over the land, to facilitate both the establishment of gold mines and the potential setting up of plantations, they failed to do so. The following pages discuss the attempts by the British government to take over possession of the land of Ghana once the takeover of the Colony and the conquest of Ashanti had been completed, and the reasons why this attempted takeover failed.

2. The Issue of Land Ownership

One of the prerequisites for the formation of capitalism in any economy is the establishment of land as private property. Individuals must be able to buy and sell land, to alienate it as they please, and to acquire as much as they can afford. Those who concentrate lands in their own hands can by so doing acquire agricultural surpluses which may (but not necessarily) then be invested in urban industrial production. At the same time, those who in the process of such concentration lose their lands through sale, rural indebtedness, or perhaps outright expropriation, are 'freed' from their land and from rural agricultural labour (either subsistence or cash-crop) and can become wage-labourers either on plantations or in the industrial centres.[34]

In colonised areas, the patterns are somewhat different from core capitalist areas. One pattern is that those who concentrate land in their own hands tend to be individuals from the colonising nation, while those who are landless are the indigenous inhabitants, as in South Africa or Kenya. Agricultural surpluses are not necessarily invested in industrial production in the colony itself; instead, a plantation economy can be established in which the surplus is either consumed or invested in the imperialist country. Such a pattern, it can be assumed, might well have been followed in Ghana had agriculturally productive land become the property of British settlers.

The defeat of the British attempt to take over land in Ghana had two results. The first was that, as private property was not established, there was no immediate transformation of the indigenous class structure in a capitalist direction. The other was that neither did a racial class structure based upon ownership or non-ownership of land evolve. The fact that Europeans did not take over land protected possibilities for the evolution of indigenous peasant production. But at the same time, possibilities for the primitive accumulation of capital based upon the concentration of ownership of land were thwarted.

A simplistic model of land tenure in Ghana would distinguish it from modern European land tenure systems by the fact that throughout the colonial period there was no private property in land, and that only usufruct was granted to the individual cultivator. Land was owned by the tribe, as a communal entity, and was not normally alienable. It was divided, in general, into tribal (stool) land (land under the control of the chief, to be used by him for his own purposes but also to earn revenue to fulfil the ceremonial needs of the tribe) and family land, which was allotted to individual families and to which the families held rights (for use only) in perpetuity.[35] Land could, on rare occasions, be alienated, but not absolutely; that is, the person or persons to whom the land was alienated could not further alientate the land; if they ceased to occupy it themselves, it reverted to the original owners.

> [A] n absolute alienation of stool or family land can only be made under special circumstances, and for a particular object, as, for instance, to raise money for the payment of a stool or family debt. Most commonly the alienation only gives a limited right; the right, namely, for the grantee and his family to occupy and live on or cultivate the land, upon the condition (often, but not always) of rendering or paying to the grantor and his representatives, as tribute, either part of the crops or an annual sum of money, and when the land ceases to be occupied it reverts to the grantor or his representatives.[36]

Indigenous agriculture was based upon a system of shifting cultivation. Such a system was a rational adaptation to soil conditions and to the level of technical development, although it seemed crazily patchwork to the Europeans who took over the colony, used as they were to clearly-defined, permanent fields. But, in fact, boundaries were relatively well-marked. Tribal property was clearly delineated and strangers occupying tribal land held certain obligations of payment to the chief which a tribal member did not hold; usually, in Ashanti and the Gold Coast, under what was known as the 'abusa' system, they were obliged to present one-third of their produce (or, in the case of cash-crop production, of the revenue of their produce) to the chief. Boundary disputes became common only after the widespread introduction of cash-crop production, not only between tribes but between individuals. Although land itself was not privately owned, the crops or trees on the land were private property; hence, it was crucial to delineate usufruct rights.

This brief sketch, however, does little justice to the complexity of land tenure in Ghana. As more and more Ghanaians were drawn into the system of cash-crop production, property rights began to undergo some change, even before the twentieth century, in the direction of private ownership of land. A number of reports compiled by various District Commissioners in 1895 indicated a wide variety of property systems, especially near the coast where, because of contract with the Europeans and the consequent desire to earn money by cultivating permanent cash-crops, private property in land was developing. In Accra, in 1895, the Attorney-General reported that it has become a common custom to transfer land absolutely for a consideration by conveyance forms. These conveyances are made at least as frequently to natives as to Europeans . . . They are generally held by the Courts to be valid instruments of title between natives, even if imperfect according to English law.[37]

The question of the right of occupancy was the key to British land policy in the 1890s. The report above quoted was specifically commissioned in order to ascertain African customs as to land rights at a time when the colonial government was considering taking over all 'unoccupied' or 'waste' land as Crown land. Although it may perhaps have exaggerated the extent of formation of private property, especially by confusing private property in cash-crops with private property in the land on which those crops were grown, the report indicated that the ownership and tenure of land was well organised. So-called 'waste' lands were simply lands being left fallow.

There were two reasons for the colonial state's interest in taking over Ghanaian land in the 1890s. One was that at the time a number of British administrators doubted that enough cash-crops could be produced without complete European takeover of the land. There was talk of establishing plantations using imported Chinese labour to produce cocoa and palm products.[38] Moreover, the Europeans regarded Africans as unreliable and they hesitated to do business with a race which they considered inferior. Controlled production, as one contemporary Ghanaian, J.E. Casely Hayford, observed, was more to their taste.

> It is [the land question] . . . that the land shall belong to the indigenes and not to foreign capitalists; or that, in the last analysis, neither the foreign capitalist nor the indigenes, but Government shall own it? To state the problem in another way, is it that the people shall be free to till the soil in their own right and sell produce thereof to the merchants abroad . . . or that Government shall step in and control private rights on the assumption that parties are incapable of managing their own business?[39]

A second and more important motive for taking over Ghanaian land was to obtain absolute control over the production of gold. The 1890s was the period of the first Ghanaian 'gold rush'; hundreds of small speculators were trying to take out concessions to prospect land in the hopes that gold might be found. Large claims on land were being granted to Europeans by Ghanaian chiefs who often had no idea of the extent of the land that they were bargaining away. The largest concession was granted to Ashanti Goldfields, which obtained a concession of one hundred square miles, with complete monopoly rights, in some of the best gold land of Ashanti.

Complaints from its competitors about the size of Ashanti Goldfields' concession convinced the imperial government that it should regulate land more carefully. It was decided to vest all waste lands in the Crown, ostensibly to protect African interests against those of European entrepreneurs who were flooding the colony.[40] In 1894, the Crown Lands Bill was introduced, its stated aim being to protect chiefs from being cheated by European concessionaires by vesting all 'waste lands, forest lands, and minerals' in the Crown.[41] But, in fact, it would seem that protection of the African was a minor consideration compared to the desire to protect the rights of both government and business concerns. In the Gold Coast Legislative Council, the Governor stated freely that 'for the past three years his attention had been directed to the establishment of a means of acquiring the waste land in the Colony for the use of the government.'[42] But the Governor's insistence on having powers to regulate concession agreements backfired; European merchants and miners feared too much control by officialdom, especially with regard to royalties, and made representations to the Colonial Office to that effect. These fears, combined with protests registered by Africans who sent memorials to the Governor asking that the Bill be withdrawn, resulted in the substitution of a new Bill, called simply the Lands Bill, in 1897.

The vesting of all lands in the Crown was dropped from the 1897 Bill, the aim being stated simply as a desire to regulate and control the use of land in the colony. However, under the new bill the government intended not only to regulate the land's occupation and use by expatriates, but also its occupation and use by Africans.

> African rights of ownership would no longer be automatically recognized. Occupiers of land would not be disturbed; but they would be entitled only to a 'settler's right', a permanent heritable right of occupancy, which could be transformed into an absolute right, on application to the Governor, by the grant of a land certificate. The Government could also declare that any piece of land had no owner, and then authorize its occupation.[43]

In the face of this promised onslaught upon their land rights,

Ghanaians were quick to organise. Many petitions were laid on the table in the Legislative Council against the Lands Bill, but with little effect.[44] The Aborigines Rights Protection Society (ARPS), formed to protect the rights of the chiefs and peoples of Ghana but consisting primarily of educated Africans, sent a delegation to England to present a petition to the Colonial Secretary, Joseph Chamberlain. The petition argued that the British had no paramount title to land in the Gold Coast Colony, especially since the colony had been obtained not by conquest but by cession.[45] It also argued that in any case lands needed for government use could be obtained under the Public Lands Ordinance of 1876, and protested that under the bill no compensation would be issued to persons whose land was granted to some other person by a Government Land Certificate. Further, the ARPS pointed out that the bill removed all rights for Africans to buy, sell, or make profit from land and retained for their benefit only the minimal customary rights; but at the same time that if Africans tried to obtain a Government Certificate to their own land they would by so doing be putting themselves under English law, and removing themselves from 'native customary' law.[46] All of these were detrimental measures, which, the ARPS argued, would both undermine traditional rule and custom, and prevent the natural evolution of proprietary relations.

At the same time as they argued that the Lands Bill would undermine traditional land rights, Africans also argued that the natural evolution or proprietary relations in land should not be regulated by the courts. The government's attempts to regulate the granting of concessions to Europeans, ostensibly so that Ghanaians would not be cheated, would also limit the rights of the developing petty bourgeoisie. James H. Brew complained of these limits to the Colonial Office.

> Am I to understand that I have not the power to dispose, in any way, of any landed property, being freehold, owned by me in the Gold Coast Colony, whether by granting a concession for the same, or leasing the same, or otherwise, as I may deem fit, without the sanction and approval of the Governor of the Gold Coast Colony?[47]

Thus, simultaneously, Ghanaians were attempting to defend both their right to maintain traditional land tenure relationships, and their right to evolve and change. But overall, their objective was to avoid British control.

The 1898 petition to Joseph Chamberlain had its desired effect, and

under his orders the Lands Bill was removed from the books. There is
no doubt that had the ARPS not organised and presented its petition
in such an articulate manner, the Bill might well have gone through.
However, it would be facile to attribute the demise of the Bill solely
to such African opposition; both prior to and after this Bill many issues
arose in Ghana on which African opposition had no effect whatsoever.[48]

It would indeed seem that a confluence of forces combined to
suggest to Chamberlain that it would be wise to rescind the Bill. First,
it was becoming obvious that even with a system of peasant proprietorship, Ghana was producing the goods needed for the world market; it
was not necessary to establish plantations and introduce forced labour
in order for British merchants to obtain the goods they needed. Moreover, the political situation in Africa was unstable; a war was brewing in
South Africa and Sierra Leone had just had a hut tax rebellion; the
Ghanaian petitioners hinted that a similar rebellion might take place
in Ghana were their needs not met.[49] Ashanti had just been conquered
and was still in a state of unrest. Not only was the opposition in Ghana
approaching a state of apprehended insurrection, but also, apparently,
some merchants were beginning to consider that the area was unsafe
for investment. One expatriate agent reported to the Colonial Office
that

> The new land ordinance was causing much dissatisfaction amongst
> both natives and Europeans, and as the Government intended to
> enforce the new law, which also operates retrospectively, open
> opposition was feared.
> This corresponds with the information we have from the missionaries,
> and also from our Company's agents on the coast . . . The natives
> look upon the Bill as one likely to deprive them of their lands by
> the imposition of heavy duties or taxes. The Bill, in its present
> form, certainly seems an unusual one, and will, I fear, stop British
> companies risking much money on the Gold Coast.[50]

The implied threat not to invest was, no doubt, also a result of
commercial objections to the provision of a 5 per cent royalty to be
paid to the state on the gross value of mineral products of the colony.[51]
But the threat of insurrection was real enough to lead Chamberlain to
consider the injurious effects of 'raising a sense of injustice and consequent hostility to the Government in the minds of the people.'[52] As
well, Chamberlain feared that the loss of land would lower the dignity
and importance of chiefs, thus threatening indirect rule in Ghana. 'This

consideration alone would, in my opinion, be enough to make us reject the proposed legislation. . . '[53]

While in the end organised African opposition did have some independent effect on the outcome of the lands policy, nevertheless by asserting their opposition in terms of the defence of their traditional rights, Ghanaians bargained away their right to change their forms of land tenure in the future. The ARPS consistently argued that traditionally land was held communally and was inalienable. Essentially, this was correct, but the system was already changing by the 1890s (if not, indeed, earlier) to accommodate itself more fully to the development of cash-crop agricultural production for the world market. After the rescission of the Lands Bill, the colonial state adopted a policy of retaining traditional forms of ownership even when the internal dynamics of the indigenous society demanded change; even when certain tribes were willing to sell land outright to members of certain other tribes, or when chiefs were willing to grant freehold to their subjects because it was recognised that freehold and security of tenure were necessary for the cultivation of cash-crops. Because the Africans' only method of defence had been to counterpoise the traditional against the new society, the internal development of Ghana's productive forces was retarded.

Once a land policy had been established for the Gold Coast Colony, a similar policy was established for Ashanti. In the Northern Territories, however, the government passed the Land and Native Rights Ordinance in 1927, under which all land was 'placed under the control and made subject to the disposition of the Governor for the common use and benefit of the natives,' and the government was responsible for the granting of rights of occupancy to both 'Natives' and 'Non-natives'.[54] As Northern Territories' affairs were not debated in the Legislative Council,[55] opposition to this usurpation of northern rights was difficult to organise. As late as 1938 the regulation of concession in the Northern Territories was not fully legislated and the government operated on an *ad hoc* basis.[56]

The last of the flames caused by direct attempts to take over control of land died, then, by 1897. The basic policy of leaving ownership of land in Ghanaian hands had been established, but land was still a political issue, as became evident when the colonial government attempted to initiate a programme of forest reserves in 1911. The reaction of the African chiefs and educated men was similar to the reaction they had experienced 14 years earlier, and as in the earlier so in the later case, the bill was watered down and eventually reformed.

In 1910 a Forest Bill had been introduced into the Gold Coast Legislative Council which

> enabled the Colonial Secretary of the Colony to grant concessions, leases or licenses on behalf of the owners of the land, and to regulate the gathering of forest produce in a forest reserve, and the sale, or export, of such produce.[57]

The intent of this bill was ostensibly to preserve forests and forest products, and concomitantly the humidity necessary for cocoa plantations, as well as both to safeguard chiefs against 'dirty deals' with European concessionaires and to safeguard the rights of the African people as a whole to use their forests. There was no argument as to the fact that forests were indeed necessary for the ecology of the country, and that without their protective roots soil would erode and water would disappear. What was at issue was the means by which forests should be protected.

The 1910 bill imposed such stringent 'protective' measures on forests that opposition was intense. One opponent, E.J.P. Brown, an African, accused the government of drafting the bill in order to acquire the privileges of compulsory acquisition of land which it had renounced in 1898.[58] Certainly, the bill was drafted in such a way as to imply this, as it provided for measures to compel chiefs to alienate, absolutely and against their will, land deemed by the government to be necessary for forest reserves. In the face of opposition, a milder bill, the Forest Ordinance, which included provisions for chiefs and their people to protest takeovers of their land for reserves, was passed in the Legislative Council on 9 November 1911.[59] This bill provided that the government could set up forest reserves and make a profit from their leasing, or from allowing concessions on them, as long as it adhered to the principles of conservation. Two-fifths of any profits the government made were to go to the owners, the other three-fifths to be retained by the government for administrative purposes.[60]

Although the bill was passed unanimously, there was a great deal of opposition to it, even within the Legislative Council.[61] Ghanaians generally felt that whatever the ostensible reasons for the bill, the government had an ulterior motive not beneficial to the African.

> It is quite evident that from the principles laid down by this Bill, it is wholly and purely a foreign element which is being imposed into Native Customary Laws and for its 'objects and reasons' it is stated

that, it is to establish 'Forest Reserves' and to enable the Government to grant licenses and leases ... but for its 'objects and reasons' where does the Native come in?[62]

The chief issue of debate between Africans and Europeans was deforestation, which in the cocoa areas was having the effect of reducing humidity. The question was whether deforestation was actually the responsibility of Africans. Ghanaians argued that the European-owned mines were as responsible for deforestation in the colony as was the constantly criticised shifting cultivation which the Africans practised. Yet it seemed that the mines were to get off scot-free while tribal authorities made the sacrifice of giving up lands for reserves. There was also much debate over whether or not a mining concession brought with it the right to timber and agricultural produce of the land on which the mine was situated. Mining companies often planted cocoa and rubber trees in cleared areas.[63] By doing so the companies denied access on mining land to Africans, either for shifting cultivation or for the more permanent and profitable cultivation of cash-crops.

By law, the mining companies' concessions granted, as a maximum, the right to use such lumber and timber as was necessary for the mine. But this was often quite an extensive need, encompassing not only construction but also fuel requirements. In 1917 it was estimated that the mines consumed 1,070 acres of forest per year, and it was recommended that 134 square miles of land should be set aside to assure an adequate supply of timber in the future.[64] Nevertheless, the idea that European miners, not Ghanaians, should be responsible for the cost of reforestation was never entertained. '[T]here is no obligation on the Mines authorities to replant. They have leased Forests for the specific purpose of using all the timber they can get out of them, without any provisio that they shall re-stock the denuded areas ... '[65] The African communities were to be responsible for the reforestation of areas which mines had denuded, even though the timber rights of those mines were none too clear in the first place. The cost of such reforestation, to be paid by Africans, was estimated at about £6,400 per square mile in 1917.[66] Further, the chiefs were to create reserves for the mines which were to be completely unproductive from their own point of view, for not only were no rents to be paid on the reserved lands, but also no crops were to be grown on them.

Because of the immense hostility to the Forest Bill, a committee under the chairmanship of Conway Belfield[67] was set up to investigate land tenure and the forest situation in Ghana in 1911. The committee was supposed to be an impartial body, and neither the European business community nor the African community was given representation on it. Nevertheless, Conway Belfield took the unusual step of making a serious effort to encourage testimony to the committee from both educated Ghanaians and chiefs. The picture they built up of the proposed administration of the forest reserve system was one of mistrust and abuse.

The educated Ghanaians criticised the government for trying to set up reserves when an adequate system of forest protection was already extant. The Timber Protection Ordinance prevented the cutting of immature trees below a certain girth and width.[68] If the government had to have timber protection, the Africans argued, the chiefs themselves could take care of the forests. Instead of enacting ordinances, the state could sponsor the education of young African men in forest conservation. Indeed, the ARPS, on its own initiative, had already sponsored such young men in the cocoa industry, but their efforts had been thwarted by the government, which refused to support the Society's candidates for training as indigenous agricultural experts on the grounds that they had only passed Standard Six in their schooling, rather than Standard Seven.[69]

Speaking for his own class of 'modernised' Africans who used land not only for subsistence cultivation but also for cash-crop production, E.J.P. Brown argued that if the government took over forest land, paying only two-fifths of the profit to the original African owners, it would in effect be depriving them of the right to make profits on their own.

> I do not consider the reservation of my land and the payment to me of two-fifths of the profits arising therefrom a matter of public interest to which must be subordinated my private interest, right, and ardent desire to work and improve my own land myself.[70]

Three-fifths of the profit would be going to a government which was free, if it saw fit, to rent out the land, technically only 'reserved' from the Africans, to European entrepreneurs. '[F]oreign speculators ... in the process of time will absorb our lands and thereby reduce us to a landless proletariat fit to work at a wage for the benefit of outsiders ...'[71] In essence, another African argued, '[T]he Forest Bill of 1911 ... introduces the same encroachments on the people's proprietary rights which were objected to in 1894 and again in 1897.'[72] Reinforcing the arguments of the ARPS, chief after chief complained to the Belfield Commission, always asking the same question, why they could not be allowed to take care of the forests themselves, with the help of their educated young men.

> We should be glad if the Government would send us instructors to teach us how to improve our forests, but we wish to manage them ourselves. I admit that we have never taken steps to improve our forests, in fact at present we do not understand the management of forest lands ... [But] I should not be satisfied with any arrangements which do not give to the people the sole control of the forests.[73]

The masses of testimony presented against the 1911 Forest Bill convinced Conway Belfield that it must be revised. He recommended that the government not be permitted to lease land, but only to employ the reserved land for its own use. Further, the state should not be allowed to retain three-fifths of the profits, but only as much of the profit as was absolutely necessary to cover the costs of administration. Finally, he recommended that a maximum be set on the percentage of stool land which could be reserved so that no tribe would find itself without a sufficient supply of common land.[74]

Because of the many submissions against it, backed up by Belfield's recommendations, the Forest Bill itself was never implemented. The 1910s were taken up by preoccupation with the European war, and the issue of forest conservation was left in abeyance until Governor Guggisberg took over the colony in 1919. Guggisberg was a strong believer in forest conservation and he decided to implement the long-delayed system of reserves. His policy was originally 'to trust the Chiefs entirely with the formation and administration of those reserves which are considered necessary by the Forestry Officers and which are set aside after mutual agreement between them and the Chiefs.'[75] However, it soon became apparent that not enough reserves were being set up by the chiefs on their own initiative, and after a great many threats, Guggisberg had a Forestry Ordinance passed on 3 March 1927. It maintained the rights of owners and did not override by-laws made by tribal authorities as long as such laws were satisfactorily administered. The government was to supervise and maintain reserves constituted either under the Forestry Ordinance or under by-laws, and one-third of the revenue was to be used for improvement. The owners could grant concessions to work minerals or timber in a reserve, but the government would supervise such concessions to ensure fairness.[76] By 1938, 5,659 square miles of some 30,000 square miles of forest land in the Gold Coast had been constituted or approved as reserve land.[77]

The defeat of the 1911 Forest Bill represented a consolidation of the African position that land in Ghana could not be usurped either by the state or by expatriate entrepreneurs, even for such an ostensibly beneficial purpose as preserving forests. Suspicion of European motives was deeply engrained. Although the 1897 Lands Bill had been defeated, legislation had been passed in 1900 by the colonial government to regulate concessions made to Europeans, usually for mining purposes. While the Concessions Ordinance preserved Ghanaian property rights, many Ghanaians felt that its provisions were too liberal and allowed too much land to be made available to Europeans, for too long, and at rents which were too low. It was the implementation of the Concessions Ordinance which perpetuated Ghanaian suspicions of European motives with regard to land as late as 1911, and indeed beyond.

The Concessions Ordinance was originally a result of pressure by gold speculators on the Colonial Office to institute regulations so that large companies such as Ashanti Goldfields (with its one hundred square mile concession) could not dominate the entire Ghanaian mining industry. It limited the size of concessions to five square miles for mineral lands, and twenty square miles for timber, rubber, or other products, with a maximum length of 99 years. (Ashanti Goldfields, however, having already obtained its lease, was exempt from these provisions.)[78] The 1900 law applied only to the Gold Coast Colony, but a similar law was enacted in Ashanti in 1903. In the Northern Territories, no Concession Ordinance was enacted; the government simply had the right to grant concessions as it saw fit; however, by 1910 the total area leased in the North was less than one acre.[79]

The limitation of lease rights to 99 years was regarded by some Europeans as a drag upon their enterprise; they felt that they should be allowed to work their lands in perpetuity. To many Ghanaians, however, 99 years was more time than they could fathom; in essence it meant that land was being signed away not only for the original owners' lifetimes, but also for the lifetimes of their children and grandchildren. The feeling among these Ghanaians was that usufruct should be returned to a man's family; that he should not be able to or required to sign away his family's rights as well as his own. 'I . . . consider the term of ninety-nine years too long because the land will not come back to the people now living.'[80] Africans also objected to the Concessions Ordinance because the limitations on land holdings to twenty square miles for agriculture and five square miles for mining were often exceeded. By law no one concessionaire, either an individual or a company, could hold more than two concessions, but the practice of setting up dummy corporations to acquire options on land to be held for future use soon became prevalent in Ghana. Even without the setting up of such dummy corporations, however, the chiefs soon began to feel that too much land was being alienated. Few had any accurate idea of what exactly a square mile was, and European administrators did not visit the Africans' lands to point out to them in detail just how much land they were alienating. In testimony to the Belfield Commission, many chiefs stated that had they known the extent of a square mile, they would never have alienated their land. Chief Esselkojo of Appinto, in the Tarkwa area, for instance, said 'I do not know what a square mile is. Sometimes I have given more land than I intended, and if I had known the true extent I would have given less.'[81] Chief Kobina Foli of Adansi agreed.

> Before signing the agreement I appear before the Commissioner to have the document explained to me. He describes the area in square miles, so we are not much wiser then. The Commissioner never visits the land. I should like a local officer to visit it and explain the boundaries to me.[82]

By 1911, concessions on land appeared to be a very serious business indeed, since in some parts of the Colony, there was more land under option (that is, to which a concessionaire had first rights if he so desired them) than there was actual land in existence. *In toto*, concessions on only about 880 square miles of land (out of 23,490 square miles) in the Gold Coast Colony had been completely validated but another 3,000 square miles were 'under notice'.[83] While some chiefs seemed deliberately to be granting options two or three times over on the same land, others simply had no idea of the extent of the land they were alienating or indeed whether the land was theirs to alienate in the first place. Boundary disputes arose with alarming frequency as neighbouring chiefs discovered that they were alienating the same land, and each wanted to retain the land as his own so that he could have payment for it. By 1923, the Colonial Office estimated that 3,000 square miles of land in the colony (or one-eighth of the total land surface) were under valid concessions.[84] But of these concessions, only

1,840 square miles were being worked; moreover, a further 6,000 square miles had been granted during the Colony's history but had then lapsed, been invalidated or abandoned. Land was being 'overalienated'; more land was being removed from the supply available to Ghanaians, either for cultivation of cash-crops or for subsistence agriculture, than was needed by the expatriates. As a result 'areas available for the casual agriculturalist are becoming more restricted and the whole tendency is towards individual ownership by native proprietors.'[85]

Fortune hunters from Europe were the originators of this practice of overalienation. Ghana was known to have large deposits of gold, although at the time, in the late 1890s and early 1900s, such land was often unworkable because of the difficulties of transport and of obtaining labour. In order that potential gold land be not lost to them, Europeans would arrange to have lease options, tying land up at minimal option rents of perhaps five or ten pounds a square mile, until they saw fit to actually lease and hopefully work it. There was no legal regulation as to how long an option could exist before it lapsed, nor was there any way a chief could compel a European either to take up the option or to forgo the land.

Land so tied up was often used for speculative purposes in Britain; gullible investors bought options thinking that the options ensured them actual ownership of Gold Coast land, unaware that by law they could never do more than rent the land in question for 99 years. Concessions granted by chiefs were being used in Europe to induce investors to finance companies when there was no proof either that the government would validate the concession or that the land contained what it was purported to contain by way of exploitable resources. In 1904 the Legislative Council passed some regulations to counteract this practice, since in that year alone there were some 3,000 'enquiries' on the Court lists, that is, concessions for which the claimants had merely filed claims and gone no further.[86]

The government feared both fraud and a sudden rush for validation of claims, but its attempts to stem such frauds were partially stymied by complaints from legitimate investors in the Gold Coast that any public announcements about fraudulent concessions could also affect them.[87] Thus during the period of this gold boom both expatriates and Ghanaians were able to make money peddling worthless concessions. There were incidents of Ghanaians' manufacturing fake samples of auriferous gold, and then requesting a fee, called 'knockdoor' money, before conducting interested Europeans to the areas where the fake gold was alleged to have been found. Other Ghanaians set themselves up as 'princes' and sold concessions over areas to which they had no legal rights whatsoever.[88] Fortunately, no sudden rush for validation of these fraudulent concessions occurred, as the Ghana gold rush declined very quickly. 'Only the failure of the expected gold mining boom to materialise saved the people from at least a century of land starvation.'[89] Had all the options on land granted by the chiefs been validated, it is possible that very little, if any land at all, would have been left for peasant cultivators. As it was, one of every eight square miles of land in the colony was under concessions in 1923.

Even on land where legitimate concessions had been granted, very little profit was made by Ghanaians after the concessions had been validated by the courts and after the boundaries had been clearly defined. Concessions rents were always very low, in order to encourage European investment and speculation. The few mines, such as Ashanti Goldfields, which made large profits were not obliged to pay proportional rents. Mines were simply obliged to pay 5 per cent of their profits in royalties to the colonial government (but such royalties were not necessarily retained in the colony for its own use). 'Consideration money', that is, money paid to Africans in order to have the right to negotiate a concession, usually amounted to about £50 for five square miles with a £10 per annum occupation fee until the concession was actually worked. In times of boom, especially during the 'gold rushes' of the late 1890s and the 1930s (when the price of gold was allowed to float on the open market) the amount of consideration money was raised and chiefs often received bribes, occasionally as high as £5000.[90] During the time that the concession was worked, rents varied from £100 to £300 per annum.[91]

Concessions were frequently worked without the consent of the government, and without government validation rents were lower than they otherwise would have been.[92] Moreover, the concessionaires frequently abused the provisions of the concessions by renting out parts of their concessions to other Europeans, for instance, for trading posts. Such extra rents were supposed to be paid not to the Europeans, but to the original African owners. Chief Esselkojo of Appinto complained to the Belfield Commission about this practice.

> I wish to complain that in the case of the Tarquah concession the concessionaires have allowed white people to build houses and shops on land forming part of the concession, and, inasmuch as their surface rights are restricted to such as are appurtenant to

mining, I think the rent should come to me instead of being appropriated by them. . .[93]

In general, concessions were viewed not as means for Africans to make profits which could then be invested in money-making ventures or self-improvement schemes of their own, but as a means to further the development of the Gold Coast through European investment. Even Conway Belfield, whose commission of investigation into land law in Ghana certainly took seriously Ghanaians' complaints of abuse, and who tried to remedy these abuses as best he could, saw the object of the Commission as primarily to 'expedite the process of alienation [of land] and reduce the expense of acquisition . . .'[94] While Africans argued that the rents charged for concessions were too low, the European companies seemed to feel that the expenses of obtaining concessions were too great. There were, for example, continual disputes between the government and prospecting firms as to who should be responsible for surveying concession land; the firms argued that by putting the onus of such work on them the government was getting a free survey of the land,[95] while the government argued that the opposite was true. Similarly, investors complained that the 5 per cent royalty was too high, and suggested that 1 per cent was a more reasonable figure.[96] The general belief of the firms was that no obstacle should be put in their way, since only through European investment would the colony develop (even though by the mid-1910s it was obvious that the economy was rapidly expanding through African investment in cocoa, rubber, and palm oil production). The state, on the other hand, was concerned to protect its own interests, to make sure that royalties on minerals were paid and to ensure that it did not itself have to pay the costs of granting concessions.

The state, moreover, had already protected its own interests with regard to the alienation of land by passing the Public Lands Act in 1876. This act permitted the government to take over lands for public purposes, such as roads, railways, hospitals or administrative buildings, without compensation to the owners. While both Europeans and Africans agreed to the need to allow the government the right to expropriate land for public purposes, there were complaints throughout the colonial period about abuses connected with this practice. In 1897 the government was obliged to pay compensation when it expropriated the land of an independent European mining company, the Ahanta Company, without going through even the formalities of the 1876 Act. Until the Company pressed its claims for compensation this practice had apparently been quite common, as a confidential circular from the Acting Colonial Secretary indicated.

> Several recent instances [have] been brought to the Governor's notice of private land being occupied, and even built on, by some Government Department, without any proper steps being taken to acquire the land beforehand, either by arrangement with the owner or under the provisions of the 'Public Lands Ordinance, 1878' [1876].[97]

Until 1919, the government not only took over land for public use without compensation but also took the liberty of disposing of it, as it saw fit, to other Europeans, often charging them rent for the use of these 'public' lands. In fact, most of the land on which the European firms erected their bungalows and trading houses was owned by the state and they paid rents for it to the state. The firms disliked this system and continually pressed for the right to hold freehold land for commercial buildings.[98] But freehold rights were never granted since they would infringe on the principle of African ownership of land. Only the state was allowed to take over ownership.

But to Africans, government use of land often meant abuse, especially when they could see that the colonial state profited from its right to occupy expropriated land. Although as late as 1932 the governor could argue that *in toto*, the state owned only 52 square miles of land in the Colony, including all the land needed for the railways,[99] some of this 52 square miles was prime urban land. Had Ghanaians had the right to rent out that land to the Europeans themselves, instead of watching the state expropriate it for 'public' purposes and then rent it out on its own terms to its European compatriots, it was felt, considerable fortunes might have been made.

As a result of frequent public protests over the state's appropriation of urban land, Governor Guggisberg changed the practice in 1919.

> We have done away once and for all with the old policy of the Government taking up land and sub-letting it afterwards and holding on to the rent themselves. The natives are going to have the benefit of land rented to merchants, for that is a fair return to them for having given the land rented to Government for Government purposes.[100]

But Guggisberg's reversal of the rental policy on public lands was again overturned. When A.W. Kojo Thompson, a consistent critic of the government on this point, questioned the Colonial Office in 1938, he was told 'Sometimes it is deemed expedient to dispose of certain portions of such [public] land by way of exchange, or to benefit public revenue by leasing Crown land which is lying unused.'[101] Had the Ghanaian petty bourgeoisie been able to bargain directly with the expatriate entrepreneurs who used urban land, instead of bargaining indirectly through the government and during long periods forgoing rent as well, they might have been able to make tidy fortunes in urban real estate which could then have been invested in other enterprises. Similarly, had they been compensated for the use of land for roads and railways, small fortunes could have been made in the countryside. The development of an indigenous bourgeoisie was inhibited, in this instance, by government restrictions on the operation of free market forces.

And indeed, the whole situation with regard to land in Ghana was anomalous. In order to prevent their complete expropriation, from 1897 on Africans were obliged to defend the preservation of traditional rights in land, successfully arguing their case in both 1897 and 1911. But in arguing for the preservation of their traditional rights against the encroachment of the Europeans, educated Africans used a defense which was already, to some extent, outmoded. The preservation of traditional property rights was at the expense of the possible developments of new forms of ownership which would have been more conducive to individual private profit for Africans participating in the world economic system. The internal economic development of the country was, therefore, retarded. A choice had to be made between allowing private property relations to develop freely, with the concomitant risk that the Europeans, with their greater resources, would then take over all property, and protecting traditional property relations into which the Europeans could not intrude, at the expense of possible internal capitalist development. The African political community chose the latter option, reflecting the continued insecurity of Ghanaians with regard to British motives, and the constant fear that their hard-won rights to ownership of land would be abrogated.

> Policy in other countries is closely watched. The native will often refer to conditions in South Africa, and will express fear that here, as there, the native landowner eventually will be displaced to make room for the European ... It is not unusual to be asked by an

illiterate native 'what did the Government do with the land in Kenya?'[102]

The basis of Ghana's peripheral economy was to become cash-crop production for the world market by independent peasants, but the very existence of this peasant class was a result of vigilant and continued defence of their rights by Ghanaians.

Notes

1. There had, however, been some contact between Europe and the West African coast in pre-Christian times. The records of Herodotus suggest that the Ancient Phoenicians rounded West Africa and reached the Gold Coast around the sixth century BC. W. Walton Claridge, *A History of the Gold Coast and Ashanti*, (Frank Cass, London, 1964, 1st edn. 1915), p. 14.
2. Sylvia Harrop, 'The Economy of the West African Coast in the Sixteenth Century', *The Economic Bulletin of Ghana*, Vol. 8, Nos. 3 and 4 (1964), No. 4, p. 23.
3. J.D. Fage, *A History of West Africa* (Cambridge University Press, Cambridge, 1969), p. 59.
4. Harrop, 'The Economy', No. 4, p. 23.
5. Quoted in Walter Rodney, 'Gold and Slaves on the Gold Coast', *Transactions of the Historical Society of Ghana*, Vol. 10 (1969), p. 19. The entire section on the incompatibility of the gold and slave trades is based on this article.
6. Eric Williams, *Capitalism and Slavery* (Capricorn Books, New York, 1966, 1st edn. 1944).
7. For a description of the concept of 'plunder', see Wallerstein, *The Modern World-System*, pp. 335–6.
8. Walter Rodney, *How Europe Underdeveloped Africa* (Tanzania Publishing House, Dar es Salaam, 1972), p. 113.
9. Robin Hallett, 'The European Approach to the Interior of Africa in the Eighteenth Century', *Journal of African History*, Vol. 4, No. 2 (1963), p. 196.
10. Sir Matthew Nathan, 'The Gold Coast at the End of the Seventeenth Century under the Danes and Dutch', *Journal of the African Society*, Vol. 4, No. 13 (1904–5). Many of the 'forts' were actually simply tiny trading stations with perhaps two or three men.
11. Sir Matthew Nathan, 'Historical Chart of the Gold Coast and Ashanti', *Journal of the African Society*, Vol. 4, No. 13 (1904–5), pp. 40, 42.
12. Williams, *Capitalism and Slavery*, p. 149.
13. John Gallagher and Ronald Robinson, 'The Imperialism of Free Trade', *Economic History Review*, 2nd. Series, Vol. 6, No. 1 (December 1953), p. 1.
14. H.J. Bevin, 'The Gold Coast Economy about 1880', *Transactions of the Gold Coast and Togoland Historical Society*, Vol. 2, pt. 2 (1956), p. 73.
15. J.B. Webster and A.A. Boahen, *The Revolutionary Years: West Africa Since 1800* (Longmans, London, 1967), p. 61.
16. Ibid., p. 71.
17. J.D. Fage, *Ghana, A Historical Interpretation* (University of Wisconsin Press, Madison, 1961), p. 61.
18. Samir Amin, 'Underdevelopment and Dependence in Black Africa: Historical Origin', *Journal of Peace Research*, No. 2 (1972), p. 113, italics in

original.
19. R. Szereszewski, *Structural Changes in the Economy of Ghana 1891–1911* (Weidenfeld and Nicolson, London, 1965), p. 5.
20. Stavenhagen, *Social Classes*, p. 65.
21. 'Grievances of the Gold Coast Chiefs', dated 9 August 1864, in G.E. Metcalfe, *Great Britain and Ghana: Documents of Ghana History 1807–1957* (Thomas Nelson and Sons, London, 1964), pp. 300–1.
22. Edward Reynolds, 'Trade and Economic Change on the Gold Coast, 1807–74', unpublished PhD thesis, University of London, 1971, p. 125.
23. 'Observations on the State of Trade at the Several British Forts on the Gold Coast, 1814–1815', quoted in Metcalfe, *Great Britain*, p. 30.
24. Bevin, 'The Gold Coast Economy', p. 73.
25. Ibid., p. 74.
26. Quoted in J.E. Casely Hayford, *Gold Coast Native Institutions* (Frank Cass, London, 1970, 1st edn. 1903), p. 366.
27. Ronald Robinson and John Gallagher, *Africa and the Victorians: The Unofficial Mind of Imperialism* (Macmillan, London, 1961), p. 462.
28. Letters from the Cape Coast Chamber of Commerce to the Manchester Chamber of Commerce, reported in ManCC, 6 February 1895.
29. ManCC, 10 January 1894.
30. H.R. Fox Bourne, *Blacks and Whites in West Africa* (P.S. King and Son, London, 1901), p. 41.
31. Statement by King Prempeh concerning mining in Kumasi, 1 March 1896. CO 879/46 no. 513.
32. CO 879/57 no. 578.
33. For a discussion of the scramble for Africa, the reader is referred to Raymond F. Betts (ed.), *The 'Scramble' for Africa: Causes and Dimensions of Empire* (D.C. Heath, Lexington, Massachusetts, 1966).
34. This analysis follows the description of the results of land alienation in early capitalist Europe by Maurice Dobb in *Studies in the Development of Capitalism* (International Publishers, New York, 1963, 1st. edn. 1947).
35. G. Benneh, 'The Impact of Cocoa Cultivation on the Traditional Land Tenure System of the Akan of Ghana', *Ghana Journal of Sociology*, Vol. 6, No. 1 (February 1970), pp. 45–6.
36. Letter from J.J. Hutchison, Chief Justice, to the Governor, 7 April 1891, in CO 879/46 no. 513.
37. 'Report upon the Customs Relating to the Tenure of Land on the Gold Coast' (Waterlow and Sons, London, 1895), p. 16.
38. Olufemi Omosini, 'The Gold Coast Land Question 1894–1900: Some Issues Raised on West Africa's Economic Development', *International Journal of African Historical Studies*, Vol. 5 (1972), p. 457.
39. J.E. Casely Hayford, *The Truth About the West African Land Question* (Frank Cass, London, 1971, 1st edn. 1913), p. 2.
40. In 1895, there were only eight gold mining companies with interests in Ghana listed in the *Stock Exchange Yearbook*. But by 1905, there were 153. *Stock Exchange Yearbook* (London, 1895 and 1905).
41. GCLegCo, 14 November 1894.
42. Ibid.
43. David Kimble, *A Political History of Ghana, 1850–1928* (Clarendon Press, Oxford, 1963), p. 340.
44. GCLegCo, May–June 1897.
45. Kimble, *A Political History*, p. 388.
46. 'Report of the Proceedings of the Deputation from the Kings and Chiefs of the Western Province of the Gold Coast' (Morris Cripp and Co., London, 1898).

47. James H. Brew to Colonial Office, 6 February 1896, despatch 3070 no. 60, CO 879/46.
48. For instance, the issue of the Sedition and Water Works Ordinances of 1934. See Francis Agbodeka, *Ghana in the Twentieth Century* (Ghana Universities Press, Accra, 1972), p. 115.
49. Letter from lawyers of the Aborigines Rights Protection Society to the Under-Secretary of State, the Colonial Office, 18 August 1898. Included in 'Report of the ... [ARPS] Delegation', p. 16.
50. R.W. Perks to the Colonial Office, 21 May 1897, despatch 10868 no. 116, in CO 879/49.
51. Omosini, 'Gold Coast Land Question', p. 462.
52. Memorandum by Joseph Chamberlain in CO 879/76, no. 513.
53. Ibid.
54. Gold Coast, *Colonial Report*, 1927–8, p. 44.
55. The Powers of the Legislative Council are explained below, Chapter 5.
56. Memorandum dated 11 February 1938, CO 98/37.
57. Allan McPhee, *The Economic Revolution in British West Africa* (Frank Cass, London, 1971, 1st. edn. 1926), p. 148.
58. 'Report on the Legislation Governing the Alienation of Native Lands in the Gold Coast Colony and Ashanti, 1911' (hereafter referred to as the Belfield Report); (London, 1912), p. 99.
59. 'Report of the Committee on the Tenure of Land in West African Colonies and Protectorates', (hereafter referred to as the Digby Report), (London, 1917), p. 284.
60. GCLegCo, 9 November 1911.
61. Although the majority of its members were Europeans, the Legislative Council had a few Ghanaian members. See Chapter 5.
62. Nene Mate Kole of Krobo, in GCLegCo, 13 September 1911.
63. Belfield Report, p. 35.
64. 'Papers Relating to Re-afforestation of Areas which have been denuded of Forest by the Requirements of the Mines and of the Railway' (Gold Coast, Government Press, Accra, 1918). Report by N.C. McLeod, Conservator of Forests, 25 March 1917, p. 4.
65. Ibid., p. 5.
66. Ibid., p. 7.
67. Cited above as the Belfield Report.
68. Belfield Report, testimony of E.J.P. Brown, p. 111.
69. Ibid., p. 109.
70. Ibid., p. 111.
71. Ibid., p. 109.
72. Ibid., testimony of J.E. Casely Hayford, p. 102.
73. Ibid., testimony of Amanhin Mensah of Elmina, p. 117.
74. Ibid., report by Belfield, pp. 7, 38, 39–41.
75. GCLegCo, 6 March 1924.
76. Ibid.
77. F.M. Bourret, *Ghana, the Road to Independence, 1919–1957* (Oxford University Press, London, 1960), p. 126.
78. R.E. Dumett, 'British Official Attitudes in Relation to Economic Development in the Gold Coast, 1874–1905', unpublished PhD thesis, University of London, 1966, p. 229.
79. McPhee, *Economic Revolution*, p. 188.
80. Belfield Report, testimony of Kobina Foli, Omanhene of Adansi, p. 97.
81. Ibid., p. 76.
82. Ibid., p. 97.

83. Ibid., p. 11.
84. Report on concessions, by the Land and Boundaries Section, dated 30 March 1926, in CO 96/6630.
85. 'Land Tenure in the Gold Coast', report signed by R.H. Rowe, Surveyor-General, 18 February 1926, in CO 96/6630.
86. GCLegCo, speech by the Chief Justice, 25 July 1904.
87. Correspondence between Mr J. Simpson and the Colonial Office, 28 November 1901, 42171 no. 176, CO 879/67, no. 652.
88. Enclosure No. 1 in 35826 no. 147, signed by C.A. O'Brien, CO 879/67 no. 652.
89. Charles U. Ilegbune, 'Concessions Scramble and Land Alienation in British Southern Ghana, 1885–1915', *African Studies Review*, Vol. 29, No. 3 (December 1976), p. 27.
90. Interview with a former British barrister, Accra, May 1974.
91. Belfield report, testimony of Giles Hunt, p. 65.
92. Digby Report, p. 141.
93. Belfield Report, p. 76.
94. Ibid., p. 25.
95. GCLegCo, speech by Mr Osborne, a European unofficial member, 17 December 1901.
96. LivCC, 48th Annual Report, 1898, p. 155.
97. GNA, file Adm. 11/1461. Confidential Circular no. 52-1906/6327, 12 December 1906.
98. JWAC, 27 November 1907.
99. GCLegCo, 1 March 1932.
100. GCLegCo, 17 November 1919.
101. Reply by Colonial Office to A.W. Kojo Thompson, 2 September 1938, CO 98/37.
102. 'Land Tenure in the Gold Coast', report signed by R.H. Rowe, Surveyor-General, 18 February 1926, in CO 96/6630.

3 THE CREATION OF GHANA'S PERIPHERAL CAPITALIST ECONOMY

Peripheral capitalism, in a colonial economy, is characterised by a high degree of integration into the world capitalist market, but a low degree of development of the capitalist mode of production internally. The economy is not 'autocentric' (to borrow a term used by Samir Amin),[1] the internal market is underdeveloped while external dependence is exaggerated. Production inside the peripheral social formation is for profit, but this profit is obtained through international trade, not through the creation of surplus-value consequent upon the exploitation of labour-power in capitalist production. Producers are not alienated from their means of production; they can continue to own their own tools and, as in the case of Ghana, their land. Capitalist social relations are incompletely formed, although new social classes begin to emerge as producers differentiate into rich and poor, and as groups of brokers and traders emerge to complement the activities of the metropolitan bourgeoisie.

Ghana's peripheral status during the colonial period was characterised specifically by its heavy reliance on the import-export trade. Production both of minerals and cash-crops was geared completely to the international world market. Consumption, while provided for at least partially by the indigenous pre-capitalist sector, became more and more dependent on foreign-manufactured imports as the period progressed. By 1915, Ghana, with its heavy reliance on cocoa exports, could be classified as a 'monocultural' economy, in the sense that although it exported more than one crop, cocoa determined its overall economic prosperity. The nature of cocoa as a consumer good, which played a relatively unimportant role in the world economic system and had no use at all in industrial production, meant that Ghana was highly dependent on economic swings in the world cocoa market.

This chapter will describe the emergence of the basic features of Ghana's peripheral economy in the early colonial period. After the land issue had been settled, it was possible to implement the system of independent peasant cultivation for the market. At the same time, European entrepreneurs could set up their mines for export production. There was very little structural change in the Ghanaian economy as a whole: it started and ended the colonial era as a peripheral economy highly dependent on imports and exports.

1. The Development of the Mining Industry

The colonial name for Ghana was the 'Gold Coast', and the name reflects the economic history of the area. The Portuguese first came to Ghana in search of gold; gold remained an important export commodity throughout the period of the slave trade; and when the British took over formal political control gold was one of their chief reasons for doing so. Throughout the colonial period, gold remained one of Ghana's major exports. Table 3.1 indicates that for 25 of the 55 years covered in this study, it constituted over 20 per cent, by value, of Ghana's exports. From 1905 to 1914 it constituted about one-third, by value, of the country's exports, as it did again in the late 1930s, at the end of the Depression era, when a rise in the price of gold was accompanied by a decline in demand for Ghana's non-mineral exports.

Table 3.1 also indicates that gold was not the only mineral export of Ghana; in 1916 Ghana began to export manganese, and from 1924 diamonds were also exported. Both these minerals soon became significant, if not major, contributors to Ghana's foreign exchange earnings. The production of manganese was controlled entirely by Europeans, but about half of Ghana's diamond production was attributable to the activities of Ghanaian 'diamond winners'. The distribution of diamonds, however, was controlled by expatriates.

The history of the gold mining industry of Ghana is the history of the takeover of an indigenous industry by a group of expatriates who, because they possessed superior technology, were easily able to displace the original producers. Gold was mined on an active basis in Ghana long before the first European entrepreneurs negotiated concessions for mines in the early 1870s, but the final result of the negotiation of such concessions in the late nineteenth century was the elimination of indigenous mining enterprises. As one British adventurer, Sir Richard Burton, wrote in his account of his Gold Coast explorations, many prospecting licenses granted to Europeans were simply licenses to take over mining in areas in which it was already known that African mining activity existed. Shaft mining was common among these Ghanaian producers, contrary to the generally held belief that their level of technical skill had not reached beyond the level of 'women's washings', or panning. Burton, for instance, saw one shaft in the centre of a concession at the Apatim valley. This African mining enterprise had shafts twelve feet square and 55 feet deep over an area 2,000 by 1,000 yards

Table 3.1: Gold, Diamonds and Manganese as Percentages of Total Ghana Exports by Value, by Five-Year Averages, 1885–1939

Years	Total Exports (£000s)	Gold		Diamonds		Manganese		Total Minerals	
		Value (£000s)	% Total Exports By Value	Value (£000s)	% Total Exports By Value	Value (£000s)	% Total Exports By Value	Value (£000s)	% Total Exports By Value
1885–89	394	87	22	–	–	–	–	87	22
1890–94	704	87	13	–	–	–	–	87	13
1895–99	927	75	8	–	–	–	–	75	8
1900–04	908	152	15	–	–	–	–	152	15
1905–09	2293	931	40	–	–	–	–	931	40
1910–14	4233	1314	31	–	–	–	–	1314	31
1915–19	6682	1489	24	–	–	37	1	1526	25
1920–24	9300	872	10	17	0	208	2	1097	12
1925–29	12769	758	6	429	3	681	5	1868	14
1930–34	9020	1616	19	582	6	435	4	2633	29
1935–39	14097	4123	29	558	4	790	6	5471	39

Sources: Raw figures for 1885–99 from Gold Coast, *Blue Books*. For 1900–39 from Geoffrey Kay, *The Political Economy of Colonialism in Ghana* (Cambridge University Press, London, 1972), Table 18, p. 325, 'Imports, exports, and the balance of visible trade, 1900–1960', and Table 21a, pp. 334–35, 'Value of major exports, 1900–1960'. NB – = no exports; 0 = some exports but less than 0.5%. Averages for 1885–89 are calculated on the basis of figures for 1886–89 only, as the figures given in the *Blue Books* for 1885 are grossly inconsistent with figures for the rest of the century and have been presumed to be in error.

62   *The Creation of Ghana's Peripheral Capitalist Economy*

square, and as many as 2,000 people had been known to work there at one time.[2] The generally held belief was that the Appolonia tribe worked these shafts, having learned the elements of this type of mining from the Portuguese centuries before.[3]

In a 1932 history of the Ashanti Goldfields Corporation, G.W.E. Turner quoted an oral account of African methods of gold mining, obtained, he stated, from 'a very old man'.

> [B]efore the White Man came to Obuasi the Appolonians used to sink pit until they found the hard rock, when they pile firewood in the pits and set fire to this. When the fire is wasted, then they carry water in big pots and pour down into the pits until the fire goes out. They wait for a day or two until the pit gets cool before they go down again and with hammer or something of the kind they break the walls, then having become quite loose and very easily broken up owing to the fire they burned. Then they bring all the stone up and divide them into three parts, one of which is given to the Chief of that land.[4]

But while Ghanaians mined gold on their own, either by the panning method, chiefly confined to women, or by shafts, their methods were hardly as sophisticated as the Europeans'. Nevertheless, they quickly picked up European techniques. Burton reported that as soon as Ghanaians learned how to 'bore and blast' from him, 'thefts of powder, drills, and fuses became every day more common,'[5] as his African employees stole off at night to use his techniques on their own shafts. For the same reason the Frenchman Bonnat, renowned in Ghanaian histories as the negotiator of the large Tarkwa mining concession,[6] deliberately refused to make pumps available to Africans when they asked for them. Bonnat, referring to the Ghanaians working the Tarkwa mines, wrote in his journal in 1879:

> This has been a very profitable year for them; but their galleries are getting very deep; and when the wet season sets in, not being able to drain them, they will have to abandon them. This will be all the better for us; for a time will come when we shall reach those galleries from our tunnel and easily drain them; all will then be in our possession...[7]

Another expatriate miner, one Major-General Wray, wrote of the African miners:

One man assured us that he estimated his daily outrun, with two others, at £40. He was most importunate in begging us to sell him a pump at any price, as of late his operations had been entirely suspended by the entry of water into his shaft.[8]

Despite the handicaps they faced, several early attempts were made by educated Africans to set up modern industrial gold mines, rather than allow the industry to fall straight into the hands of the Europeans. The Tarkwa gold area, later to house several European firms, was originally taken as a concession by Dr J. Africanus Horton, an African physician in the employ of the West African Medical Service, in conjunction with one Mr Fitzgerald, British publisher of the *African Times* and an enthusiastic supporter of indigenous African enterprise.[9] These two entrepreneurs formed the Gold Coast Mining Company in 1880, after Horton had already spent over two years going 'round the country inland from Axim persuading rulers to grant him mining concessions.'[10] But the Company failed for want of technology. At a meeting of the Society of Arts in London in 1882, Horton pleaded for technical aid to save the African Gold Coast Company and the Effentua Company, both his own concerns. The first company, he said, 'did its work well, but unfortunately they had not the machinery which would bring good dividends to the shareholders.'[11] At Effentua, 'They had four different places, and shafts in another place, and it was only the want of proper machinery to raise the water from the valley up to where the stamping machinery was, which prevented their paying large dividends . . .'[12] Because of his inability to obtain machinery and financial backing, Horton, like other African entrepreneurs, was obliged to stand aside and watch as Europeans quickly made concessions over all the gold land of Ashanti.

The Europeans who first made concessions for gold mining did so in areas where mining already was taking place, and they reached these areas not through their own intrepid exploring, but rather with the help of hired African guides.[13] The chiefs who negotiated concessions were accustomed to receiving tribute from the indigenous miners, but some concluded that the rents which the Europeans were willing to pay would be more than their indigenous miners, with their less sophisticated methods, would be able to pay. Referring to the Apatim concession, Burton wrote:

Its lessor had forbidden his fraudulent people to prospect or to mine, because, as usual, they systematically robbed him of his royalty. This universal practice has made the kings and chiefs throughout the country ready and even anxious to sell mining lands for small sums which will be paid honestly and regularly.[14]

But although it would have suited the purposes of the British to be able to contend that all chiefs willingly rented their gold land to expatriate concessionaires, such was not the case. As already observed in Chapter 2, it was necessary to fight a war of conquest to obtain access to the almost mythologically famous Ashanti mines, which King Prempeh adamantly refused to give up.[15]

By the 1890s, gold mining in Ghana was an exclusively expatriate enterprise. A two-tiered arrangement of mines quickly developed and was the pattern until the Second World War. The two tiers consisted of a few large, consistently profitable firms, and a large number of small, unprofitable, almost 'fly-by-night' firms. A plethora of small companies emerged at about the turn of the century when a false report on the gold-mining prospects of Ghana combined with the South African war to divert much mining capital to investment in the former colony. In the Annual Report of the Gold Coast for 1898 the government, probably influenced by fabulous reports of the legendary wealth of Ashanti, stated that there was enough gold in the Western Province for £40,000,000 worth to be extracted in ten years, at an annual profit of one and one-quarter million pounds. A 'jungle boom' ensued and over 400 companies were formed to exploit Ghana's gold by 1901.[16]

Although the 400 companies registered in 1901 represented a high point in gold speculation in Ghana, they were typical of the many small firms which were to emerge and re-emerge throughout the colonial period, often dissolving themselves and then re-forming under slightly different names. Their subscribed capital rarely approximated their declared capital, and investors frequently lost their entire investment. An investigation of the Stock Exchange Yearbook at ten-year intervals reveals that while there were only eight public gold mines listed for 1885 and only three for 1895, in 1905 there were 153, in 1915 sixty-seven, in 1925 forty-three, and in 1939 forty-nine companies registered as having interests in mining gold in Ghana. Aside from these companies there were many others which were never listed as public concerns.

Many of these mines failed because they were no more than prospecting ventures which never actually struck gold. For example, the Gold Coast Selection Trust Limited spent a total of some £108,000 on prospecting its concession; but no gold was ever found.[17] Other mines failed because they simply did not have the capital necessary for their investments; operating often on shoestring budgets, one major loss could break them. The important Abontiakoon Mine, for example, was liquidated in 1927 after the mine flooded because the crank shaft on the main engine broke and there was no money for repairs.[18] Only Ashanti Goldfields and the mines which had very large holdings in the Tarkwa area of Ghana were able to make any substantial profits in the industry. Over the 19-year period from 1912 to 1931, only four mines produced over £3 million worth of gold.[19]

The first mining boom, around 1900, was followed by a second 'boom', somewhat more subdued in style, in the 1930s when the fixed price of gold was removed and profits rose dramatically, causing many formerly unremunerative mines to re-enter production.[20] Also during the 1930s the gold-mining industry as a whole became somewhat more organised. A consortium known as the Finsbury Pavement House Group bought up many of the Tarkwa mines, which were included in holdings which at one point comprised over 400 companies.[21] The Finsbury Group's chairman, H.G. Latilla, was also a director of mines in Nigeria, South Africa, and Rhodesia.[22]

More order was introduced into the mining industry with the formation of the 'London Advisory Committee' in 1936, which comprised all the chairmen of the major mining interests and made all of the important decisions for the industry.[23] Its first chairman was J.H. Batty, who was also chairman of Ashanti Goldfields as well as of several other mines, and was, moreover, former chairman of the African and Eastern Trade Corporation,[24] one of the largest import-export firms in West Africa.

Ashanti Goldfields was the largest mining company in Ghana, with the most consistent record of profits throughout the colonial period. Much of its success it owed to the fact that it was a far more productive mine than others; whereas the Tarkwa group of mines was located in the low-producing banket areas, Ashanti was a high-producing quartz mine. In the 19-year period from 1912 to 1931 Ashanti produced some two million fine ounces of gold at a total value of eight million pounds sterling. Ashanti's dividends were consistently high after 1910; between 1911 and 1919 they varied between 62½ per cent and 87½ per cent; between 1920 and 1929 they varied between 25 per cent and 65 per cent, with the exception of 1922 when there were no dividends, and between 1930 and 1938 they varied between 75 per cent and 95 per cent.[25] Overall, Ashanti's dividends averaged 57 per cent per year between 1903 and 1938.

Some of Ashanti's success might, however, be attributed to its 100-

square-mile concession over some of the richest gold land of Ghana.[26] Although Ashanti Goldfields did not use all of this land for mining, its concession prevented competitors from moving in. Further, the concession gave the mine exclusive rights to the use of timber in the 100-square-mile area, thus effecting considerable savings in the costs of fuel and construction. With such a large concession, it was able to exert a considerable amount of influence over the colonial government; specifically, to make an agreement with the government to extend the railway to its minehead at Obuasi in 1903.[27]

A further privilege which accrued to Ashanti Goldfields under the terms of its lease was a complete monopoly of trading rights within the concession area. In conjunction with the three companies of Millers, Swanzy, and the African Association (which were later to become the mainstays of the African and Eastern Trading Corporation and then of the United Africa Company), the mine ran the Ashanti-Obuasi Trading Company.[28] This enterprise was on the whole very successful and paid dividends as high as 40 per cent.[29] Because the concession's trade monopoly had been granted by the government, there were some constraints on the Ashanti-Obuasi Trading Company's activities, specifically, that it was not permitted to charge Europeans more than 10 per cent above cost on imported goods. However, no such constraint was placed upon dealings with Africans. A report by the Ashanti-Obuasi Trading Company to its headquarters in London in 1928 shows how jealously its monopoly of trade was guarded.

> This business has the *sole monopoly* to trade on the 100 square miles of the Concession belonging to the Ashanti Goldfields Corporation... The Trading Rights have been the subject of litigation... [I]n 1917 we on the Gold Coast brought a Case in the Ashanti Courts for infringement of our rights against an African trader, and as a result this man was turned off our property. The question of these Rights turns up from time to time and the Government know they have to support us as if they did not they would probably have to compensate us to do away with the Rights. We undertake to supply Europeans working on the Mines at an agreed 10% upon cost, but we are free to do the African trade without any such arrangement. We purchase annually about 2,500 tons of Cocoa. Here again Africans have infringed our Rights by attempting to buy Cocoa on the Lands, and the Government usually remove them without action being taken ... as we claim to have the Sole Right here also ...[30]

The Creation of Ghana's Peripheral Capitalist Economy 67

Although the government could have removed its monopoly of trade on the grounds that Ashanti Goldfields did not actually have the right to transfer the monopoly to the Ashanti-Obuasi Trading Company, a separate concern, it did not choose to do so. The injunction against and expulsion of an African trader in 1917 was one of several incidents in which the company destroyed the businesses of Africans trading on its concession land; in general it only permitted Africans to trade if they originally bought their goods from Ashanti-Obuasi.[31]

The question of Ashanti Goldfield's monopoly was brought to the attention of the Colonial Office not in defense of Ghanaians' rights, but rather in pursuit of equal opportunity for other British traders. In 1927 a Manchester firm, J.J. Horsfield and Company, complained that one of the largest shareholders in Ashanti and Obuasi was the African and Eastern Trading Corporation, its competitor in West Africa.

> We always thought that our Colonies were for the benefit of trade development [sic] and supposed to be open Markets. Why this concession should be given to the above [Ashanti Goldfields] company we are at a loss to understand, and according to an abstract from their Annual Return we see that one of the biggest shareholders is the African and Eastern Trading Corporation Ltd. . . who have 57,068 shares. This Trading Corporation is [our] . . . competitor, and as already stated why the above privilege should be granted, we should like to know.[32]

In this case, the Colonial Office looked into the matter and decided that in fact Ashanti Goldfields did not possess a monopoly of trade, although it did legally have a monopoly of the land on which the trade was conducted. The Colonial Office decided that it would be 'impolitic' to inform the Company that it did have such a legal claim.[33] But neither did the Colonial Office take any action against the monopoly, thus Ashanti Goldfield's activities in Ghana remained undisturbed.

Ashanti Goldfields was rivalled in its profit-making capacity by only two other Ghana mines, the African Manganese Company and Consolidated African Selection Trust. The former was the first to exploit the manganese deposits discovered by a government geologist during the First World War;[34] the latter was to become the most prominent diamond mine in Ghana. As shown in Table 3.1, the discoveries of manganese and diamonds marginally diversified Ghana's export economy. The reason for the discovery of manganese, however, was not the imperial state's concern with monocultural dependence, but rather its increased need for mineral supplies in wartime. Manganese was a strategic material and as soon as it was discovered in 1914 the state made plans to exploit it. Bauxite was also discovered during World War I and was immediately preempted by the government, over the protests of certain African members of the Legislative Council,[35] for the use of the Empire, But the bauxite was not actually exploited until after World War II.

Government policy with regard to the new mineral resources, combined with the technological inability of Africans to exploit them, quickly pushed both manganese and diamonds into British hands. As early as 1860, Africanus Horton had speculated that there were diamonds in Keta, in the eastern province of the Colony.[36] When the diamonds were eventually found by Europeans in Akim Abuakwa, however, Africans could not exploit them on any large scale. Consolidated African Selection Trust, registered in 1924, quickly acquired 'alluvial diamond mining concessions over about fifty-four square miles in the Akim district',[37] and immediately began to pay dividends which, with the exception of low years in 1931/2 and 1937/8, varied from 35 per cent to 90 per cent from 1925 to 1938, averaging 55 per cent per year.[38]

Only about half of the diamonds exported from Ghana were mined by the Consolidated African Selection Trust; the rest were found loose in the soil.[39] Africans who wished to sell these diamonds were obliged, even if the diamonds were found on their own soil, to purchase licenses to act as 'diamond winners'. Such licenses were granted at the absolute discretion of the District Commissioner, a discretion which was limited only in 1926 when he was obliged to grant the license if he was satisifed that the landowner was the true owner of the diamond.[40] The capacity of individual Africans to export found diamonds was seriously hampered by the fact that they had to enter into a bond to ensure that they could pay the export duty. Few diamond winners could afford to pay the 15 per cent of the value of the diamond required as a bond,[41] hence, they sold their found diamonds to expatriates inside the country. In areas covered by diamond concessions, African diamond winners were not permitted to operate and 'the holder of the mining concession possesse[d] certain rights of search and power to prohibit unauthorized persons from entering therein.'[42] Moreover, until 1934, Ghanaian landowners were prohibited from carrying out mining operations 'by methods other than native methods'.[43]

This brief exposition of the development of diamond, manganese and gold industries in Ghana highlights the dependence of the Africans on European technology to exploit these resources, a dependence which resulted in the almost total takeover of the industry by the Europeans. Such dependence, however, was not complete. Expatriates had to deliberately restrict Ghanaians' access to advanced technology in order to push them out of gold mining. The state defended expatriate interests by reserving the right to mine diamonds by modern methods to Europeans. Moreover, the integration of the mining industry into the tight network of international mining consortia served to exclude Africans. Thus, while the incursion of Europeans into Ghana served to rapidly develop its mineral resources, it did so in the context of an externally-oriented peripheral economy, and in the interests of a metropolitan bourgeoisie which deliberately excluded any Ghanaian competition

Fortunately for Ghana, however, it was only in mining that production, as well as distribution, was taken out of indigenous hands. Export agricultural production remained in the control of African farmers, but the increasingly monocultural nature of export agriculture, combined with an ever-increasing dependence on imported consumer goods, meant that Ghana's economy became ever more dependent on, and vulnerable to, the capitalist world market.

2. The Creation of the Agricultural Export Industry

Table 3.2 presents the percentage figures for the major agricultural exports of Ghana from 1885 to 1939. From this table it can be seen that the major exports, aside from minerals, were cocoa, palm oil, palm kernels, rubber and timber. Palm oil, palm kernels, rubber and timber, while constituting signficant percentages of Ghana's exports in the early colonial period, dropped sharply after 1905 and had virtually disappeared by 1915, leaving cocoa as the only agricultural export of any significance.

The last two decades of the nineteenth century witnessed a concentration on palm oil, palm kernel and rubber production to the exclusion of other Ghanaian exports. Certain products which had formerly been minor sources of revenue lost their importance; these included ivory, monkey skins, gum copal and kola nuts. Animal exports such as ivory and monkey skins declined as the supply was depleted, while other exports such as kola, which was used by Africans in other parts of West Africa, especially Nigeria, suffered as the direction of trade reversed from the north to the south.

Palm oil and kernels had been important Ghanaian crops since the abolition of the slave trade had compelled indigenous entrepreneurs to search for something new to sell. After 1850, a large market for palm products arose in Western Europe. The new machine-based factories

Table 3.2: Major Agricultural Products as Percentages of Total Ghana Exports by Value, by Five-Year Averages, 1885–1939

Years	Total Exports (£000s)	Cocoa %	Palm Oil %	Palm Kernels %	Rubber %	Timber %	Total Agricultural Exports %
1885–89	394	–	37	14	14	–	65
1890–94	704	0	26	13	30	5	74
1895–99	927	0	16	9	46	8	79
1900–4	908	9	23	12	23	6	73
1905–9	2293	19	5	4	13	5	46
1910–14	4233	41	3	4	5	5	58
1915–19	6682	59	1	2	1	2	65
1920–24	9300	73	0	1	0	n.d.	74
1925–29	12769	78	0	1	0	n.d.	79
1930–35	9020	60	0	0	0	1	61
1935–39	14097	47	0	0	0	1	48

Sources: Raw figures for 1885–99 from Gold Coast, *Blue Books*. For 1900–39 from Kay, *Political Economy*, Table 18, 'Imports, exports, and the balance of visible trade, 1900–1960', pp. 325–6, and Table 21a, 'Value of major exports, 1900–1960', pp. 334–5. N.B. – = no exports; 0 = some exports but less than 0.5 per cent; n.d. = no data. Averages for 1885–89 are calculated on the basis of figures for 1886–89 only, as the figures given in the *Blue Books* for 1885 are grossly inconsistent with figures for the rest of the century and have been presumed to be in error.

used palm oil for lubrication; and the rising prosperity of the middle classes and skilled workers provided a market for palm-based soap and candles. From the palm kernels, oil for margarine was extracted. Palm oil was an especially expedient product as it was also used locally; hence, its production did not impose on traditional ways of life or cause major reallocations of farming priorities. Palm kernels, however, were produced primarily for export.[44]

Until about 1902, the combined production of palm oil and palm kernels constituted about 40 per cent of Ghana's exports. It is interesting to note that the export of palm products seemed to vary inversely with that of rubber, suggesting that these were probably alternative lines 'between which traders could switch their interest according to where their best advantage lay for the time being.'[45] The decline in palm oil exports after 1902 appears to have been caused by a combination of poor production conditions and falling prices on the world market. Transportation costs based on head-load carriage were excessively high in Ghana, and palm oil and kernels were high-weight, low-priced goods which gave little return per mile compared to more expensive goods such as gold, or even rubber.[46] More crucial was the fact that methods of purification of oil in Ghana were primitive, and the oil produced often could not compete with oil from other areas such as Lagos, let alone with substitutable products such as tallow, petroleum by-products or whale oils. The process of fermentation employed in Ghana produced low-quality, 'hard' oil, whereas 'soft' oil commanded a better price.[47] The problem was exacerbated by persistent adulteration of the product; palm oil was mixed with adulterants as various as red earth, overripe plantain and sour kenke.[48] The idea of quality control for palm products was entertained by the government as early as the 1890s, but no efforts to legislate such controls were made until the 1930s.

The combination of poor quality and lack of competitiveness with substitutable products resulted in lower prices for palm products between 1885 and 1905.[49] Since, simultaneously, the demand for cocoa rose, many farmers switched their efforts from palm trees to cocoa trees, despite the fact that palm trees grew 'naturally' whereas cocoa trees had to be planted and tended for a good five years before they could bear fruit. In later years, it became a frequent preoccupation of the colonial government that Ghanaian peasants refused to cultivate palm products because they were too concerned with cocoa, and it was often charged that fine supplies of palm trees were brutally cut down to make way for cocoa farms.[50] Such charges, it would seem, were exaggerated, especially as palm trees were used by farmers to provide the necessary shade for the growth of young cocoa plants. In any case, palm trees were also exploited locally for oil and palm wine. The government's sporadic attempts through the 1910s and 1920s to encourage Africans to cultivate and export more palm products failed to recognise the realities of the international market.

The cultivation of rubber began for reasons similar to those for the cultivation of palm oil and failed for much the same reasons. Between 1890 and 1905 Ghana was not only the largest rubber producer in the British Empire, but also fourth of the world's five leading producers.[51] According to R.E. Dumett, the rise of rubber exports was a result of African responsiveness to international market conditions, at a time when the government was trying to encourage non-profitable crops such as coffee and tobacco. Dumett maintains that rubber production in Ghana began in 1883 as a response to an attempt by an international ring of speculators to corner all existing supplies of Parà rubber, mainly from Brazil. Gold Coast Africans quickly saw opportunities for new suppliers of rubber to sell to those buyers who were not part of the Brazilian ring.[52]

But, like palm oil, rubber suffered from inferior methods of processing and preparation, resulting in a product which was wet, heavy and difficult to transport. The rubber trees were also over-exploited, as their trunks were often cut down in order to obtain rubber, rather than simply being tapped.[53] As soon as alternative sources of supply were found, Ghana's rubber lost much of its market. It was wild, not cultivated; as such it could not compete with the organised plantations which arose early in the twentieth century in South-east Asia, where the rubber had a higher caoutchouc content.[54] Given the competition from Asian rubber, and the obvious opportunities for investment in cocoa, the demand for which increased rapidly in the 1900s and 1910s, it was rational for Ghanaian rubber producers (and oil palm producers) to use the money they had earned to invest in new cocoa plantations.[55]

Before going on to discuss the cocoa industry, a look should be taken at the timber trade in Ghana which, although it did not provide a very large percentage of Ghana's exports, nevertheless is unique in that much of its distribution, as well as production, was in African hands. The timber industry was never as large, during the colonial period, as one might have supposed it to be from the amount of wood, especially mahogany, available. In fact, during the 1880s and 1890s, Ghana was importing timber from the United States because of the difficulty of obtaining it in the colony.[56] Transportation difficulties were the main reason for the slowness of development of the industry. The heavy logs were cut as near to rivers as possible, and then floated down; hence, the Ankobra river and the port of Axim were the centres of the earliest timber export trade. As logs near the rivers were depleted, it became necessary to move further inland; logs were cut near railway lines as these were built, and later near roads. After World War I, lorries were introduced to carry the logs. Until 1939, all logging was conducted by manual extraction and dragging of logs to transport facilities, although a very few tractors were introduced to replace hauling gangs in the 1930s.[57]

The logs which were exported were usually owned by Africans. No expatriates, except for one American company from Louisville, the Mengel Mahogany Logging Company,[58] had timber concessions in

Ghana prior to World War II. Many mines, of course, possessed timber rights on their concessions, but they did not avail themselves of these rights for exporting purposes although they complained bitterly about Ghanaians who trespassed on their land to obtain logs.[59] African entrepreneurs could obtain 'concessions' for logs from chiefs; to the chagrin of certain Europeans, these were not subject to the 1900 Concessions Law as they were the object of dealings between 'natives'. 'Pa' Grant, a legendary figure in Ghanaian history and one of the most important indigenous entrepreneurs of the colonial period, obtained his logs from concessions, and he is said to at one time have had as much as 700 square miles of concession land.[60] Other entrepreneurs obtained logs simply by buying them, one at a time, from the owners of the trees, and shipping them to the coast in whatever manner they could.

For many years, even after logs had arrived at the coast for shipment, facilities at the surf ports were unable to handle them, and the older ships were not able to lift the logs and their hatches were unsuitable for their transport.[61] With the exception of the German line, Woermann, the regular shipping lines refused to handle logs at all.[62] Prior to World War I much Ghanaian timber went to Germany while British brokers complained that it was unobtainable.[63] 'Pa' Grant was often unable to obtain shippers. After World War I he bought and converted two German minesweepers for carriage of his exports, but in the face of this competition the large British companies agreed, at last, to ship his logs.[64]

The timber industry as a whole did not reach large proportions until after World War II. The transportation infrastructure had to be completed before it was worth the while of Europeans to invest in the trade. Africans, with the exception of such persons as Grant, generally did not have enough capital to exploit the industry; they certainly did not have the contacts in Europe and America which would enable them to obtain credit for exporting. Moreover, there were difficulties in proving ownership of trees.[65] Timber exports, like palm kernels, palm oil and rubber exports, declined to almost nothing in percentage terms after 1915 as the production and export of cocoa expanded.

The export of cocoa from Ghana began in minute quantities in the 1890s, rising considerably after the turn of the twentieth century to become the foremost export of the colony, vastly overshadowing all others, by 1910. Cocoa had been grown in Ghana by the Basel Mission as early as 1858, but as there was no market for the crop at that time its cultivation did not spread.[66] In 1876, cocoa was introduced into the

Mampong area by a Ghanaian named Tetteh Quarshie who had worked on the cocoa plantations in Fernando Po, but there was still a very small market for the crop.[67] The market for Ghana's cocoa increased dramatically after 1900, however, especially when the Quaker firm of Cadbury decided to buy its cocoa from Ghana rather than from the slave plantations of Sao Thomé and Fernando Po.

The government agriculture department, unaware of the market for cocoa, did not begin to promote its cultivation until well after the industry was established through the enterprise of African peasants. Ghanaian response to the demands of the international market for cocoa was independent; in no way was it government induced. Nor, indeed, did the government's early transportation policy encourage the development of cocoa. Transportation in the 1890s and early 1900s was geared towards opening up gold-mining territory; cocoa farmers were compelled to build their own roads or carry their cocoa crops on their heads if they wished to sell to the European buyers.

The type of cocoa grown in Ghana was in high demand on the international market as a base for chocolate production. Cocoa production on a world scale was divided into 'fine' cocoa, known as Trinitarios or Criollo and cultivated chiefly in the West Indies, certain Latin American countries, Ceylon and Java, and 'basic' cocoa, known as Forastero and grown chiefly in West Africa and Brazil.[68] The price offered for basic cocoa was, obviously, never as high as that offered for fine, but on the other hand the demand for basic cocoa was far greater. The export of fine cocoa shrank from 78 per cent of the world's total cocoa exports in 1895 to 13 per cent in 1933.[69] The two types were not competitive, although higher quality Forastero than Ghana produced was often in demand (that is, Forastero free of defects and properly cured).

The beginnings of cocoa cultivation in Ghana represented a dramatic change in the organisation of production, inasmuch as, for the first time on a large scale (except for some palm tree 'plantations' in Krobo), exports were the result of organised, planned, cash-crop cultivation, not simply of the extraction of naturally growing produce from the land. Cocoa 'plantations', or farms, were established over most of Ghana except the Northern Territories, starting first in the Eastern Province of the Colony, spreading into Ashanti, and moving later into the Western and parts of the Central Provinces of the Colony. Most cocoa farms were very small; in 1938 the Nowell Commission on cocoa estimated the average Ashanti farm at two-and-a-half acres, although multiple farm ownership was common.[70] Often Ghanaians who had already saved capital through trade or professional work bought cocoa farms; in such cases the size of their farms was considerably larger, in some cases reaching as high as 24 or 45 acres.[71] Investments in cocoa involved a considerable amount of waiting time, as cocoa trees did not bear fruit until they were five years of age. An acre of cocoa land produced on average, in 1938, about nine head-loads (of 60 pounds each) of cocoa; it was estimated that in 1938 a million acres of land in Ghana were under cocoa, using approximately one-sixth of the total potential labour force of the country.[72]

The cultivation of cocoa as the major export crop had one particular advantage; it did not preclude the growing of other crops on the same land. Cocoa trees needed shade, which palm trees could provide, and underneath the cocoa trees, during their first few years of existence, nursing plants, such as yams and cassava could be cultivated. The other crops grown on cocoa farms could be eaten by the farmers and their families, or they could be sold to provide income. The peasants who were investigated in a 1930 study by an official of the Gold Coast Department of Agriculture sold maize, coco-yams and plantain from their farms while waiting for their cocoa crops to yield.[73]

By 1915, cocoa was the dominant export crop of Ghana; by the late 1920s, as indicated in Table 3.2, it constituted 78 per cent of Ghana's total exports. This reliance on cocoa was, obviously, a double-edged sword; in times of boom it resulted in high revenues not only for Ghanaian peasants, but also for the expatriate traders who organised its exports, and through them for the state (in the form of export duties); but in times of depression it considerably reduced the overall revenues of Ghana. All sectors of Ghanaian society were dependent on cocoa and its price vagaries on the world market.

After 1915 Ghanaian governments became increasingly aware of the monocultural dependence of the colony, but only sporadic attempts were made to modify such dependence. Attempts to rectify the dependent nature of Ghana's economy took two forms; the encouraging of new crops for export, and infrequent efforts to start processing and manufacture within the colony, both to reduce reliance on imports and to try to export higher quality products. The problem, however, was that attempts by the state to encourage diversification normally took place when the economic situation was good and revenues (based mainly on cocoa exports and the consequent ability to import more) were high. But in such periods of boom, Ghanaian farmers, content with high cocoa prices, were not interested in changing crops. In periods of depression, when it looked for new products to relieve

Ghana's overdependence on cocoa, the state had no revenues for new diversification schemes of any consequence.

One example of an abortive attempt at diversification was a sisal plantation set up by the colonial government in 1925 on the Accra plains.[74] This was an ambitious endeavour, involving two to three-year investments before the plants were ready for cultivation, and projecting not only a factory in Accra to process the sisal into hemp, but also a tramway from the plains to the factory.[75] The first exports of sisal hemp in 1925 earned profits of between £22 and £23 per ton;[76] but these profits coincided with abnormally high prices on the world market; when the market for hemp returned to normal the following year, the Accra industry was found to be unprofitable. The government tried to sell the plantation to a private buyer,[77] but none was ever found, since it was obviously not in the interests of either expatriate or indigenous businessmen to invest in a new, unprofitable industry when profits could be made through the export of simple raw materials. In 1930 the colonial government discontinued its experiment with sisal at a loss of some £14,000.[78]

Another option for diversification of exports, rather than starting state-organised production, was to negotiate with private firms to begin exporting new products. In this respect, the history of Ghana's banana export industry is of some interest. Banana exports were first proposed to the government in the late 1920s by the firm of Elders and Fyffes, a subsidiary of Elder Dempster, the most important shipping line in British West Africa. Since 1907 Elders and Fyffes had been party to an agreement on the world banana trade with the United Fruit Company, which had purchased £550,000 worth of shares in the former company in 1913.[79] The banana export industry was, therefore, oligopolistically owned, and Elders and Fyffes were only willing to export Ghanaian bananas if the state would assure them that competition would not be tolerated.[80] When such assurance was not forthcoming, Elders and Fyffes discouraged the industry, arguing that attempts by the government to set up fruit canning and storage in Ghana would not be viable.[81] The most that the government could do with respect to setting up a fruit export industry was to negotiate with Elder Dempster for carriage of bananas in special cooling chambers in 1936.[82]

A second attempt to improve agricultural exports through state negotiation with private firms came with proposals by Lever Brothers to set up palm nut processing in Ghana, but only on condition that Lever be granted a monopoly of such enterprises. Lever had tried to obtain a monopoly of oil palm processing in Ghana as early as 1912,[83] considering it advisable to begin processing the nuts in Africa instead of Europe because although freight charges for processed oil were higher than for unprocessed palm nuts, the quality of the oil processed in Europe after a long journey on the high seas was very low.

Lever began negotiations with the Colonial Office for the right to set up a processing factory in Ghana and obtain a monopoly, over an area within a ten-mile radius of its factory, of all mechanical oil-palm processing. Africans within that ten-mile radius could bring their palm nuts to the factory for processing but they could not give their nuts to any other Europeans for processing nor could they use any mechanical means of processing themselves.[84] To facilitate the acquisition of such monopoly rights, in 1912 the Gold Coast Legislature passed the Palm Oil Ordinance, which empowered the government

> to grant to any person, within such area not exceeding a circle within a ten-mile radius and for such period not exceeding twenty-one years . . . the exclusive right to construct and work mills, to be operated by mechanical power, for expressing or extracting oil from the pericarp of palm fruit.[85]

This ordinance, however, was passed with considerable opposition. Some members of the government objected to it because they were suspicious of Lever's possible influence in the Colony, and they were joined in their opposition both by Lever's European competitors and by Ghanaians. The former argued that if Lever were to have a monopoly of palm processing, it would be impinging on the established nut export trade.[86] The latter objected because the governor, not the chiefs in charge of the land, would have sole authority to grant processing monopolies, without even consulting the native authorities.[87] The Ghanaian opposition also viewed the monopoly as a threat to any future plans by Africans to process their own palm fruit by mechanical means. It so happened that in 1912, coincidentally just when the processing monopoly Ordinance was being approved by the government, one W. Essuman Gwira, an African employee of the Government Agricultural Service, invented a machine which was cheap, easily manufactured, and easily operated, and which could have been used for small-scale palm processing by Africans. The Aborigines' Rights Protection Society pressured the government to invest funds in perfecting this machine for African use, and even went so far as to have its potential verified by an independent expert in London. The government, however, not only refused to invest funds in the machine, but also denied its inventor leave from his job to perfect it.[88] At the same time the government argued that concessions such as demanded by Lever, and as provided for in the Ordinance, were necessary because the 'natives' had not yet reached the stage at which they could process oil themselves.

Opposition to the processing monopoly Ordinance was so intense that it lay dormant for several years. In 1917, the Digby Commission investigating land law in West Africa recommended that the Ordinance be repealed.[89] However, it was not repealed, but remained law, and was used in 1930 to grant a palm oil processing monopoly in the Manya Krobo area to Lever's successor, the UAC. The government in this instance not only granted UAC a monopoly of all processing within a radius of ten miles of its factory, but also agreed that if the projected supply of 3,000 tons of palm nuts per year could not be obtained, it would, once the supply fell to less than 80 per cent or 2,400 tons, pay UAC £1 16s for every ton of fruit lacking.[90] This monopoly project eventually failed for lack of supplies: Africans simply did not bring in their palm nuts for processing but rather continued to sell them in their unprocessed form. The government on its part refused to pay the promised subsidy because it maintained that low world prices, not lack of supply, actually caused the eventual closing of UAC's processing mills.[91]

The willingness of the state in the 1930s to encourage Lever's processing scheme indicates its preoccupation with export diversification during the Depression era, when the price of cocoa was much lower than previously. But such preoccupation was tempered by the decline in government revenues during the same period; without the revenues supplied by cocoa exports, there were few funds to invest to eliminate over-reliance on cocoa. State policy wavered between encouraging diversification and deciding to invest even more in cocoa so as to improve its position on the world market. Certainly, insofar as the colonial government did interest itself in diversification, it confined itself to finding new agricultural products for export. As one official stated 'A country's wealth can be increased either by manufacture, that is to say, by converting raw products into finished articles, or alternately, by production and exportation. Of these two, the latter is, obviously, the Gold Coast's métier.'[92]

There were, then, on the whole few changes in the basic structure of Ghana's export economy during the colonial period. Neither the state, the expatriate firms, nor the indigenous peasant producers were willing to divert attention towards export diversification in periods when the cocoa price was high, and when the cocoa price was low, funds for diversification were unavailable. While sporadic attempts were made by the state to introduce new export crops, the overall problem of Ghana's dependence on exports was determined by its position in the world economy. Complete restructuring of this world economy, or else Ghana's complete withdrawal from it, would have been necessary to reduce its dependence either on exports or on imports.

3. Ghana as a Market for European Capitalist Production

In return for the minerals and agricultural products which they produced for the world capitalist market, Ghanaians were sold a variety of manufactured goods which changed surprisingly little over the period 1885–1939. Ghanaians consumed mostly light manufactured goods which were for personal use; textiles, foodstuffs and provisions, ornaments, liquor and tobacco, and arms and ammunition. Very few of their imports were investment goods of any description.

Table 3.3 presents figures for 1900 to 1939 of the major imports into Ghana, divided roughly into consumer and investment goods. It can be seen that in 1900 only about 20 per cent, or less, of Ghana's imports were for investment purposes. After about 1905 the percentage varied around the 30 per cent mark. The investment-oriented imports consisted primarily of construction goods, fuel, machinery and transport supplies. Construction goods were used by both Europeans and Africans; by the former to build mines, government buildings, storage sheds and individual residences; by the latter primarily for their own housing needs and secondarily for retail shops. Fuel, which varied around a constant figure of about 5 per cent of imports, was used for rail and lorry transport. Machinery had several uses, one of the most important of which was in the expatriate mining sector. Only transport supplies could be considered major investments for Africans in the sense that they encouraged the development of an indigenous transport business alongside the larger European transport concerns.[93] Very few of the so-called 'investment' goods imported into Ghana had any long-term uses, or could be used to further economic development by providing basic infrastructure. Their purpose was to facilitate the export of minerals, cocoa and other goods from the coast, by providing transportation and storage facilities. African investment in transport was of some use in building up capital which

The Creation of Ghana's Peripheral Capitalist Economy

Table 3.3: Consumer and Investment Imported Goods, Per Cent of The Total by Value, by Five-Year Averages, 1900–39

Year	Tobacco, Food, Drink	Clothing, Leather, Textiles	Other Consumer Goods	Total Consumer Goods	Construction	Fuel	Machinery	Transportation	Total Investment Goods
1900–4	38	18	19	75	7	5	4	4	20
1905–9	30	16	16	62	13	5	7	9	34
1910–14	34	14	19	67	10	3	6	11	30
1915–19	30	15	16	61	12	4	7	11	34
1920–24	28	25	14	67	10	7	4	8	29
1925–29	25	31	12	68	8	6	5	7	26
1930–34	30	19	15	64	9	6	6	10	31
1935–39	26	21	14	61	10	4	7	15	36

Source: Raw figures in Kay, *Political Economy*, Table 20a, 'Value of imports by commodity group, 1900–1960', pp. 327–8. The totals for these imports do not coincide with the figures given by Kay as total imports in his Table 18, 'Imports, exports, and the balance of visible trade 1900–1960', pp. 325–6, presumably because only major import groups are considered in Table 20a. Since it is the relative percentages of imported consumer and investment goods which are of importance here, it is assumed that the discrepancy in totals can be overlooked, and the table is calculated on the basis of the totals given in Kay's Table 20a.

could be used for other purposes, but African investment in houses, while fulfilling consumer needs and acting as much-needed collateral for credit from European banks and trading companies, had little effect in terms of promoting a more active or independent economy.

Consumer goods also changed very little during the colonial period. In 1886 the total value of imports of major consumer goods was some £183,000, while the importation of 'investment' goods was about £26,000, or barely 14 per cent of the total consumer goods, even when such expendable items as bags, sack, cord and twine are included as investment imports. The largest single group of imports was liquor, tobacco, and arms and ammunition; with rum alone accounting for £59,000 worth of imports. This group was followed by textiles and wearing apparel, which in turn was followed by provisions.[94] With the exception of the categories liquor, tobacco, and arms and ammunition, which declined drastically in importance after the turn of the twentieth century, the composition of imports in 1939 was very similar to 1886.

The decline in importance of arms and ammunition followed quickly upon the final subjugation of Ashanti in 1900 when the colonial government passed a law forbidding the indiscriminate importing of arms and ammunition and their sale to whichever Ghanaians, friend or foe, wished to buy them. It would seem reasonable that it wished to deny arms to Ashanti, a nation which had just been conquered, but by 1902 the business community in the Gold Coast was complaining of the loss of revenue occasioned by the prohibition. In 1905, therefore, the government removed some restrictions and drew up a list of selected Africans who were to be allowed to buy arms.[95]

The decline in importance of arms imports after 1900 was paralleled by a decline in the importance of liquor imports. Although in 1875 the value of liquor imports was about £59,000, in 1895 £121,000 and in 1910 £176,000, its importance as a percentage of total imports declined drastically from 19 per cent in 1879 to 15 per cent in 1894 to 7 per cent in 1910.[96] Europeans were inclined to attribute to Africans an incapacity to 'hold their liquor' and to assume that the 'demon rum' was destroying the fabric of African society; hence, at a later date the state began to impose stringent controls on liquor imports. Between 1913 and 1923 the import duty on liquor was raised over 400 per cent,[97] ostensibly to discourage drinking but also, one suspects, for revenue purposes. In 1919 a prohibition was placed on the import of low-quality trade spirits (a prohibition which, incidentally, seriously affected the American trade in rum which had formerly been one of the staples of the Swanzy Company's business), but by this time some Africans were earning enough money to be able to afford beer and better quality liquor. The decline in percentage consumption prior to 1913 indicates that as their incomes rose, Ghanaians spent less on liquor and preferred to buy other goods, such as cloth.[98]

Indeed, as is well known, textiles were one of the mainstays of the West African trade, enabling many a Manchester merchant to make his fortune. Generally speaking, clothing, textiles and leather were responsible for about 20 per cent of Ghana's total import bill, although it is worth noting that during the prosperous 1920s the figure was closer to 30 per cent. Much of what was imported was actually second-hand European clothing, a fact disguised by the statistics which listed clothing according to type, as dress, shirt and so on. Second-hand clothing from America, where the southern climate more closely approximated that of Africa, was a booming business in which most of the British expatriate firms engaged with some considerable success.[99] But although the trade in second-hand clothes was large, the bulk of the textile trade was in lengths of printed cotton which Africans could use to make up clothing of their own. The large firms such as the predecessors of the United Africa Company had their own mills in Manchester where cottons were printed to order. Any cloth pattern which became popular was jealously guarded by the firm which owned its patent. At the end of the nineteenth century a great deal of controversy occurred within the West African business community over extending the Merchandise Marks Act to the African coast, in order to protect these patterns. The Colonial Office was finally induced to provide protection in the colonies, thus granting future competitive advantages to the expatriate firms who had already cornered large sections of the textile market.

While the firms were concerned to protect their own privileges, however, they were less concerned to protect the African consumer. Occasionally both the Colonial Office and the government in Accra attempted to institute measures of quality control over imports. During the 1890s, for example, the government was obliged to institute a law known as the 'Folded Woven Goods Ordinance'. Africans were accustomed to buy European cloth by counting the number of folds, to determine the length of the piece. The Europeans, however, had adopted the custom of folding the last fold short, so that many 12 yard pieces were in fact only about 11½ yards long. The British business community, while it acknowledged that 'falsely folded goods' were prevalent, complained bitterly against the passage of controls which would leave them with short pieces of cloth which they could not sell.[100] Lest it be thought that business morals improved after trade became more regularised, it should be noted that the same sorts of arguments, that they would not be able to sell their produce, were made in 1931 when the Chief Commissioner of Ashanti tried to introduce regulations over a broad range of imported goods, including short-weighted bags of rice and corrugated iron sheeting so thin that it was ruinous for Africans to invest in it for their houses. The London Chamber of Commerce argued against regulation on the grounds that '[the] native[s] should not be barred from obtaining cheap goods if they were unable to afford the better quality.'[101]

The large amount of money spent on European-manufactured consumer imports in Ghana[102] indicates the increasing wealth of the Ghanaian community which followed upon its rapid and ever-closer integration into the world economic system. It also indicates, however, an increasing dependence on foreign goods to the detriment of local industry and production. The point must not be overstated; in some cases foreign goods were provided which Africans could not have provided for themselves; in other cases, new wants created new indigenous enterprises. Everything which was imported into Ghana was used; singlets were made out of flour sacks, wooden cases were used for construction, iron hoops holding together packing cases could be converted into knives.[103] New opportunities for consumption and a higher standard of living resulted from the income from cocoa farming.

But at the same time European-manufactured products replaced a range of indigenous products. Imported enamelware and brassware, for example, partially replaced the indigenous pottery industry. Moreover, while it cannot be argued that the large amount of textile imports replaced an indigenous cloth industry, inasmuch as the cheap, mass-produced textiles catered to an enlarged market which the indigenous, narrow-weave Kente cloth industry would not have been able to supply, nevertheless, it would seem that there was some decline in African-made textiles as a result of the influx of imports. Traditional centres of African weaving lost their role in the Ghana economy. In 1939, for example, an anonymous witness wrote of the decline of the Keta cloth industry as follows:

> Notes on Changes in West Africa
> Keta Native Cloth Industry
>
> The cloth is made from yarn generally imported from Manchester. Up to the war [WWI] there was an enormous trade in this cloth. Practically every family along the lagoon had primitive native made looms. The main income then was derived from cloth making. This industry has practically disappeared. European imported prints and garments are replacing the locally made article.[104]

A more serious criticism of the pattern of imports into Ghana is that many foodstuffs and provisions began to be imported which Ghanaians could have produced for themselves. Many cash-crop farmers preferred to buy imported foods rather than devote time to subsistence farming. While some farmers did produce foods both for subsistence and for the local markets, patterns of transportation, especially prior to World War I, were such as to facilitate the movement of imports on railways rather than the movement of indigenous foods by road.[105] But transportation patterns alone do not suffice to explain why, for example,

Ghana imported rice, which could have been grown in the Northern Territories, sugar, which could have been produced locally from cane, or salt, which had been produced for centuries in the salt flats at Ada. As early as 1889, the 'Report of the Commission on Economic Agriculture in the Gold Coast' pointed out the irrationalities of Ghana's food dependence, stressing among other arguments that the rice grown in Ghana was more nutritious than the excessively cleaned rice brought in from Europe.[106] This report, however, was never acted upon by the government, concerned as it was with promoting palm oil and cocoa production.

Given its hesitance, if not its refusal, to encourage the production of indigenous foodstuffs, it is not surprising that when it came to the question of investment in light industry the colonial state also took a very conservative stance, reflecting its interests in preserving its revenue from import duties on industrial and consumer goods. As shown in Table 5.1, a very high proportion of government revenue was derived from import duties. Although this proportion declined steadily from the inception of the colony until 1918, it remained high, varying from 45 per cent to almost 60 per cent of the revenue, until World War II. If indigenous industry were allowed to develop, imports and import duties would decrease, and the state would be obliged to find an alternative tax base, no easy task in a country which had steadfastly refused all forms of hut tax, head tax or income tax since 1852. Merchants had constantly to try to persuade the government to support the few private industries in which they did invest. In 1930, for example, the two merchant members of the Legislative Council urged the government to support the infant mineral water industry, arguing that it would have important linkage effects, providing jobs, paying import duties on ingredients and using public railways.[107] But the state, protective of its customs revenues, was unwilling to make concessions to encourage either the mineral water industry or the new brewery, owned by Overseas Breweries, which was started in Accra in 1932 and which was to employ 100 to 120 Africans.[108] Even though the brewery was one of the few industries in Ghana, the government expected it to pay the same duties and contribute as much to government revenues as imported beer.[109]

The case of the Overseas Breweries investment was unusual, however. In general the government's reluctance to consider diversification into light industry was matched by a similar reticence on the part of the expatriate investors in the colony. Most of the companies' investments in Ghana were in the form of buildings and transport equipment.

Buildings were necessary to house their goods, to store their cocoa, and for the conduct of retail trade. As well, the expatriate firms had to provide for the fairly extensive housing requirements of their own European staff. After World War I, there was also significant investment in fleets of lorries to carry cocoa and other exported and imported goods in competition with the state-owned railways which were often not as able to reach far into the 'bush' as were the light lorries.

In 1959, the United Africa Company argued that no investment in industrialisation had taken place in West Africa under its aegis prior to World War II because it would have been untimely.

> In the early 1930s every industrial country in the world was concerned with avoiding unemployment and not duplicating existing manufacturing facilities, with the result that the time was not propitious for introducing industrialisation into tropical Africa. Indeed it is questionable whether at that stage the local population would have had the necessary skills or whether government finances could have tolerated the consequent loss in import duties.
>
> A further important factor was that prior to 1939 African purchasing power was so low that local markets were seldom large enough to sustain an economic manufacturing unit . . . Criticism of the lack of industrialisation in the past has largely arisen from ignorance of such factors as these.[110]

It was, in the Company's own words, simply uneconomic to start factories in West Africa when goods could be produced much more cheaply in Europe, where a trained labour force used to factory work already existed. The UAC saw itself 'primarily as a merchant'.[111] As a merchant company, it promoted imports and exports; and in so doing, it followed the state's policy towards Ghana's role in the world economy.

4. A Peripheral Economy

The concentration on colonial Ghana's import-export trade which characterises this analysis of its economy reflects its dependence on the world capitalist system. What internal economic growth occurred in Ghana was a function of its position in the world capitalist market as a primary producer. As more was sold to this market, so more could be bought. Table 3.4 indicates the growth of both imports and exports in Ghana between 1885 and 1939. Although the long-range trend was for a steady growth in the import-export trade, the Ghanaian economy reflected world economic trends and slumped considerably during the Depression of the 1930s. During the war years of 1917 and 1918, as also in 1921 after the world market for cocoa slumped, imports and exports declined considerably. But the general trend was not only for a dramatic growth in both imports and exports (imports multiplied 37-fold and

Table 3.4: Ghana: Total Imports and Exports by Value, by Five-Year Totals, 1885–1939

Years	Imports (£000s)	Exports (£000s)	Balance of Visible Trade (£000s)
1885–89	1614	1577	−37
1890–94	3356	3522	+166
1895–99	5178	4633	−545
1900–4	9281	4539	−4742
1905–9	10333	11463	+1130
1910–14	20744	21165	+421
1915–19	25096	33409	+8313
1920–24	47476	46502	−974
1925–29	56119	63845	+7726
1930–34	29752	45100	+15348
1935–39	59846	70485	+10639

Source: 1886–99: Gold Coast, *Blue Books*; 1900–39: Kay, *Political Economy*, Table 18, 'Imports, exports, and the balance of visible trade, 1900–1960', pp. 325–6. Averages for 1885–89 are calculated on the basis of figures for 1886–89 only, as the figures given in the *Blue Books* for 1885 are grossly inconsistent with figures for the rest of the century and have been presumed to be in error.

exports almost 45-fold between the late 1880s and the late 1930s) but also, after the turn of the century, for an almost consistently positive balance of trade. Unfortunately, the implications of a positive balance of trade in a peripheral economy differ from those in a developed capitalist economy. The surplus revenue from Ghana's export trade was not invested in the country; rather, profits were repatriated to Great Britain and large reserves were kept by the state. While the general expansion of trade can be taken as a sign of Ghana's transition from a pre-capitalist to a peripheral capitalist economic entity during the colonial period, the uses to which profits from that trade were put indicate its continued underdevelopment, vis-à-vis the capitalist core.[112]

The Creation of Ghana's Peripheral Capitalist Economy

The varied composition of Ghana's agricultural exports from 1885 to 1910 gave way to an almost completely monocultural situation after 1915. The only major export from Ghana which could in any way compete in value with cocoa was gold. But the price of gold was subject to controls on the world market, and it was only in the 1930s, when gold was allowed to float after Britain went off the gold standard, that its price rose sufficiently to make any serious inroad on Ghana's export composition. In any case, although gold was important to Ghana's economy, its importance on the world market was very small; from 1891 to 1931 it contributed only between 0.04 per cent and 1.88 per cent of the total world supply.[113] With such a miniscule percentage of the world gold market dependent on it, Ghana had no room to manoeuvre, especially as expatriate mines controlled gold production.

Other mineral exports, while they had some importance to the Ghanaian economy, did not become items of trade until the post-World War I era. Manganese rose to constitute at its highest point some 8 per cent of Ghana's exports, while diamonds rose to 6 per cent. Neither could make any significant change in the basically monocultural pattern pattern which developed after 1915. Rubber, timber, palm oil and palm kernels, once important exports, declined to miniscule amounts. Ghana was left almost completely dependent on cocoa as an export crop. While in percentage-value terms its importance varied as the price of gold rose or fell, it was the only major employer of labour, land and capital in African hands. The internal development of Ghana depended almost totally on the cocoa export trade. But as an agricultural export industry, cocoa cultivation had few linkage effects. Tools were simple, labour unsophisticated. Investment in farms consisted almost completely of extension to new areas of cultivation. Because Ghana produced saleable cocoa at all times, even though it was not always of the best quality, the government saw little need to invest in its production.

The reliance of Ghana on cocoa, moreover, left her dependent for most of her trade on Great Britain, Western Europe and the United States. From 1900 to 1939, France, Germany, Switzerland, the Netherlands, Great Britain and the United States imported over 80 per cent of the total world supply of cocoa. Ghana's share of this total world supply rose steadily until the mid-1930s when competition from Nigeria began to assume some importance, but at its peak it was never more than 45 per cent. A higher percentage of Ghana's cocoa than the world average went, of course, to the United Kingdom, because of colonial, political and economic ties.

Table 3.5: World Net Imports of Raw Cocoa as Percentages of the Total, by Five-Year Averages, 1900–1939

Years	United Kingdom	United States	France	Germany	Netherlands	Switzerland	Total % of World Supply
1900–4	17	20	16	18	8	5	84
1905–9	14	24	14	21	8	4	85
1910–14	12	26	11	21	11	4	85
1915–19	19	20	13	n.d.	7	5	84*
1920–24	11	37	10	18	8	2	86
1925–29	12	38	7	15	9	1	82
1930–34	12	36	8	16	9	1	82
1935–39	16	38	7	11	10	1	83

Source: Gill and Duffus Limited, *Cocoa Statistics* (London, February 1970), Table 7, 'World Net Imports of Raw Cocoa', pp. 21–23.
*Excepting Germany

At its peak, Ghana produced a significant percentage of the world's cocoa. But because the marketing of cocoa was controlled by Europeans, it benefited the expatriate commercial class more than it benefited the African farmers. Even the expatriate traders, however, were limited in their power by the fact that cocoa was not a necessary commodity. The demand for cocoa was more or less inelastic in an upward direction; it was an everyday luxury and consumers did not buy more of it when their income was raised. On the other hand, the demand was elastic in a downward direction, since in times of economic recession or depression it could be easily eliminated from the consumer's diet.[114]

Ghana was dependent to a very high degree on Britain for its trade. From 1895 to 1924 an average of almost 70 per cent of its trade was with the 'mother country'; after 1924, more of its trade was with Western Europe and the United States. This pattern owed itself, not to imperial preference, but rather to expatriate control of its import-export trade. As long as the trade remained largely in British hands, Britain would absorb most of its products. Even when imported goods originated in other countries, they arrived in Ghana through British intermediaries. Some non-British firms had branches in Ghana, but these were of Western European origin; no American firms traded in the colony. The control of trade by the expatriates, who also had considerably more access to the colonial government than did Africans, meant that some opportunities for trade outside the imperial network were not exploited and Ghana's dependence on the colonial power was increased.

The perpetuation of Ghana's original peripheral position in the world system throughout the colonial period was, however, not simply a result of the impersonal operation of universal economic forces. It was also the result of the gradual evolution of an oligopolistic system of control

Table 3.6: Ghana: Direction of Trade in Percentages, by Five-Year Averages, 1885–1939

Years	United Kingdom	US and Canada	Other Commonwealth	Western Europe	Total
1885–89*	81	5	1	14	101
1890–94	75	2	2	20	99
1895–99	69	2	5	23	99
1900–4	62	4	7	25	98
1905–9	74	1	5	17	97
1910–14	69	3	6	19	97
1915–19	66	17	6	9	98
1920–24	56	16	4	18	94
1925–29	42	19	4	29	94
1930–34	50	15	4	23	92
1935–39	50	23	4	16	93

Source: Raw figures for 1885–99 from Gold Coast, *Blue Books*. For 1900–39 from Kay, *Political Economy*, Table 22a, 'Direction of Trade, 1900–1960', p. 341. Categories for 1885–99 include 'U.S.', and 'British Colonies' rather than 'U.S. and Canada' and 'Other Commonwealth'.

*Figures for 1885–89 are based on raw data for 1887–89 only; figures given in the *Blue Books* for 1885 are presumed to be in error and no figures are available for 1886.

of trade, banking and shipping on the West African coast. Such an oligopoly was in a better competitive position than large numbers of equally competitive small firms could be; it also had more power when dealing with the state, and it was able to take deliberate steps to exclude Ghanaians who tried to break down expatriate control of commerce. It is to the development of this oligopolistic structure that

90 *The Creation of Ghana's Peripheral Capitalist Economy*

we now turn.

Notes

1. Amin, *Accumulation*, Vol. I, p. 288.
2. Richard F. Burton and Verney Lovett Cameron, *To the Gold Coast for Gold* (Chatto and Windus, London, 1883), p. 159.
3. G.W. Eaton Turner, 'The Ashanti Goldfields Corporation', *The Mining Magazine*, Vol. 46, No. 6 (June 1932), p. 329.
4. Ibid.
5. Burton, *To the Gold Coast*, p. 246.
6. For a biography of Bonnat, see H. Bevin, 'M.J. Bonnat: Trader and Mining Promoter', *The Economic Bulletin of Ghana*, Vol. 4, No. 7 (1960).
7. Quoted in W.F. Holmes, 'Notes on the Early History of Tarkwa as a Gold Mining District', *Gold Coast Review*, Vol. 2, No. 1 (1926), p. 81.
8. Quoted in ibid., p. 84.
9. The story of Horton's gold mining venture is found in Christopher Fyfe's *Africanus Horton: West African Scientist and Patriot* (Oxford University Press, New York, 1972), pp. 129–32.
10. Ibid., p. 131.
11. Reported in *Journal of the Society of Arts*, Vol. 30 (2 June 1882), p. 782.
12. Ibid.
13. For instance, Mr Sam of Cape Coast, mentioned in Burton, *To the Gold Coast*, p. 113.
14. Ibid., p. 122.
15. CO 879/46 no. 513. 9893 no. 90.
16. GCCMines, 'Gold in the Gold Coast' (December 1950), p. 7.
17. Ibid., pp. 12–13.
18. Interview with an English metallurgist involved in mining in Ghana from 1919 to 1968, Liverpool, November 1974.
19. GCCMines, *Fourth Annual Report* (1931), p. 13.
20. GCCMines, *Seventh Annual Report* (1934), speech by the president, p. 16.
21. Interview with a former Chairman, Gold Coast Chamber of Mines, Accra, May 1974.
22. *Directory of Directors* (1935).
23. Interview with a former Chairman of the Gold Coast Chamber of Mines. The author was unable to obtain access to any records of the London Advisory Committee, nor to locate any records of its assumed predecessor, the West African Chamber of Mines, which is mentioned frequently in the Minutes of the British Chambers of Commerce.
24. *Directory of Directors* (1935 and 1925).
25. *Stock Exchange Yearbook* (London, 1910, 1939).
26. *Stock Exchange Yearbook* (1939), lists Ashanti as follows: 'Registered 25 May 1897. Owns (*inter alia*) the lease (until Dec. 1986, subject to a Government royalty of 5% on gold and other metals) of 100 square miles in the district of Bekwai and Adansi, Ashanti, West Africa.'
27. For details of this agreement, see Chapter 5.
28. See Chapter 4 for details of these companies.
29. J.J. Rankin, *The History of the United Africa Company Limited to 1938* (mimeo, United Africa Company, London, 1938), p. 87.
30. UAC Rankin File: Report 55. (Italics in original.)
31. UAC: Document 393, Ashanti-Obuasi Trading Co. Ltd.

32. Letter from Messrs. J.J. Horsfield and Company to Colonial Office, 6 May 1927, in CO 96/674 (1927) despatch 4346.
33. CO 96/647 (1927) despatch 4346.
34. Its discovery was announced in GCLegCo, 25 October 1917.
35. Ibid.
36. Fyfe, *Africanus Horton*, p. 128.
37. *Stock Exchange Yearbook* (1939).
38. Ibid.
39. *Ghana: Five-Year Development Plan* (Ministry of Planning, Accra, January 1977), Part II, p. 238.
40. This licence system was discussed in GCLegCo, 22 February 1926.
41. GCLegCo, 16 August 1920.
42. N.R. Junner, 'Gold in the Gold Coast' (Government Printer, Accra, 1935), 'Appendix', by R.P. Wild, p. 73.
43. The question of changing this law was discussed in the Gold Coast Executive Council, 19 November 1934. CO 98/69.
44. Bevin, 'The Gold Coast', p. 73.
45. H.J. Bevin, 'Some Notes on Gold Coast Exports 1886–1913', *The Economic Bulletin of Ghana*, Vol. 4, No. 1 (January 1960), p. 16.
46. 'Report of the Commission on Economic Agriculture in the Gold Coast, 1889' (manuscript), GNA Adm. 5/3/7, p. 57.
47. Ibid., pp. 46–56.
48. Ibid., p. 51. Kenke is a staple food of Ghana made from fermented corn (maize).
49. Bevin, 'Some Notes', p. 15.
50. For example, a report by W.S. Tudhope, Director of Agriculture, 23 September 1910. 'The destruction of the oil palm trees in making clearings for cocoa and other agriculture crops is quite unnecessary and should be discontinued.' In GNA SNA Case no. 87/1911.
51. R.E. Dumett, 'The Rubber Trade of the Gold Coast and Asante in the Nineteenth Century: African Innovation and Market Responsiveness', *Journal of African History*, Vol. 12, No. 1 (1971), p. 79.
52. Ibid., p. 81.
53. 'Report . . . 1889', p. 90.
54. Dumett, 'The Rubber Trade', p. 100.
55. Ibid., p. 95.
56. The Gold Coast Legislative Council, for example, decided in 1892 to spend £2,650 on timber from the US, GCLegCo, 24 June 1892.
57. The description of the timber industry is taken from 'Gold Coast Timber Industry: Report of a Fact-Finding Committee Appointed by the Minister of Commerce, Industry and Mines' (Accra, 1951), p. 29.
58. Interview with a former European Barrister, Accra, May 1974.
59. See statement by Mr Hunt, European Unofficial Member, in GCLegCo, 29 April 1907.
60. Interview with George Grant Jr, son of 'Pa' Grant, Takoradi, July 1974.
61. Royal Commission on Shipping Rings (RCSR), Cd.4668 (1909), testimony of Sir Ralph Moore Q.7055.
62. See Chapter 4 for a description of the shipping industry in Ghana.
63. Charlotte Leubuscher, *The West African Shipping Trade* (A.W. Sythoff, Leyden, 1963), p. 22.
64. Interview with George Grant Jr.
65. 'Timber Supply, Consumption, and Marketing in Gold Coast', undated, report included in GNA, Cape Coast, Adm. 23/1/801.
66. 'The story of the Basel Trading Company Limited, 1859–1935', supplement

to the *West African Review* (November 1935), p. 14.
67. The story of Tetteh Quarshie can be found in M.J. Sampson, *Gold Coast Men of Affairs* (Dawsons of Pall Mall, London, 1969, 1st edn. 1937).
68. United Africa Company, 'What Cocoa Means to the Economy of the Gold Coast', *Statistical and Economic Review*, No. 2 (September 1948), p. 2.
69. C.T. Shephard, 'Report on the Economics of Peasant Agriculture in the Gold Coast' (Government Printing Office, Accra, 1936), p. 10.
70. 'Report of the Commission on the Marketing of West African Cocoa' (hereafter referred to as the Nowell Commission), Cmd. 5845 (1938), p. 17.
71. T. Hunter, 'Cost of Establishing Cacao by Ashanti Farmers', Gold Coast, Department of Agriculture *Year Book* (1930), included in Cad:289/24.
72. S. Herbert Frankel, *Capital Investment in Africa* (Howard Fertig, New York, 1969, 1st. edn. 1938), p. 323.
73. Hunter, 'Cost'.
74. 'Despatch of First Consignment of Sisal Hemp from Accra Sisal Plantation to Europe', *Journal of the Gold Coast Agricultural and Commercial Society*, Vol. 3, No. 3 (April 1924, to March 1925). p. 204.
75. Ibid.
76. Speech by the Governor to GCLegCo, 3 February 1925.
77. Speech by the Governor in GCLegCo, 22 February 1926.
78. Speech by the Governor in GCLegCo, 17 February 1930.
79. P.N. Davies, 'Sir Alfred Jones and the Development of West African Trade', unpublished MA Thesis, University of Liverpool, 1964, p. 272.
80. ManCC, 12 February 1931.
81. ManCC, 29 July 1931.
82. Governor to GCLegCo, 20 February 1936.
83. Digby Report, p. 248.
84. Ibid., p. 252.
85. Ibid., p. 245.
86. A statement to this effect was made by Mr Grey, of the 'Combine' firms, in GCLegCo, 28 January 1913.
87. Digby Report, p. 250.
88. Documents concerning this invention can be found in GNA Adm.11/1/223.
89. Digby Report, p. 270.
90. Statement by the Governor to GCLegCo, 17 February 1930.
91. GCLegCo, 1 March 1932.
92. Quoted by Nana Ofori Atta in GCLegCo, 19 March 1935. The author was unable to identify the original speaker.
93. The indigenous African transport business is discussed below, Chapter 5.
94. Gold Coast, *Blue Book* (1886).
95. LivCC, 30 October 1902, 5 August 1906.
96. Raymond E. Dumett, 'The Social Impact of the European Liquor Trade on the Akan of Ghana (Gold Coast and Asante) 1875–1910', *Journal of Interdisciplinary History*, Vol. 5, No. 1 (Summer 1974), p. 77.
97. 'Report of the Royal Commission on Trade and Taxation', Cmd.1600 (1921), Q.2254-57.
98. This point is made by Dumett, 'The Social Impact', p. 94.
99. Interview with several former British agents of G.B. Ollivant, Manchester, November 1974. The centres of the second-hand clothes trade were in London, New York, Philadelphia, Detroit, Chicago, Houston, Los Angeles and San Francisco.
100. ManCC, 10 April 1894.
101. Meeting of the London Chamber of Commerce with Mr H.S. Newlands, Chief Commissioner for Ashanti, LonCC, 22 June 1931.

102. For figures on total imports into Ghana, see Table 3.4.
103. Interview, G.B. Ollivant, Manchester, November 1974.
104. Anonymous report found in UAC Rankin File. The Keta cloth industry is also mentioned in W.M. Macmillan, 'African Development', in C.K. Meek (ed.), *Europe and West Africa* (Oxford University Press, London, 1940), p. 80.
105. J.C. de Grant-Johnson, *African Experiment: Co-operative Agriculture and Banking in British West Africa* (Watts and Company, London, 1958), p. 117.
106. 'Report . . . 1889', p. 36.
107. Speech by Mr Youngman, a European unofficial representative, to GCLegCo, 17 February 1930.
108. Governor to GCLegCo, 1 March 1932.
109. GCLegCo, 23 March 1933.
110. United Africa Company, *Your Company* (London, 1959), p. 23.
111. Ibid.
112. Investment patterns in Ghana are discussed further in Chapter 5, section 2.
113. GCCMines, *Fifth Annual Report* (1932), p. 23.
114. Interview, Gill and Duffus (cocoa brokers), London, December 1974.

4 OLIGOPOLISATION OF THE GHANAIAN ECONOMY

It is in the nature of mercantile capitalism to organise to protect its supplies and its markets. Its profits are made, not from the efficient organisation of the factors of production in order to increase the rate of exploitation, but rather from trading goods of equal value for unequal prices. The inequality of the pricing of such commodities implies inequalities in power relationships between traders; these inequalities are safeguarded by organisations of commercial co-operation, which have as one of their conditions the exclusion of outsiders. Thus, in Europe during the transitional stage between feudalism and capitalism merchant capitalists organised to protect their access to markets abroad.

While the oligopolistic exclusivity of merchant capitalists was broken down in Europe once industrial capitalism became ascendant, this form of organisation did not become outmoded in the periphery. The periphery was not industrialised; hence, there was no indigenous industrial capitalist class to compete for power with the merchant capitalists. 'Buying cheap and selling dear' was still the order of the day. In effect, the elimination of mercantilist policies in Europe had only been necessary for its dealings with other capitalist states; not for its dealings with the colonies.

It is not meant to imply here that the quasi-mercantilist control of oligopolists in underdeveloped areas was structurally equivalent to the mercantilism of early capitalist Europe. Rather, monopoly capitalism in the core required protection in the periphery; during the period of colonial rule, such protection was guaranteed both by organisations of commercial firms and by political overrule. The purpose was to increase the flow of wealth out of colonial areas to the core, where such wealth could be converted into capital for industrial production, into raw materials, or into food for the reproduction of workers.

1. Co-operation and Oligopoly in the Import-Export Trade[1]

Probably the best way to describe the process of oligopolisation of trade in Ghana is to take as one's starting point the United Africa Company (hereafter referred to as UAC). It is no doubt anachronistic to refer to the UAC as the most important of the companies trading in Ghana between 1885 and 1939, as the Company was not actually formed until 1929. Nevertheless, the reference is appropriate since, although the Company itself did not exist until 1929, those companies which eventually united to form it thoroughly dominated the Ghana trade from the early nineteenth century. This section will, therefore, briefly review the history of the UAC and its predecessors and then consider what competitors they had in trade.

The UAC was formed as a conglomeration of several companies which had dominated the British West African trade, especially in Ghana and Nigeria, since the turn of the nineteenth century. Originally, on the Gold Coast, there had been many small trading firms; competition was easy to enter because there were few advantages of scale. In the first half of the nineteenth century the major British firm in Ghana was that of Forster and Smith, with that of F. and A. Swanzy, a firm which began trading in 1789, a close competitor. Swanzy made agreements with Forster and Smith after 1852, when the invention of the steamship facilitated the regular carriage of small lots of goods and therefore the entrance of more small firms into the trade, but despite these agreements by 1873 Forster and Smith had disappeared from the coast, leaving Swanzy a free hand.[2] Swanzy's imports into Ghana during these early years included such goods as rum, tobacco, lumber, medicines and sewing machines, while its exports included gum copal, rubber, palm oil and sometimes more unusual items such as parrots and monkeys.[3]

By the beginning of the colonial period the main rival to Swanzy in Ghana was a Glasgow-based firm, Millers Limited. It had originally started as Alexander Miller, Brother and Company, and had been operating in the Gold Coast and the Niger area since 1868.[4] The two firms quickly began to come to agreements on prices and market distribution. Miller reorganised in the early twentieth century, forming Millers Limited, which traded in Ghana, in 1904, and Miller Brothers (of Liverpool) Limited, which traded in Nigeria, in 1907.[5] In 1904, Miller also moved to take over control of Swanzy, which as a result of over-investment in gold mines was then in financial difficulties. Thereafter the two firms remained nominally distinct but they cooperated very closely both at home and in Ghana.

The main competitor to Miller and Swanzy in the late nineteenth century was the African Association, a conglomeration of companies which had been formed into one group in Nigeria in 1889, the better to compete with the Royal Niger Company. The object of the formation of the Association was to obtain a charter in the Oil Rivers similar to that which the Royal Niger Company held, up to 1899, for the Niger River. In this object the company failed; it did, however, manage to reach a *modus vivendi* with the Royal Niger Company without which no doubt the several small companies would have gone under completely. This *modus vivendi* was doubly important because of close connections between Miller and the Royal Niger Company.

Although the African Association was originally formed to compete both with the Royal Niger Company and with the Miller-Swanzy group, by 1919 it had joined with the two latter companies to form the African and Eastern Trade Corporation. The reason for this new organisation was not simply that more co-operation was deemed necessary, but rather that by this point all three firms were worried about a new competitor, Lever Brothers. It seemed logical for the three firms to unite, as in fact their competition had been mitigated by a series of trade agreements, starting shortly after the African Association had opened its first store in Ghana in 1896.[6] In 1899 an agreement was made between the Niger Company, the African Association, Alexander Miller, Brother and Company, and the Company of African Merchants that they would not intrude upon each other's territory and that they would pool their profits and divide them in specified portions. This agreement, investigated by the Colonial Office and approved in 1900,[7] was followed by a 1901 agreement between Millers, Swanzy, and the African Association to fix prices on imported merchandise. In March 1904, an agreement was made to pool net profits and to divide them according to each company's capital worth. Later on, the three original companies joined with the Basel Mission Trading Company, J.J. Fischer and Company, and the German West African Trading Company (which was to disappear during the First World War) in an agreement to fix prices and pool profits on all staple exports.[8] The path to unity was further smoothed by co-operation during World War I, when 'a series of trade agreements started whose purpose was to regulate the purchase and division of produce. Nearly all the produce-buying houses entered into them.'[9]

The final impetus to unity, however, was provided by the entrance of Lever Brothers into the West African Coast, with its consequent threat of monopoly and destruction of all the carefully-organised trade patterns built up by the older trading firms over the late nineteenth and early twentieth centuries. Lever had had interests in West Africa from 1896, when it had first entered the palm oil trade in order to increase its control over the world supply of edible fats, which it used in its soap and margerine manufacture.[10] Realising that Lever Brothers was out to acquire as much control of oil palm supplies as it could, the African Association, Miller and Swanzy united in 1919 to form the African and Eastern Trade Association to protect their own interests. In July 1920, Lever Brothers bought the Niger Company. According to a former director of Lever Brothers, Lever wanted to make sure that it would obtain a certain portion of its requirements for the soap firms.

> He may have paid too much for it but the Niger Company strengthened Lever's hand by the quantity of produce that they were able to buy and import as against opposition. They had land and a monopoly; the land belonged to them. If you wanted to establish on the river Niger, you couldn't do it then without the Niger Company ... He [Lever] had a monopoly ... [A]n organisation such as Unilever, should not depend upon the market for raw material ...[11]

Although Lever Brothers originally entered the African trade in order to guarantee supplies of palm oil and kernels to itself and its sister companies, Jurgens and Van den Berghe of the Netherlands, it soon became evident that it would enter other aspects of the trade, particularly, in Ghana, the import-export trade based upon cocoa. The slump in cocoa prices in 1920 enabled it to very quickly buy up some of the smaller firms which had been trading in Ghana independent of the African and Eastern Trade Corporation. It immediately tried to buy out African and Eastern as well. In 1929, with the onset of the Depression, African and Eastern lost its financial backing, while the Niger Company was able to continue because of its 'fairy godmother', Unilever.[12] Without credit, African and Eastern was forced to join the Niger Company and form the United Africa Company on 3 March 1929. Originally, the two companies entered the union on equal terms, each holding 50 per cent of the United Africa Company shares. But in its first few years the United Africa Company faced serious financial difficulties from which only Unilever could bail it out; consequently, by 1932 Unilever, through the Niger Company, had 80 per cent control, and African and Eastern's originally equal voice had been reduced to only three directors.[13] By 1929, therefore, a large number of independent British firms which had traded in the Gold Coast over the space of 140 years, had succumbed to the forces of oligopoly and had been joined together under the umbrella of the

United Africa Company, which to the time of political independence was to remain the single most important firm in Ghana.

The UAC's holdings were extremely extensive. Aside from the firms already mentioned above, African and Eastern at the time of its incorporation included 26 other West African companies, which in 1929 were merged with the 29 West African firms owned by Lever Brothers. Between 1929 and 1938, the UAC acquired another 29 enterprises.[14] These holdings included interests in motors, lighterage, mineral waters, machine shops and chemists' shops, as well as in palm oil estates, mines and timber companies (not all in Ghana, however). Where the UAC did not have its own monopoly holdings, it often made agreements as to restrictions of trade with other companies. In 1930, for example, it made an agreement with Maypole Dairy of Accra that Maypole would submit to certain restrictions of its trading rights in return for shares in UAC.[15] This agreement was a continuation of practices which had been common prior to the UAC's formation. The A&ETC had had a monopoly of the distribution of petrol, kerosene and packet candles in Ghana during the 1920s.[16] It had also owned various manufacturing companies in Europe which provided it with diverse goods for the West Africa trade, such as oil palm casks, and which processed goods from West Africa; and it had owned factories which produced goods such as cotton cloths, preserves, dried fish and cosmetics for the West African market.[17] All of these firms had been incorporated into the UAC.

Lest it be thought, however, that the UAC maintained complete control of the trade at all times after its formation, it should be noted that it never managed to incorporate into its empire the independent manufacturing firms which were buying in Ghana; that is, the chocolate companies which bought cocoa primarily for their own use and were engaged only to a limited extent in the import-export trade. The three most important chocolate manufacturing firms which became direct buyers in Ghana were Cadbury Brothers Limited, J.S. Fry and Sons Limited, and J. Lyons and Company. The latter was a giant concern which included many hotel and restaurant interests in England, while the former two were more strictly concerned with the manufacture of confections. Cadbury Brothers and J.S. Fry amalgamated their business on the Gold Coast as of 1918, buying also for Rowntree.

Cadbury Brothers Limited was formed in England in 1900 and moved into the Gold Coast in 1907. Cadbury, a business owned by Quakers, professed interest in establishing fair practices in Ghana so as not to be guilty of some of the trade abuses practiced by its competitors at the time.[18] A recommendation made by their first Gold Coast agent condemned the business practices of firms such as Miller, Swanzy and the African Association, who paid for cocoa in 'chits' rather than in cash.[19] Cadbury also made a strong resolution to buy only good quality cocoa, and to encourage cash-crop farmers, by the payment of higher prices, to invest more time and money in their produce. This policy, however, did not succeed, as the producers found that Cadbury was rejecting poor quality cocoa which they had often travelled miles to sell, and as a result they were embittered against the company.[20] Cadbury did continue, however, to try to encourage farmers to grow better quality cocoa by giving grants to be spent on tools and insecticides, and by providing scholarships so that the more progressive farmers could study.[21]

There was stiff competition against Cadbury as a result of its policies not to pay by chits and not to buy poor quality cocoa. A transport boycott against the firms was instituted on its entrance into Ghana, but it was soon broken and by 1911 Cadbury was a leading cocoa buyer. After the sudden downswing in the cocoa market in 1920 (as a reaction after the post-war glut) 'tempting offers were made to manufacturing firms and blatant attempts were made by trading companies to jeopardise the position of the Cadbury-Fry agency on the Coast . . .'[22] When the United Africa Company was formed, yet another attempt was made to oust Cadbury from the Ghana trade. The company was obliged to charter its own ships because UAC pressure on the shipping companies resulted in its being denied space; further, the UAC outbid Cadbury for cocoa by as much as 1s 6d per cwt., then undersold it on both the Liverpool and the New York cocoa markets. (Cadbury and the other manufacturing firms customarily sold surplus supplies on the open market.) As a result negotiations took place in 1932–33, and an agreement was made on prices to be paid in Ghana and on a system of regulating supplies in Europe.[23]

The competition against the UAC and its predecessors by the chocolate manufacturing firms was supplemented by the few other British trading firms which were able to compete effectively and retain their independence. These firms included John Holt and Company (Liverpool) Limited; W. Bartholemew and Company; Busi and Stephenson Limited; Paterson, Zochonis and Company Limited; and G.B. Ollivant Limited. They were the largest of the myriad firms which were scattered all over West Africa during the colonial period, eking out, for the most part, a meagre existence, and often ending up by being incorporated into the oligopolistic structure.

John Holt entered the West African trade in the 1860s, beginning with the export of cheap manufactured goods to Nigeria and branching from that into produce buying. The company did not enter Ghana until 1935, although it had a 'factory' at Keta, near the Togoland border, from the early 1920s.[24] Its expansion was rapid, however, and by 1938 it had 61 stores and 27 cocoa-buying stations in Ghana.[25] The firm of John Holt had been a founding member of the African Association in 1889, but quarrels with the other members of the Association had resulted in its withdrawal in 1896.[26] Thereafter, the firm remained independent, although its role as a check on monopolistic tendencies was somewhat modified by its participation in price-fixing agreements.

W. Bartholemew and Company was formed in 1926 and entered Ghana in the same year, specialising not only in cocoa-buying and merchandise selling, but more specifically in the importing of motor cars.[27] Like Bartholemew, the firms of both Busi and Stephenson and Paterson Zochonis entered Ghana quite late, the former in the late 1920s or early 1930s, the latter about 1933.[28] But whereas Busi and Stephenson was a new firm, Paterson and Zochonis was, like Holt, a firm which had traded in other West African colonies for a considerable period of time, having begun in Freetown, Sierra Leone, in 1890.

It should be noted that many firms entered Ghana in the late 1920s and 1930s. The thirties was also a period of entry for Lebanese traders and for a number of independent Continental Europeans. This entry of new firms contradicts the theory that in times of economic depression small firms are pushed out of trade in favour of larger firms. In Ghana, more firms competed for a diminished world cocoa market. One possible explanation for this phenomenon could be that, in order to keep their profits up, firms such as John Holt sought to expand. Another explanation could be found in the fact that even during the Depression, comfortable dividend rates were being paid by the firms investing in the import-export trade in West Africa. Oligopolistic organisation, into which some of the newer firms joined, counterbalanced the effects of the Depression.

One of the oldest independent British firms to compete with the UAC was G.B. Ollivant (GBO), a Manchester-based concern which was started in 1858. GBO was the firm which imported the most Lancashire cottons into West Africa. In 1923, it was recorded as having three branches in Ghana, at Accra, Winneba and Keta.[29] In 1934, it became financially associated with UAC, but it continued to compete with the actual UAC organisation until the 1960s; there was, in other words, 'regulated' internal competition.[30] GBO was perceived as a separate organisation by its African customers.

Those few foreign (that is, non-British) firms which were able to establish themselves over significant periods of time in Ghana, also co-operated with the UAC. Both the French Compagnie Française de l'Afrique Occidentale (CFAO) and the Swiss Société Commerciale de l'Ouest Africain (SCOA) had extensive networks in Ghana, the former having entered the Colony in 1909, and the latter in 1914. They engaged, as did the British firms, in general import and export trade, concentrating on cocoa. Like the British firms, they shipped through the Elder Dempster and Woermann lines. The only substantial difference they had with their British competitors was that they tended to be financed by European banks and a higher proportion of their goods and produce came from or was destined for the Continental market. They suffered no discrimination on account of their national origins.[31]

A smaller continental company, the Swiss African Trading Company, which entered the Gold Coast in 1922 specifically as a cocoa-buying firm with its headquarters in Kumasi, was bought out by the UAC in 1936,[32] although it remained nominally distinct after that date.

Until the 1930s when the Depression induced a certain amount of protectionism, the policy of the government was to allow all companies equal access to Ghana. In the case of French firms such as CFAO, this right was guaranteed by the Anglo-French agreement of 1898. There was, in fact, only one Continental company which suffered any discrimination in Ghana as a result of its national affiliation. The assets of the Basel Mission Trading Company, a Swiss firm with some German personnel, were confiscated in 1918, but after a long legal battle the company, under the new name of the Union Trading Company, was awarded £250,000 remuneration and allowed to re-enter Ghana in 1928.[33]

Discrimination against non-British companies in Ghana was unusual, because informal, extralegal means of control were on the whole sufficient to guarantee that a large percentage of the trade was kept in British hands. The government confined its role to bland statements that it could not interfere in arrangements made among the firms to regulate trade; it did not actively forbid outsiders or Africans from trade. In fact, the primary aim of the colonial state, in regulating its trade policy, was to encourage as much trade as possible, with whatever country, in order to increase the revenues which it obtained from import and export duties.[34] Only during the Depression was there significant pressure to close Ghana to foreign traders, and this pressure was aimed not at England's real rivals, that is, America, France and Germany, but against the relatively weak rivals of Japan and Russia. Any pressure for restriction of imports from the three former countries would have resulted in retaliatory measures by their governments against Gold Coast exports.[35]

The hostilities which existed in Europe between Germany and Britain were, however, reflected in Gold Coast policy. During World War I all German traders and their agents were expelled from the colony, and their property was auctioned off to British traders only, thus effecting a redistribution of commercial properties in the eastern Gold Coast adjoining Togoland. After World War I the German traders were allowed to re-enter the colony under strict immigration procedures. No hostility was evinced against them until the 1930s, when European unofficial members in the Legislative Council began to protest generally about the presence of foreigners. The Germans were accused of paying their European staff lower wages than the British, of hiring few Africans, and of selling British goods at lower prices than the British themselves could manage.[36] No expulsion of German citizens took place, but after the declaration of war in 1939 they were interned.

Rumblings were also heard in the West African trade community during the 1930s against several other nations, all of whom were infringing on the now closely-guarded empire of the large British firms. The Liverpool Chamber of Commerce tried, without success, to persuade the home government to place a prohibitive duty on Russian and Norwegian whale oil imports to Britain as whale oil was competing with palm oil.[37] The Sheffield Chamber of Commerce, through Manchester, tried to persuade the Gold Coast government to place a tariff on Continental manufactures so that Sheffield could export more agricultural machinery and road and mine building equipment to Africa.[38] Manchester, concerned for its textiles, pressured the government for protection against Russian greys.[39] None of these petitions was successful, however, as in each case the fear of retaliatory measures which would affect the empire as a whole pre-empted the interests of the British African traders.

The only successful move against foreign competition was that against the import into Ghana of Japanese textiles, which began to increase during the mid-1930s. In 1932, Japan was responsible for only 1 per cent of the cotton piece goods imported into Ghana, but by 1934 its share had increased to 18 per cent.[40] Since Japan was not a customer for British exported goods, it was easy enough to impose a quota on its imports, on the grounds that the economy of Ghana, and also of the empire, would suffer if those who sold to Ghana did not also buy from it. The Textiles (Quotas) Ordinance was passed in 1934, with the object 'to restrict the annual imports only of certain textile goods manufactured in Japan.'[41]

During the 1930s, pressure also began to be generated inside Ghana to restrict the number of non-Africans immigrating into the colony. Specifically, this pressure was directed against Italians and Lebanese. Italians were becoming a significant force in the internal Ghanaian economy as, unlike the English, they were not afraid to perform manual labour and they were engaged, not in trade, but in contracting work. In 1931, 43 per cent of the government's small contracting work was given to Italians and Syrians, and 48 per cent to Africans.[42] Because the Italians charged less than the British, certain Europeans felt that they must be doing shoddy work and paying poor wages to their employees. The government, however, argued that a significant percentage of large railroad contracts still went to British firms, and moreover, that for all government work contractors were obliged to use British materials, and therefore refused to move against the Italians.[43]

Similar objections were made against the Syrians (Lebanese), who began to move into the colony in increasing numbers in the 1930s. Always ready to invoke African interests when it helped their own case, the London Chamber of Commerce expressed the fear that Syrians would take over opportunities from 'the African trader, the African clerking class, the African Property Owner and the European Merchant.'[44] Africans also complained against the Syrians, whom they accused of unscrupulous pawnbroking and of denying opportunities for employment to Africans.

> Parents in this country feel that certain Syrians are ruining the youths of this country, and the youths must be protected ... These Syrians do not scruple for a moment to take or pawn anything even from an infant; and the amount of gold which is carried away from this country, illegitimately, is enormous ... [45]

I came across during my travels a Syrian who was a cook for himself, and who, one occasion, was unloading a lorry containing yams, pepper, and onions which he had bought for himself from another place. He would not even pay a farthing to a labourer to remove the things from the lorry. A man like this leaves nothing to the country. He is taking all the money away to a foreign country, and we get nothing from it.[46]

The government was indeed concerned with the influx of Lebanese into the colony, but more for cultural reasons, one suspects (since Lebanese were certainly not black and yet not quite white) than for economic. Their incursion into petty trade did not immediately affect the large European firms. In 1938 the executive council considered the possibility of either a quota or a total prohibition on the immigration of Syrians, but no action was taken on the matter.[47]

On the whole, then, the policy of the Ghana government throughout the colonial period was one of relatively free access to all traders, of whatever nation. Restrictions on trade were imposed by the firms themselves, through their monopoly agreements, not by the state. There were only two exceptions to this policy; the exclusion of Germans during and immediately after World War I, and the imposition of quotas on Japanese textiles after 1934. In both of these cases hardships resulted for the indigenous population. The removal of German traders from eastern Ghana left trade there in the hands of a few British, who found it easy to collude against the African middleman trader. The removal of Japanese textiles from the market in the 1930s imposed an additional hardship upon the already squeezed African consumers. There was some opposition among Ghanaians to the move, especially as they suspected that after the imposition of the quota they would be sold the same Japanese goods under a British label at a higher price.

> It is confidently felt that the Government cannot, after appealing to the people to join in putting this embargo on the Japanese, hesitate to bring down to the lowest ebb our present inflated import duty — the only cause for the rush after Japanese goods . . . It is stated that the Empire is analagous to a large family, the members of which should watch with jealous care the interests of each other. That being so, it cannot be conjectured that immediately the Gold Coast Market is relieved of Japanese imports of cheap prices, then the same goods re-appear with different labels, and, with extortionate value in the same market.[48]

In cases in which the interests of African consumers conflicted with those of British traders, the interests of the latter took priority. It was more important to protect British textiles (and Lancashire textile workers, whose political clout was far more potent, during the

Depression, than that of African peasants) than to supply cheap cloth in Ghana. But where the interests of British traders conflicted with those of the empire as a whole, the latter took precedence. Trade patterns with other nations had to be considered *en bloc*, and protection for Ghana might mean retaliation against another part of the empire. It was left to the business community to make its private agreements to ward off competition, agreements which were neither influenced by, nor the responsibility of, the colonial government, and of which it could deny knowledge were it accused of not acting in the best interests of the African.

Ghanaians, well acquainted with the fact that despite their different names, the British firms were often legally amalgamated or at least acted in concert, referred to the original firms of African and Eastern, Miller and Swanzy, as the 'Combine' firms. They were aware that the Combine firms and their descendant, UAC, could not simply impose prices either for produce or for imported goods, since there were still a number of fairly large independent firms, both British and Continental, trading in Ghana. However, it was known, although difficult to substantiate, that it was common practice for the Combine firms to make agreements both among themselves and with their major rivals. Such agreements usually covered both the prices to be paid for agricultural goods produced by Africans and the prices to be charged to them for imported manufactured goods.

The list of agreements made by the European firms to control import and export prices, as well as the share of the market to be allotted to each participating firm, extends from the early twentieth century to 1939. Table 4.1 presents a partial list of these agreements, but it is by no means meant to be complete. It includes, for example, few agreements during the 1910s, yet an unofficial history of the UAC states that during World War I most of the large companies entered into agreements on the purchase and division of produce.[49] The Nowell Commission in 1938 reported a series of agreements which more or less coincide with the list presented below; it concluded that periods of co-operation were interspersed with periods of intense and damaging competition.

> We have had described to us in evidence a cocoa Agreement entered into in 1903 ... Although the 1903 Agreement was apparently limited to one year, subsequent agreements were made in 1903 [sic], 1905, and again for a period of five years in 1906. From 1910 there followed a period of cocoa buying and selling agreements

[i.e., agreements including provision for the pooling of sales as well as of purchases] which lasted until 1917. After the War, probably owing to the efforts at amalgamation between the two largest concerns [A&ETC and Lever], agreements were less common, but a cocoa Agreement of the earlier type was in force between 1925 and 1927; and a cocoa buying and selling Agreement operated during the first three years of the United Africa Company's existence . . .

[I]t appears from admissions to us in evidence that agreements have tended to be regarded as 'breathing spaces' between bouts of fierce competition, and that they have invariably broken down through competitive forces reestablishing themselves.[50]

The companies argued that competition was irrational in West Africa; that there was a limited amount of trade available, which could not be expanded, and that therefore it behooved them to organise and share out that limited amount among themselves rather than allow a dog-eat-dog situation to develop in which the weak would suffer.

The Firms do not co-operate to make exorbitant rates of profit. They well know it to be impossible. What they seek is to stabilise trade and create such conditions as will enable them to obtain a modest but fairly steady return on their capital.[51]

The point of the agreements which were made, according to the firms, was not to be able to make excessive profits, but rather to be able to guarantee a certain percentage of the trade to each firm and to guarantee a certain return. The prime aim was to create stability in a limited trade which, at least on the export side, was subject to extreme fluctuations in the world market. When the world market could not be controlled, the firms tried to establish control of the local market.

During the 1930s, the UAC, in concert with a number of its major rivals, formed a Merchandise Agreement group; that is, a group of firms who agreed on prices and shares of the market for a number of major imports into Ghana. This group of cooperating firms became known as the Association of West African Merchants (AWAM).[52] Surviving into World War II and beyond, the Association was the centre of power in the Ghana (and Nigeria) trade. Again, Africans were

Oligopolisation of the Ghanaian Economy

Table 4.1: Trade Agreements in the Gold Coast

No.	Date	Description
1.	1 May 1900	Agreement for pooling produce of West African business between the African Association, the Niger Company, and others.
2.	1 October 1901	Pooling agreement between the African Association Limited, Alexander Miller and Company, and F. & A. Swanzy Limited.
3.	20 February 1902	Agreement regarding palm kernels, etc., between the African Association Limited, Alexander Miller, Brother and Company, and the Germany West Africa Company.
4.	3 November 1903	Pooling agreement between Messrs. F. & A. Swanzy Limited and Millers Limited.
5.	1 March 1904	Agreement regarding sharing in proportion to the capital of each party the net profits of the businesses of the parties carried on in the Gold Coast and the German Colony, between F. & A. Swanzy Limited, Millers Limited and the African Association Limited. Expired 31 December 1913.
6.	10 May 1906 11 July 1910 22 May 1913	Agreements between F. & A. Swanzy, Millers Limited and the African and Eastern Trade Corporation Limited (the African Association).
7.	1905	Accra Produce Agreement between F. & A. Swanzy Limited, Millers Limited, the African Association Limited, J.J. Fischer and Company, the [Basel] Mission Trading Company and the German West African Trading Company.
8.	13 February 1906	Volta Produce Agreement for pooling purchases of cocoa, rubber, palm oil and palm kernels between the [Basel] Mission Trading Company, F. & A. Swanzy Limited, Millers Limited, and Chevalier and Company.
9.	1905, 1909, 1914	Sundry timber pool agreements between the Gold Coast Machinery and Trading Company Limited, F. & A. Swanzy Limited, Millers Limited and the African Association Limited.
10.	27 July 1912	Agreements regarding staple articles between the Basel Mission Trading Company, the African Association Limited, Millers Limited, and F. & A. Swanzy Limited.
11.	1925/1926	Cocoa pool agreement. African and Eastern Trade Corporation and others.
12.	7 January 1930	Agreement for the purchase and sale of palm oil and palm kernels between the UAC, John Holt and Company (Liverpool) Limited, G.B. Ollivant and Paterson Zochonis.

continued . . .

Table 4.1 continued

No.	Date	Description
13.	27 July 1934	Gold Coast Merchandise Agreement (and Supplement 18 June 1937).
14.	18 May 1935	Agreement regarding the Gold Coast Motor Business between Cie. Française de l'Afrique Occidentale, Société Commerciale de l'Ouest Africain, Union Trading Company, W. Bartholemew and Company, and UAC.
15.	30 November 1936	Agreements covering the sale of palm oil and palm kernels between UAC, John Holt and Company and G.B. Ollivant Limited.
16.	10 November 1937	Agreement between W. Bartholemew and Company, UAC and others for division of cocoa in the Gold Coast (the Cocoa Pool).

Source: This table is taken from listings of the United Africa Company archival holdings in London. Unfortunately, the author did not obtain access to the actual agreements. It is presumed that the list is incomplete.

well aware of the existence of the Association, and often referred to it as the chief power behind the colonial government.[53]

Although it is difficult to ascertain the exact profit rates of the companies operating in Ghana during this period, what little evidence is available does suggest that the firms' argument was basically correct; that in fact their profits were not excessive. Nevertheless, the profits were steadier, especially during the Depression period, than the firms maintained. Much of their profit came not from the cocoa crop but from the sales of imported goods, which could be bought at a consistently cheap rate from the suppliers but sold at whatever the market could bear. Prices of imported goods varied directly with the prices paid for cocoa; if the latter rose, the former rose, and if the latter fell, the former fell.[54] But losses on the cocoa crop could nevertheless be made up by profits from imports. While the prices of raw materials fell between World War I and the Depression, prices on processed goods such as cotton cloth (one of Ghana's most important imports) rose.[55] Indeed, it would seem as if although Ghana produced raw materials which were necessary for industrialism in Britain and Europe, the mercantile capitalists who were the original buyers of its raw materials actually made their profits from the resale back to the Ghanaian producers of manufactured goods.

Although data on profit rates are difficult to obtain, the author was able to locate some indications of profit rates in the mid-1920s from private archives. The data refer to companies which were branches of the African and Eastern Trade Corporation, later incorporated into the UAC. Between 1924 and 1927, the Tarquah trading company made between 2.3 per cent and 8 per cent profit per year; the Gold Coast Machinery and Trading Company made between 5 per cent and 10.5 per cent; McLaren Brothers ranged between a loss of 1 per cent and a profit of 9 per cent, and Crombie Steedman made between a loss of 1 per cent and a profit of 5 per cent. On the other hand, the African and Eastern Trade Corporation made overall between 10 per cent and 12 per cent profit in the same time period.[56] The United Africa Company made low profits for the first few years after its initial formation in 1929, but in 1934/35, 1935/36 and 1936/37, it made 8, 10 and 11 per cent profits, respectively.[57]

Table 4.2 presents dividend rates in five-year averages for several companies including the African and Eastern Trade Corporation, the Niger Company and Unilever. Dividend rates are, of course, not a completely accurate reflection of profits, especially because payments are made according to decisions on reinvestment policies; moreover, in poor periods dividends can be paid out of reserve funds. Furthermore, in the cases of J. Lyons and Unilever, the dividend rates reflect their overall business, not simply their business on the West Coast of Africa. It should be noted that the African Association/African and Eastern managed to pay consistently high dividends, with the single exception of 1921 (following the cocoa market failure of 1920), until the Depression. And the UAC, although it was formed on the verge of the great Depression, nevertheless managed to pay some dividends, increasing slowly from one-half per cent in 1931 to 11 per cent in 1937.[58]

To keep these profits and dividend rates up the large British and Continental firms in Ghana made a series of agreements, listed partially in Table 4.1, which were rigidly enforced. The agreements (which never included any African firms) covered produce, including cocoa, palm products, rubber and timber, as well as imported merchandise. During the 1930s, the share-distributing agreement, confined to members of the Association of West African Merchants, covered many popular brands of goods imported in large quantities, including salt, sugar, dried fish and dyes.[59] Agents of each firm kept a sharp eye upon one another and informed their principals whenever there was any infraction of share-setting or price-fixing rules.

An employee of one major firm was dismissed in 1939, for example,

110 *Oligopolisation of the Ghanaian Economy*

in what became known inside his firm as the 'Club Beer price cutting case'. As his superior reported:

> I had no idea whatsoever that Mr ——— was cutting prices in the Shop. I had caught him only four days previously in Bergedorfbeer and told him in rather strong terms that this is against my instructions. Yet when the Local Committee investigated matters ... it found out that seven [cases] had been sold at 39s instead of 40s ... The only remedy is to replace this man, since I have caught him again undercutting the sale price of soap (agreed) after the incident.[60]

Table 4.2: Ordinary Dividend Rates for Selected Companies, by Five-Year Averages, 1886–1939

Year	Niger Co.	African Association/A & ETC	Unilever	J. Lyons	Commonwealth Trust	Bartholemew
1886–89	3	–	–	–	–	–
1890–94	6.3	6	–	–	–	–
1895–99	10.4	8.1	12.5	10.1	–	–
1900–4	8	12.6	15	27.8	–	–
1905–9	10	12	11.1	32	–	–
1910–14	10	10.6	14.	40.5	–	–
1915–19	8	23	14	28.5	–	–
1920–24	0	8.3	12	32	1	–
1925–29	1	4.4	4	22.5	8	57.7**
1930–34	1	0	13	22.5	1	4
1935–38*	n.d.	4.6	n.d.	22.5	8.3	0

Source: Raw data from *Stock Exchange Yearbook* (1895, 1905, 1915, 1925, 1935, 1939). NB n.d. = no data. In several cases, fiscal years, not calendar years, are listed in the *Stock Exchange Yearbook*. For the sake of simplicity, in such cases the figure is listed under the last calendar year, e.g., 1893/94 is listed under 1894.
*No figures available for 1939.
**Excluding 1925.

In this case the superior officer was particularly upset because an employee of UAC had complained to the 'general Manager's Committee', a local committee of all the firms which periodically set prices, that his particular firm was deliberately undercutting the agreement. Reports of this kind could endanger a small firm's chances of being included in price-fixing and share-distributing agreements.

Most of the evidence of price-fixing in Ghana came to light in the 1930s when several attempts were being made by Africans to break loose of European control.[61] The fact that such evidence came to light at this late date may indicate that price-fixing became more prevalent after the formation of the UAC; or it may simply indicate that Ghanaians became more sophisticated in their dealings with Europeans and more perceptive of the actual trade practices being employed in the colony. In the absence of free access to private company archives, it is impossible to determine the actual incidence of price-fixing over a long time period.

In 1930 Nana Ofori Atta, protesting against the existence of a cocoa 'pool', brought two pieces of evidence before the Legislative Council to prove his charges of price-fixing. The first was a reference to a statement reported in *West Africa* by Major-General William Henry Grey, a director, at the time the statement was made in 1925, of the A&ETC. He 'stated that they [the Combine] fixed the buying price in Africa and the selling price in Europe, and the companies followed the policy dictated by the committee.'[62] Nana Ofori Atta also referred to a specific piece of evidence in a telegram which indicated not only that prices were fixed, but that prices could have been higher had the firms been freely competing. In the telegram, a Mr Youngman complained to SCOA headquarters in Lome that their Saltpond agent had increased the prices paid for cocoa, causing losses to other firms, and invoking the wrath of Cadbury. Nana Ofori Atta commented:

> According to this we got to know that even if a European who may be in the Group or otherwise to-day attempts to offer a price a little more than agreed upon by the Pool, he is arraigned before his superiors, and I do not know what would be his fate. That shows that the Group were in a position to offer more than what they were offering at the time. I do not think a man coming out here would be so foolish as to do something deliberately which he knew would bring loss. I believe, he knew he could offer a little higher price with profit to himself. It means there is something which has been kept from the knowledge of the African farmer.[63]

Not only did this telegram reveal the absence of free competition in the cocoa market, but it also indicated that Cadbury, although it had not signed the actual agreement, was co-operating in price-fixing activities. If, as was often claimed, price-fixing was a method of protecting the farmers by shoring up prices in a declining market, it was no doubt difficult for Ghanaians to understand why one firm should be disciplined for offering an even higher price.

Ghanaians were unwilling to accept the contention put forward in the 1930s that it was the international economic crisis which had, in the final analysis, facilitated both the formation of a monopoly structure in the Gold Coast, and the decline in the cocoa price. Rather, they concluded that the congruity in time of price agreements and price declines indicated that the latter had at least partially been caused by the former. At the same time, there was a great deal of evidence indicating that prices of consumer goods were systematically being kept higher than competition would have permitted by the use of oligopolistic agreements.

In one report, filed by the Acting District Commissioner of Saltpond in 1938, it was clearly demonstrated that there was a correlation between the prices being paid for cocoa and the prices charged for imported goods in the shops.

> A comparison between cocoa and store prices shows a connection. Merchants admit that it is their practice to raise store prices when cocoa prices rise. Merchants meet once or twice per month in Saltpond and fix prices for their principal goods. An 'Approved Price List' is produced, and merchants are expected to adhere to these prices.
>
> The total trade of each district is divided amongst the merchants, and a firm is allowed to sell a certain percentage only of the total district sales of any of the principal goods.
>
> | e.g. flour | UAC | 60% |
> |---|---|---|
> | | GBO | 10% |
> | | UTC | 10% |
> | | SCOA | 5% |
> | | CFAO | 5% |
> | | remainder | 10% |
>
> If at the end of the trading year any firm's sales have exceeded this fixed percentage, and other firms have not sold up to their percentage, the former pay a penalty to the latter. This adjustment is made in London.[64]

This same District Commissioner later reported a case of price fixing by the UAC, in which the Company tried to undercut a competitor, presumably an independent Syrian, who was selling sugar at less than the monopoly price.

Tate and Lyle Sugar:
UAC have been unable to get Tate and Lyle to agree to their terms for sugar, and could not put pressure on a firm of such standing. Bikhazi Brothers buy Tate and Lyle's sugar for cash and UAC are attempting to stop this. Last month the case price for sugar in Saltpond was 21/6, the price is the same this month in Accra, Nsawam, Swedru, etc. The case price of UAC sugar has been reduced to 16/6. The reason for this drop in price is that Bikhazi Brothers are landing a few thousand cases of sugar at Accra shortly and by forcing down the price UAC hopes to leave this consignment on Bikhazi's hands.[65]

Local government officials were more willing to investigate and report price fixing of consumer goods than of cash-crops, because not only Ghanaians, but also they themselves were affected by consumer prices. The Chief Commissioner for Ashanti, for instance, was very upset when in early 1938 he sent his servant to buy iron sheeting, and discovered that a bundle which in 1937 had cost 37s 6d now cost 65s. 'His boy [servant] told him that the price was the same at all stores and the reply to his query was — the price is fixed by the UAC.'[66]

The growing awareness of the existence of price-fixing agreements in the late 1930s reflected practices of which many educated Ghanaians and chiefs had been aware for some years. Both of these classes knew of the amount of monopoly in Ghana and frequently raised objections to it. The progressive amalgamation of so many firms into what eventually became the UAC was viewed not as a benign development, but as a means both of limiting free competition and of squeezing out the indigenous African trader.

Our interests demand that the trade of the Colony be open to as many competitors as possible, and I therefore strongly urge that anything tending to strengthen or to lend support of the Government to the monopolistic policy under which the natives have suffered during the past years should be seriously deprecated and discouraged.[67]

The above speech by Nana Ofori Atta was made in 1918, well before any of the larger amalgamations of firms had taken place; already, however, the African community was aware, even if only vaguely, of the many agreements which were made in restraint of trade, and was accustomed to refer to the large firms as the 'Combine' firms. When the formation of African and Eastern was in the wind, Ofori Atta questioned:

> Whether the designed amalgamation of the already existing large trading firms [into the A&ETC] should not be viewed with grave apprehension from the point of view of the future of the countries wherein such firms are going to carry on their activities?[68]

T. Hutton-Mills, a representative of the educated Ghanaian community, was concerned that the European firms would squeeze the African community out of trade, and felt that the government should assume obligations to make sure that the different commercial sectors should all have opportunities in trade.

> There are three classes [in Ghana] who are virtually entitled to participate in the trade of this Colony; the European merchant, company, corporation or firm on the one hand, the native trader on the other and the native chiefs with the concurrence and assent of their councillors. In distributing trade amongst the inhabitants I would ask that the monopoly should not be given to any particular class and to avoid complication and unsatisfactory murmuring the educated classes should always be recognised – some of them at any rate – as being entitled to a share of the trade in their own country.[69]

These early criticisms of the oligopolised structure of Ghana's trade were echoed frequently in the next two decades, always with the same refrain, that competition had declined, that prices were being systematically fixed, and that (in later years) the creation of the UAC had had adverse effects on the Ghanaian people. In 1933 the Provincial Council of Chiefs of the Central Province took it upon itself to complain directly to UAC about the situation. While its complaints were ignored, and both UAC and government explained repeatedly that the world economic situation was responsible for current problems internally, the evidence presented above suggests that the assessment of Ghana's economy by the chiefs had some accuracy.

> [I]t is interesting for the Gold Coast people to ask ... [the] British

combined Firms whether they can point out to the British West
African commercial world a single beneficient act conferred by
them on the Gold Coast for any useful public purpose . . .
[I]nstead, it has become most painful for the Ruling Chiefs and
their people to have reasons to believe that the present unstable
and most unsatisfactory condition of the local Cocoa market is
due more or less to the sharp commercial manipulation of the
UAC . . . [I]nformation has reached this Council . . . that several
independent Cocoa merchants in Europe, who usually send out
their representatives to the Coast to buy Cocoa for them, by
which the usual healthy commercial competition is infused into
the local market, have ceased to do so on account of it is believed
the UAC Ltd offering to supply their requirements cheaper . . .
[I]t is the intention of this . . . Council . . . to point out to the UAC
Ltd with particular reference to their three principal Gold Coast
associated firms of F. and A. Swanzy Ltd, and the African
Association Ltd, and Millers Ltd that the existing financial distress
throughout the cocoa farming district of this country is due to the
local low price that during some years past, they have engineered
for cocoa and induced others to follow them. . . [70]

But far from responding to these requests and objections from the
Africans, the government made no attempt at all to restrain the
increasing oligopolisation of the Gold Coast economy. Britain was, on
the whole, less concerned with problems of monopoly than other
countries, especially the United States; certainly within the colonies
she would make no move to restrain any developments which might
guarantee a higher share of trade to British firms. No matter how
the African members of local legislative councils might object, the
British firms, with regular access to the Colonial Office in London,
were in a position to push their own point of view much more
effectively than the Africans. Price-fixing agreements, crop-sharing
agreements, and monopoly distribution of goods were not matters
for investigation by the state in a colonial situation.

As the next two sections will demonstrate, monopoly agreements
and preferential treatments for large firms were as prevalent in the
shipping and banking sectors as in trade. Again, the state intervened
very little in these activities, although the shipping industry was investigated by a Royal Commission in 1909. Essentially, shipping
and banking existed to provide finance and transport for the import-
export sector in a way most advantageous, not to the economy of

the colony as a whole, but to the expatriate entrepreneurs who dominated it.

2. Oligopolisation of the Shipping Industry: The West Africa Conference

By the turn of the twentieth century, shipping over most of the world was organised into a group of 'Conferences', which set prices for shipping, organised scheduled services, and arranged which lines should be allowed to enter which ports. The West Africa trade was no exception: agreements on the control of shipping to West Africa were being made as early as the 1870s,[71] and in 1895 an actual Conference was established.

With the advent of the steamship in 1852, the need for regulation of the shipping industry had become evident. Steamships were fast and regular; they did not depend on the wind. With their speed they were able to transport previously unconveyable perishable commodities. But they also required large investments, which most merchants could not afford. A new industry, that of shipping agencies, developed and more and more merchants began to abandon their fleets of sailing ships and rely on the regular steamship lines to transport their produce. The advent of shipping lines facilitated competition because merchant houses could now send small, regular packages to the west coast of Africa; instead of sending large shiploads comprised completely of their own goods, which if they sank, would bankrupt the actual merchants. Small traders who could not afford even to buy their own sailing boats were also able to ship by the regular steam lines.

The roots of the West Africa Conference are found in the division (in 1870) of the British West Africa trade between the Africa Steamship Company, incorporated in 1852, and the British and African Steam Navigation Company, incorporated in 1869.[72] Both businesses were run by the agency of Elder Dempster Ltd, in Liverpool, which in 1894 took over ownership of both firms. Elder Dempster was to remain the single most important British shipping firm in the Gold Coast until 1939, and the only British firm within the West Africa Conference. Between 1896, when it established the Bank of British West Africa,[73] and 1929, when the UAC was formed, it was arguably the most important expatriate firm in the whole of Ghana.

Elder Dempster's most important rival in the West Africa trade was the Hamburg-based (German) African Steamship Line, otherwise known as the Woermann Line, formed in 1885.[74] Woermann was the recipient of German state subsidies, so that although it had far fewer connections in the West African trade than did Elder Dempster, and although there were fewer established German colonies, it managed to build up a large fleet in a relatively short time. In 1913–14 Woermann carried 25 per cent of the shipping tonnage between Northern Europe and West Africa as opposed to Elder Dempster's 75 per cent; in 1924–25 Woermann, with its partner the Hamburg-West Africa Line carried 20 per cent of the total tonnage; and in 1938–39 the two German companies carried 29 per cent of the Conference tonnage.[75] Throughout the period, however, as these figures make obvious, Elder Dempster was the 'senior' partner in the Conference.

It should be noted that Woermann lines had complete access to British colonial ports (but not, as will be elaborated below, to metropolitan British ports); the British government never confined access to its colonies to its own nationals but instead relied on informal controls and cartelisation to guarantee British priority in shipping. Agreements between British and German shipping lines were first negotiated in 1888, 'to stop a mutually disastrous competition . . .'[76] The trade at this time was characterised, as it was to be throughout the colonial period, by an over-supply of tonnage. Both Germany and Britain predicated their tonnage needs on wartime, not peacetime, requirements; they encouraged their shipping industries accordingly, with the result that except during wartime, too many ships were on the high seas.[77] Because of over-competition, world-wide freight rates had declined by about 40 per cent between 1889 and 1895.[78]

In 1895, therefore, Elder Dempster and Woermann Line joined together in a shipping conference designed to ensure them adequate patronage and, with this patronage, adequate return on their investments. Apparently concern over the world-wide decline in freight rates was exacerbated in their case by demands from the African Association that Elder Dempster grant it preferential treatment. Elder Dempster was able to forestall these demands by making agreements with its major competitor.[79] Following the pattern of similar shipping conferences established elsewhere, the two firms used the 'rebate system' as their main weapon in the control of trade. This was a system whereby traders who shipped only on Conference lines were guaranteed a 10 per cent rebate on their shipping charges at the end of every six months' period. The traders had to guarantee to ship only on Conference lines and no other; that is, not to ship either on their own boats or on 'tramp' steamers. They also had to wait a total of two shipping periods, or twelve months, for each rebate. In return for their loyalty to the Conference system, traders were guaranteed regularity of service, which the tramp steamers could not provide. A Conference steamer, whether it had its full load or not, would sail according to its scheduled dates. The traders were also guaranteed security of rates; charges no longer fluctuated wildly as they had done under the system of free competition; calculations of costs could, therefore, be made on a long-term basis.

The Conference system also included one or two rather discriminatory clauses, however. One was that 'loyalty' was required on all goods shipped, i.e., that goods for which rebates could not be obtained must nevertheless be shipped only on Conference lines, even though rebates would be paid only on outward-bound goods (from Europe), and on returning loads of palm kernels and palm oil.[80] Another, which gave differential privileges to the British line, was that British ships could sail from Continental ports but that Continental ships could not sail from British ports.[81] This affected both the Woermann line and the Hamburg-America Line.

The question arises as to why the large European firms were willing to accept such a blatant transport monopoly. In reply, it should be noted that the Conference was introduced more or less as a *fait accompli*, with only one month's notice to the traders.[82] They had no choice but to agree as, if they had not, they would not have had shipping space for the cargoes they were planning to send out in the months ahead. Once they had agreed, they had no choice but to remain within the system, as they soon had thousands of pounds tied up in rebates, held without payment of interest by the shipping companies. In 1909, A Royal Commission investigated West African shipping. John Holt, in his testimony to the Commission, estimated that at any one time Elder Dempster probably held £6,000 in rebates for Holt alone, and a total for all companies of about £50,000.[83] The companies were willing to pay high shipping charges and lose interest on rebates if in turn they could be guaranteed regular shipping dates.

> [W]e have no love for the rebate system at all; we do not care about it, and we do not like it, but if it is the only means of getting regular sailings, then as long as it is not abused, we consider that regular sailings are of even more importance ... than low rates of freight.[84]

When the practices of the Conference system were investigated by the Royal Commission on Shipping Rings in 1909, and by its successor commission, the Final Report of the Imperial Shipping Committee on the Deferred Rebate System, in 1923,[85] it was discovered that although there were no reported cases of rebates actually having been forfeited owing to nonadherence to Conference regulations, the system was open to attack on several counts.[86] The first of these was that while 'loyalty' was required on all goods shipped, that is, no goods could be shipped by other than Conference steamers, homeward rebates were paid only on palm oil and palm kernels, the two products which comprised the bulk of homeward shipping at the time that the Conference was established.[87] But by 1909, when the investigatory commission was set up, goods such as cocoa comprised a far higher percentage of the homeward cargo. These goods were still being shipped at rates imposed when they were only a small percentage of the cargo; fifty shillings a ton, for example, was being charged for cocoa and no rebates were allowed.[88] The articles for which rebates were not enjoyed were all shipped at rates higher than the rates for palm oil and kernels.[89] To many merchants, in any case, all that the rebates meant was that they paid ten per cent 'primage' to the shipping companies at the beginning of a trip, which was returned to them six to twelve months later without interest: not, certainly, that they received an actual refund. The primage was being paid for goods such as cocoa without the refund.

Many firms opposed to the Conference wanted to have a 'free period' during which they would be able to charter ships or ship on non-Conference lines without forfeiting their rebate. In other words, after each six months' accounting period, they wanted a breathing space in which they could, if they wished, re-evaluate their methods of shipping.[90] But such a breathing space would allow the large firms to break out of the system while the small firms, which could not charter entire ships, were still tied into it, something which would give the larger firms an advantage. It was almost unanimously agreed that the one advantage of the rebate system was that small firms were given an equal opportunity; it was assumed that large shippers and small all paid the same rates, and all could take advantage of regular shipping dates.[91]

This assumption, however, was based on incomplete knowledge. The small traders were not, in fact, granted the same rights as the large; secret bargains were made by Elder Dempster with its largest customers simply in order to prevent them from branching out and acquiring their own ships. Preferential contracts were given to firms who were willing to guarantee that they would ship by Conference lines for the next five years. Such guarantees, of course, could also be made by small shippers, but were less likely to be regarded as of any significance. Moreover, the 1909 Commission found that the liners did 'make contracts for the carriage of large quantities at net rates considerably lower than those which would be charged to the general merchant shipping similar goods in small quantities.'[92] The John Holt Company, for example, had decided soon after the Conference system was established to buy and outfit its own ships. In order to prevent it from becoming a general shipper, Elder Dempster agreed that Holt could fill its own ships with its own produce and still send the bulk of its cargo on the Conference lines at preferential rates.[93] Similarly, from 1925 to 1929, the African and Eastern Trade Corporation bought and began shipping by its own steamers; not only did Elder Dempster tolerate this practice but an agreement was reached that whatever leftover cargo was carried by the Conference for African and Eastern would be given 'most favoured' terms.[94]

Not only were small traders, both European and African, in practice discriminated against in favour of the large, but the existence of such favourable contracts served to discourage tramp or charter steamers which might otherwise have been able to undercut the prices charged by the Conference. One might presume that some of the larger companies would have been willing to forgo six months' rebate if they could charter tramp steamers to carry their bulk cargo, especially considering that prices for carriage of goods such as cocoa were for so long inflated. But Daniel Marx argues that in fact this would not be the case because liner and charter, or tramp, rates fluctuated in the same direction during most of the colonial period; from 1873 to 1908 there was a downward trend in both kinds of shipping, followed by an upward trend until 1918 and then another downswing until 1937.[95] Leubuscher argues, moreover, that in any case the West African trade was unattractive to tramps, as they had to call at a large number of very poor harbours to get a full load, and they were dependent on surf boats, owned and operated by the Conference lines, to load and unload their cargoes.[96] Nevertheless the merchants did feel a need for tramps' services, especially during the heavy cocoa export season when the liners could not fulfil the demand for immediate bulk transport.[97] But by the end of World War I, many tramps had been absorbed or bought out by regular lines; in some cases Elder Dempster effected such absorption by undercutting its competitors' freight charges.[98] There was no longer an available pool of shipping which could undercut this structure.

The fact that all lighterage (that is, the surf boats which carried cargo between the large ocean-going ships and the Ghana shore) was controlled by the Conference system further discouraged competition. It was Elder Dempster's policy at the time of the Royal Commission's investigations to charge an extra five shillings per ton for lighterage services to its customers, whether or not they actually used the Elder Dempster service.[99] Under such circumstances, there was no point in any of the firms' maintaining their own lighterage fleets, and indeed they rapidly sold what fleets they possessed to the monopoly shipping companies. Only the firm of Swanzy maintained its own lighterage company, performing all lighterage work for the Woermann line as of 1908.[100]

Through its control of lighterage, the Conference controlled which ports could be used in West Africa. Similarly, the Conference controlled ports in use in Europe. The provisions of the Conference were that Elder Dempster could call at British and European ports, but that Woermann could call only at European ports and not at British ports. Hence anyone shipping into or from Britain had to ship by Elder Dempster, which implied shipping via Liverpool. Many traders, especially those based in Manchester, complained that they could not use any other harbour in Britain without forfeiting their rebate. If a tramp were going from Ghana to Bristol, and the destination of a firm's goods was Bristol, it could not use that tramp. It would have to ship to Liverpool by a Conference liner and then trans-ship to Bristol. Cargo, similarly, which was ultimately destined for France had to be trans-shipped, since Elder Dempster landed only in England and Germany.[101]

While British firms paid for trans-shipment costs, moreover, they had to endure the spectacle of American firms shipping to Ghana from America, on Conference lines, for the same price as British firms shipped from Britain.

> The object of such rate is to prevent either the establishment of a direct line under the American flag or the chartering of steamers for service between the ports concerned. The result is that American Manufactures are thus placed on the same footing as British Manufactures in the markets of British West Africa ... [102]

While some argued that because preferential rates were granted to Americans, African consumers benefited by having cheaper American goods available, it was evident that the real reason for this concession was to prevent any American line from competing with the Conference. This tactic was only partially successful, however, as the American Bull

Line did enter the West Africa trade after the Great War. But the Conference lines were successful in forcing the Bull Line to give up its New York to Manchester run.[103] In the 1930s, the Barber Line began to cross the Atlantic to West Africa, with the support of the UAC which was attempting to reduce its dependence on the Conference.[104]

The colonial government did little to oppose the shipping conference, even though there were complaints against it by the powerful trade lobby, as it was itself benefiting from the system. The Crown Agents often complained because the system was so designed that the government of all four West African colonies was regarded as one customer for rebate purposes; thus, if one colony was 'disloyal' in its shipments, all colonies would suffer a loss of rebate. On the other hand the Crown Agents were charged lower rates than other customers.[105] In return, the government made it its policy to conduct all its shipping by British lines, which, of course, meant Elder Dempster.[106] An order was also made that when 'any part of the cost of a passage to and from West Africa is borne by public funds, the passenger must travel by a British steamship.' In return for having passed this order, the colonial state demanded a 10 per cent rebate from Elder Dempster.[107]

Until the publicity of the Royal Commission on Shipping Rings forced the discontinuance of the practice, the government also countenanced a system whereby all cement imported into the West African colonies was monopolised by Elder Dempster, ostensibly to prevent competition from 'foreign' cement. As the firm of John Holt complained,

> [T]here is only one cement that is allowed to be taken by the local government, and that must come from the Burham Cement Company ... We [John Holt] used ourselves to buy from that company, and we shipped several cargoes out before this rebate system was on, until one fine day we found out that we could get it no longer from them. We made inquiry why, and they said 'Because we have given Elder, Dempster and Company the monopoly of this brand.' So we are in this position, that we could not offer any other brand, because the Burham Company's brand is the only one allowed by the Crown Agents, and Elder, Dempster and Company had the monopoly of that one brand; therefore we were out of it.[108]

A similar monopoly on the carriage of coal was held by Elder Dempster from 1895 to 1905;[109] even after this monopoly ceased to exist Elder

Oligopolisation of the Ghanaian Economy 123

Dempster could, and did, outsell all of the merchant firms in coal because it owned collieries in the Canary Islands and transported coal from there, charging itself only cost. The firms constantly complained about this practice of 'trading on ship's account', that is, of shipping companies' acting as traders as well as transporters.

The various abuses or inconveniences suffered by European traders under the Conference system were, of course, felt much more keenly by the African traders. It was contended by many that better opportunities were provided for Africans under the Conference than formerly, as they could be assured of regular shipping times. But none of the independent Ghanaian firms was big enough to qualify for the special treatment afforded to large European firms; certainly none was big enough to disregard regulations and charter its own ships. The extra expenses of trans-shipment from Conference ports and overpriced freight charges bore hard on African entrepreneurs. In addition, as the Royal Commission on Shipping Rings discovered, the African often did not even receive his legitimate rebate. Generally speaking, British agents acting for Africans retained their rebates, although officially, rebates were only supposed to be paid to principals. The British agents argued that 'native' businesses were so unstable that by the time that the six months waiting period for a rebate was up, they would have difficulty in locating the African who was entitled to it.[110]

Aside from the abolition of the cement monopoly, none of the Conference practices complained of to the 1909 Royal Commission was rectified. The Conference carried on in its monopoly until the outbreak of the First World War, when the assumption of hostilities between Britain and Germany precluded any further collusion between the two shipping lines. Elder Dempster was thus in the enviable position, during the whole of the war, of being the only liner agency travelling to West Africa, and, therefore, of also being able to charge what rates it pleased. The records of the London, Liverpool, and Manchester Chambers of Commerce during the Great War are full of letters of complaint to the Colonial Office about Elder Dempster's exorbitant rates. Some companies went so far as to charter sailing boats to escape Elder Dempster's monopoly.

For a few years after the end of World War I, Elder Dempster continued to have the field clear for itself. But German shipping was rebuilt quickly, and at the same time, Dutch shipping had been strengthened during the war (as Holland had been a neutral country) and now had to be taken into consideration. Following a rate war in the earlier 1920s, a new Conference was established in 1924. The terms of the 1924 agreement were never published, but they contained essentially the same features as the pre-war Conference. The two Continental lines were still forbidden to use British ports, although they were permitted to embark and disembark passengers at Southampton. The deferred rebate system was changed and confined only to outward voyages from Europe, but in effect this made little difference as non-Conference ships had trouble getting outward cargo and in any case 'each shipper had to enter into a contractual agreement to use only conference ships for homeward-bound cargo too.'[111] Thus, 'loyalty' was still demanded, even where no rebates were awarded.

Nevertheless, the Conference monopoly on shipping was never as complete after as before World War I. There had always been hostility to the Conference and various efforts had been made to circumvent it, hence, for example, the special arrangement mentioned above with John Holt. The smaller traders had also organised into various associations to try to have some bargaining power with the Conference lines. The Manchester Association of Importers and Exporters, for example, was formed in 1908 to counteract the influence of Liverpool in shipping and to press for shipping services through the Manchester Ship Canal.[112] The 1923 Commission on Shipping Rings regarded the establishment of such organisations as the only effective means of negotiating with and controlling the Conference. On its recommendation the Association of West African merchants set up, in March 1930, the West African Merchants Freight Association, which made yearly agreements on behalf of its members with the Conference. '[I]t may be inferred . . . that the principal concession which the Merchants Freight Association obtained, was an assurance that its members would be charged freight rates no higher than those payable by other shippers. . .'[113] Such an assurance, then, was merely a guarantee that no large shipper would be granted a privileged position.

In 1930, the United Africa Company set up its own shipping line, drastically affecting the competitive position of the Conference lines. As early as 1909 the 'Combine' firms, who were later to form the UAC, had united to try to buy out Elder Dempster, without success. The other half of the UAC empire, Lever Brothers, had started the Bromport Shipping Line in April 1916, but in 1922 this line was taken over by the Conference. 'In return for an exclusive freight arrangement, the shipping companies undertook to carry Lever's cargoes at a rate which was to be no higher than that paid by their rivals.'[114] But in 1930 the Elder Dempster empire was rocked by scandal and imminent financial ruin, after the conviction of its chairman, Lord Kylsant, for financial mismanagement in 1929. A major reorganisation of the company followed. At the same time, UAC, under the control of Lever Brothers, was just beginning to consolidate its strength. It demanded several privileges from the Conference, including a special rate for its bulk-shipped palm oil, priority over other traders for cargo space, and the handing over of all Elder Dempster's West Coast agencies and lighterage facilities to itself.[115] At this point UAC already owned five steamers and it would seem probable that it deliberately made such exorbitant demands so that the Conference's refusal could provide it with an excuse to set up its own shipping company. The smaller traders opposed any takeover by the UAC of these facilities as they would then be completely in the hands of their conglomerate rivals.[116]

For a short period of time the rivalry between UAC and Elder Dempster forced the latter company to reduce its rates to all merchants to ensure that UAC would not enter the West Coast trade as a general carrier and take away its custom. By 1931, however, the rates were raised again when the two companies reached a compromise in which it was agreed that UAC could continue to use the Conference ships for goods which it could not handle itself, and get rebates on this cargo, although it would not be given any preferential rates.[117] Thus, the establishment of a rival line did little to benefit the small traders, especially as most of UAC's space was taken up by its own empire.

Whereas as late as 1924/25, 100 per cent of the North Europe to West Africa shipping had been controlled by the Conference, by 1939, with the entrance of the two new lines, owned by UAC and John Holt, this had fallen to 80 per cent. Although the monopoly had been broken, it nevertheless continued to preclude independent shipping by small European or African entrepreneurs. Moreover, insofar as the monopolising shipping firms granted preferential privileges to the large expatriate trading companies, the Conference helped to retard the development of an independent trading class, and especially of an African trading class.

Conference policies also reinforced the peripheral nature of Ghana's economy in a number of ways. Since, ultimately, most extra costs in international trade were passed on to the consumers of imported goods or the producers of exported goods, the high transport rates and the 10 per cent extra for 'primage' were eventually passed on to Ghanaians. Under the Conference system, Ghanaians paid more for their store-bought belongings and received less for their produce in return.

Moreover, the shipping pricing policy tended to reinforce the international division of labour.

> The policy often followed by liners, of charging what the traffic will bear, usually has the effect of requiring finished goods to pay higher rates than semi-finished articles ... [L]ow ocean freights have benefited European industry by permitting raw materials to be imported at delivered prices only slightly higher than those which have prevailed at their sources.[118]

The two shipping lines in the West Africa Conference had a joint policy of charging higher freight for processed than for non-processed goods, encouraging merchants to ship as much produce as possible in an unfinished state. Unfortunately, however, this policy did not work in reverse and merchants did not ship unfinished manufactured goods to Ghana to be finished there.

The evolution of monopoly in shipping was a result of structural needs in the world economy. Competition on a free market could not fulfil the need for regular mass transportation of raw materials to the core capitalist countries. Mercantile capitalists were willing to accept an oligopolised structure if it facilitated planning and the capacity to make long-range forecasts of prices, and ensured that regularity of deliveries which was essential to ensure a constant supply of goods to the factories of Britain. Not until the competitive mercantile structure had consolidated into an equally oligopolistic structure could the shipping oligopoly break down; vertical integration partially replaced horizontal integration.

Oligopoly carried with it the capacity to undercut or eliminate those smaller competitive firms which refused to join the new structure. Just as the choice for many small trading firms was to be incorporated into the UAC conglomerate, so also the choice for many shippers was to accept Elder Dempster conditions or disintegrate. Many small European firms fell by the wayside, as also did those African firms which could not afford the strictly controlled, non-competitive pricing system. Oligopoly reinforced the structure of dependence created in the nineteenth century; high transport prices had 'an effect similar to the imposition of a tariff'[119] raising costs to consumers and lowering prices paid to producers. The net result of these developments was, not only the constraining of the Ghanaian entrepreneurial class but also the constricting of resources which could be used for mercantile or even industrial capital. Such a constriction in supplies of money

3. The Underdevelopment of Currency and Banking

capital was further exacerbated by the extension of the metropolitan banking system into Ghana.

In financing the development of Ghana as a peripheral economy, the colonial state was faced with a dual problem. First, it had to encourage the introduction of a uniform and easily available coinage, with which Africans could both be paid and make their payments for imported goods. Second, it had to encourage a banking system which would cater to expatriate, but not necessarily to indigenous, needs.

During the late nineteenth century one of the government's principal tasks was simply to institute a uniformity of coinage, doing away with the somewhat chaotic system of multiple currencies which had resulted from European and African participation in the slave trade. European currencies other than British were gradually demonetised, either by outright banning or by imposition of *ad valorem* import duties of 10 per cent or 12½ per cent which made their costs prohibitive.[120] Gold, an indigenous currency, was demonetised as early as 1889,[121] apparently to free the maximum amount of gold for export to Britain. Without gold Africans had an additional incentive to enter cash-crop production so that they could acquire European currency, which could then also be used in the 'traditional' sector.

Although Ghanaians still managed to obtain gold for their own uses even after it had been demonetised, a number of legislative enactments limited its supply. The African custom of using gold for ornaments and jewellery was considered irrelevant, as the state wished to ensure that as much gold as possible was exported. No gold produced in the mines could be sold inside Ghana and anyone found with mined gold was presumed to have obtained it illegally. While in 1908 a law was passed permitting Africans free dealing in gold won by 'native methods',[122] the government consistently refused to publicise the bill or to advise Ghanaians as to this right. '[T]he interests of the Colony would best be served by issuing no official notification to native landowners that they are allowed to offer for sale Gold Dust collected on their own lands.'[123]

Goldsmiths' shops were often searched for illegally obtained gold, and Ghanaian members of the Legislative Council often complained of the practice, but they received little redress until 1926 when goldsmiths were at last given the right to buy a certain amount of gold from the banks so that they could continue their trade.[124] But in 1932, to curb the industry, the government passed a regulation that all goldsmiths must pay licence fees;[125] and in 1938 another bill was passed shifting the onus of proving that gold had been legally obtained onto the possessor.[126] At the same time, the Executive Council was considering allowing the importing of gold into the colony to satisfy the needs of the goldsmiths.[127]

After the demonetisation of gold and of foreign European currencies, the colonial government's next task was to provide a sufficient amount of coins of very small value, that is, one-half, one-quarter or even one-tenth pence, for use in village markets.[128] While not all Ghanaians engaged in cash-crop production, almost all bought some imported goods, even if it were only one small cigarette tin of sugar at a time, or a few matches at a time. Hence, in order for the European firms to recover the cash which they spent on export crops every year, coins had to be provided in small enough denominations to encourage buying even in the poorest and remotest villages. The need for small units of currency was a perpetual problem; even as late as 1931 a director of the UAC could complain that there were not enough pennies or half-pennies in circulation, causing merchants to either over-price or under-price their commodities.[129]

The proliferation of small denomination coins put heavy demands on the Royal Mint in England. The demand was further exacerbated by the refusal of many Africans to accept any but new coin. The British assumed that the reason for this refusal was that Africans used the coins not only for exchange, but also for decoration. Another possibility was that some Africans could not distinguish between the intrinsic value and the exchange value of worn currency; hence, once a coin had lost weight through constant use, they thought that it would not be able to buy the same amount of goods. But it was also possible that Africans were wary of old coins because they could not recognise them and worried that they might be receiving demonetised foreign currency, or forged currency, instead of legal tender. New coin, therefore, had constantly to be shipped to Ghana from England.

The need to increase the available amount of coin as the pre-capitalist sector in Ghana became more and more dependent upon the exchange economy, combined with the heavy African demand for new coin, resulted in a very rapid expansion of the amount of West African coin in comparison with the supply of coin in Britain itself. Whereas between 1886 and 1890 West African coin equalled only 3 per cent of the supply of British coin, between 1906 and 1910 it equalled 85 per cent.[130] The actual expense of supplying such currency was prohibitive: without paper notes all currency had to be shipped to

Ghana in coin form. Moreover, the government was preoccupied with
the fact that the coin was immediately repatriable to England; as
British currency, it could leave the colony and return to England at
any time. In the event of depression in West Africa, it was felt, the
need for a supply of money would shrink and the coin would be
repatriated, causing inflation in the mother country.

This fear of possible inflation was an important reason for the
eventual establishment of the West African Currency Board (WACB)
in 1912,[131] after an unsuccessful attempt to set up a separate West
African Currency in 1900. Currency in Ghana and the other West
African colonies would now be separate from British currency; while
it was freely exchangeable at par for pounds sterling, it could not
simply be transported to the British Isles. Moreover, the WACB was
obliged to keep 100 per cent backing of its coinage in sterling or
British securities, thus also preventing inflation in the colonies. The
reserves of the WACB between 1926 and 1939 were always above
100 per cent; indeed, in 1935 they reached as high as 120 per cent.[132]
Obviously, then, it was not the purpose of the WACB to act as an
agent of monetary policy in Africa. Its function was not to expand the
money supply, at however conservative a rate, in order to encourage
investment; rather, its function was solely to guard Britain against any
danger of inflation occasioned by an over-supply of coin in the colonies.
There was no danger of monetary inflation in Ghana; with the constant
expansion of African involvement in the exchange economy, any
currency supplied would be used. The anti-inflationary ruling of 100
per cent backing (or more) of currency had the further effect that it
constituted a drain on colonial revenues; monies which might have
been better spent in the colonies had to be exported to Britain
instead.

One reason why the colonial governments had originally pressed for
the establishment of the WACB had been so that they would be
entitled to the seignorage profits from the currency the Board produced.
Seignorage profits were the difference between the cost to the Board
of minting the coins and the price at which the coins were sold. In
the late nineteenth century, the Royal Mint, because of a sudden fall
in the price of silver, had been making very large seignorage profits,
but the Treasury had rejected the Colonial Office's request for a
separate currency board because it feared that the Colonial Office
might over-issue coins, causing inflation in the colonies (and possibly
also at home, if the coins were repatriated) in order to make profits.[133]
The Colonial Office, calculating that between 1901 and 1910 the

Treasury had made two million pounds in seignorage on West African coins,[134] continued to press for a separate board. Yet when the battle for redistribution of seignorate profits to the colonies was finally won, it transpired that the actual returns were very small. The Ghana government received no returns at all from the WACB until 1923; between 1923 and 1939 its receipts averaged £103,000 per year, peaking at £194,000 in 1929.[135]

The low revenues from seignorage profits, however, were of little significance compared to the effects of the ruling that the WACB must keep 100 per cent reserves, and that it often kept more. The result of this policy was that it was not even creating the amount of West African currency which it was legally allowed. Yet both Ghanaians and Europeans in Ghana periodically suffered from a shortage of coin which impeded free trade while allowing large profits to go to those who could 'corner the market', as it were, of coins.

During World War I there was a chronic shortage of coins in Ghana, caused by the conversion of the Royal Mint to the production of arms and ammunition. Because of the shortage, cocoa farmers were obliged to sell their crops at lower prices than they had originally expected; and some smaller British firms, which did not have any cash on hand, had to step aside and watch the larger firms which controlled the cash supply buy out the crops at prices which they practically dictated. These larger firms had managed to acquire cash through their sales of imported goods to Africans. One British administrator complained that as a result of their control of the scarce supply of currency, 'the Combine [firms] . . . are likely to get for one-quarter of a million the remainder of the [cocoa] crop which they apparently were prepared to take at about 2 millions.'[136]

In 1919 the situation with regard to silver was so bad that the colonial government decided to take drastic measures and introduce a bill to render illegal the melting down or hoarding of silver coin.[137] Seemingly, the British administrators were unaware that the local economy absorbed large amounts of currency which were not automatically returned as payments for imported goods to the European firms as soon as the cocoa-buying season was over. Rather, the administrators attributed the scarcity to irrational uses of silver on the part of Ghanaians. During World War I, as well, paper money had been introduced for the first time, and the government was discovering to its chagrin that Africans were refusing payment in notes. The problem here was that although notes might be considered a useful and logical solution to the shortage of coin in the eyes of Europeans, they were

Oligopolisation of the Ghanaian Economy 131

not so in the eyes of Africans. Without a country-wide system of banks, there was literally nowhere to keep the notes they acquired.

> [T]he natives had no proper means of storing the notes. If they placed them in their dwellings there was great risk of fire; if they buried them the white ants would probably destroy the notes; and there was no means of carrying them on their persons ... A case was cited of a European carrying notes in his sun helmet throughout a journey, with the result that the notes were reduced to pulp at the end of it.[138]

Very soon after the issue of notes in Ghana began, the habit of 'discounting' began as well. This was a practice whereby a money-changer would pay perhaps 15s 6d in coin for a £1 note. The practice was declared illegal in 1918[139] but it nevertheless spread rapidly and continued throughout the colonial period, whenever and wherever there were shortages of coin. In 1919 the situation was so grave that in some parts of the colony farmers paid for cocoa in silver were receiving less than eighty per cent of the price of cocoa in notes.[140] As late as 1932 the London Chamber of Commerce expressed concern to the Colonial Office about a rumour (later found to be untrue) that the French were going to introduce silver money into their colonies. The Chamber was afraid that this would divert trade away from the British West African colonies where producers were paid in notes.[141] Cocoa would be smuggled out of Ghana to be sold for silver.

Thus the general policy of the WACB was not designed to meet the needs of Africans in Ghana. The actual supply of currency was insufficient to meet the needs of a growing economy, and the fact that Ghanaians were often unwilling to accept notes instead of coin meant that they had to discount their assets. Although it did supply currency to the growing economy of Ghana, the Board's policy of keeping 100 per cent or more reserves limited the money supply. The export of colonial revenues to Britain to back the currency further depleted possible investment resources in Ghana.

On the other hand, the introduction and organisation of a separate West African currency did benefit the expatriate trading community in the colony. The introduction of notes was especially important for import-export firms who dealt with millions of pounds worth of produce and consumer goods every season. For Europeans, with access to banks, notes were more mobile and convenient than coin.

> [T]he man who has to sell the goods and buy produce . . . is strongly in favour of the note issue with a view to relieving, or . . . reducing the cost of transport of the silver . . . In parts of the Gold Coast, it is impossible to move silver about from one town to the other without a police escort. When the produce season is at its height you may have to wait three to five to seven days before your police escort is provided, and when it is provided it becomes very costly. With these notes, it will be possible to send up . . . half the amount in notes, and the specie itself might be able to wait for two or three days.[142]

Moreover, while Africans found it difficult to convert notes into the coin they so desperately needed, Europeans found it easy to convert their West African notes into English notes. Indeed, it was only on condition that West African currency would be so easily exchangeable for British currency that the expatriate business community had accepted independent West African currency in the first place. It was much easier for a European than for a Ghanaian to change the notes, since the European generally was based in Europe, often in London, while the African had few outside contacts and could not easily bank his British notes, or indeed use them, even if he presented currency for redemption into pounds sterling in West Africa. The sterling he received in exchange for West African notes was paid to him in London, not in Ghana. 'Holders of coin of the new currency and of the silver Imperial coinage will have the legal right to tender them in British West Africa for conversion at a fixed rate of exchange into sterling money issuable in London.'[143] Lacking easy access to London, the Ghanaian's access to sterling was also blocked. In essence he was limited to 'soft' currency while his European competitors moved easily between 'soft' and 'hard' currency.

Decisions made by the British government with regard to the institution of West African currency were responsible for the overall shortage of currency in Ghana. These decisions were also partly responsible for the Ghanaians' inability to use notes when they were instituted. But the banking system in Ghana was also partly responsible for the latter problem, insofar as it was geared to the needs, not of the indigenous African community or indeed of the trading, entrepreneurial sector thereof, but rather to the needs of the expatriate traders in Ghana.

Samir Amin argues that banking systems in the presently underdeveloped countries were deliberately established to accommodate the expatriate export-import trade.

> The fact is that the banks in the underdeveloped countries have a history that is closely linked with that of the installation of peripheral capitalism in these countries. The European banks established branches in these countries when international trade had reached large-scale dimensions, and with the intention of facilitating this trade. Historically, moreover, most of the expatriate banks were set up in the ports, in order to carry out foreign-exchange operations.[144]

Certainly, Amin's remarks pertain to the establishment of the banking system in Ghana. Banking was closely tied in with other expatriate interests and functioned as a resource for the European, not the African, community. Until 1897 no banks at all existed in Ghana and all transactions were carried out by individuals or firms with their banks in London, entailing a great deal of inconvenience and expense. Ghanaians without European contacts had no access to banks; any credit they received was dependent on 'trust' or on loans from European trading firms.

The first bank to be set up in Ghana was a creation of the Elder Dempster shipping company. The colonial government employed Elder Dempster to ship out the vast amounts of coin needed in the West African territories to buy each year's cash-crops. It was becoming more and more inconvenient, however, for the government to provide silver direct to the trading firms; to remedy this problem it suggested to Elder Dempster in the early 1890s that the shipping firm also act as the government's agent for the distribution of coin. As a result Elder Dempster entered the banking business and established the Bank of British West Africa (BBWA) in March 1894. Three years later the Bank entered Ghana, establishing branches in Accra (1897), Cape Coast (1900), Sekondi (1901) and Axim (1901).[145]

During the early period of its history, the BBWA did not have enough branches to supply the needs of all its customers, although it did its best to open branches anywhere there was a large number of expatriate firms. Consequently, to fill the gap in services, it employed the larger trading firms as its agents and authorised them to carry out banking services in its name. In 1905, for example, Millers agreed to act for the BBWA in Kumasi, Tarkwa and Winneba for a payment of £300 per year in Kumasi and Tarkwa and £10 per month in Winneba. The arrangements were made on the strict understanding that the firms, in return for their payments, would help to ensure the BBWA's monopoly of banking in West Africa. In an agreement made between Millers and the bank in 1903, it was stated that neither the company nor the bank would:

> directly or indirectly a) assist any third firm or company to commence conduct or be interested or concerned in banking business in the said colony [Ghana] and b) will not so assist or themselves conduct or be interested in a banking business in the West African colonies of the Gambia Sierra Leone and Lagos nor of any bank in the United Kingdom to compete with the Bank in the said colonies.[146]

Although it was to their advantage to have regular banking services set up in the colonies, both the expatriate trading firms and the government resented the BBWA's monopoly of West African banking, especially because of its ties to Elder Dempster, the most important West African shipping line. In 1909, the Royal Commission on Shipping Rings investigated the ties between the bank and the shipping firm. One accusation made against the bank was that it exerted power over its customers by threatening to have Elder Dempster withdraw shipping services if they did not comply with its regulations. A further accusation was that the bank took advantage of its monopoly situation by levying high charges for its services. Even the government was afraid to protest against these charges, because if it did so, the Elder Dempster freight charges for specie would be raised.[147]

The banking system, then, was heavily aligned with the shipping system in Ghana. Any independent businessman, whether European or African, who wanted credit to ship his goods abroad, found himself obliged to hire Elder Dempster freight. As one expatriate complained:

> [T]he bank ... is one of those systems by which a shipowner who is also a banker can keep to himself a great deal of freight ... Supposing I am a poor man, and I want an advance of 80 per cent, or 90 per cent or 100 per cent, on my goods, the bank who owned [sic] the ships says 'All right, I will give you the advance, but you are to ship the goods by my steamer.'[148]

The upshot of this connection was that the shipping line had its monopoly ensured by the monopoly of the bank. One can assume that for Ghanaians as well, any use of BBWA services was contingent on paying the high Elder Dempster freight charges.

A more serious complaint against the bank, from the African point of view, was simply that it monopolised the distribution of currency in Ghana. According to its 1896 agreement with the government, the bank was allowed complete monopoly of the import of specie with the stipulation that it would charge no more than one per cent commission to its customers.[149] But there were claims that the bank was, in fact, charging more than one per cent for importing currency[150] and also that it put pressure on its customers by delaying or withholding currency.[151] Such complaints were more likely to be made by small traders, whether expatriate or Ghanaian, than by the larger firms with whom the bank had made special agreements. Complaints of this nature continued until 1912 when, with the establishment of the WACB, the bank lost its monopoly of specie distribution.

In the light of the complaints which persisted against the BBWA and its connections with Elder Dempster, it is surprising that no new bank rose to challenge it in Ghana until 1917, when the Colonial Bank (whose name was changed in 1925 to Barclays Bank, Dominion, Colonial, and Overseas) opened its first branch in Accra. Other branches followed in Kumasi, Koforidua, Nsawam, Winneba (all in 1919), Bekwai (1921), Takoradi (1930), Oda (1932), Tarkwa (1935) and Dunkwa (1939).[152] The branches were opened in areas where expatriate trade flourished, where there were large cocoa-buying centres, and in the largest mining centres. Again, branches were not opened in such a way as to encourage African use, and as long as the banks were confined to the areas of European penetration, notes could not easily spread among the African community.

Richard Fry, the historian of the BBWA, does not indicate what might have prompted the Colonial Bank to enter West Africa, other than to refer the presence as deputy chairman of the bank of 'that unique human engine', Sir Maxwell Aitken, later Lord Beaverbrook.[153] Fry does indicate that the Colonial Bank originally provided active competition to the BBWA, 'poaching' both staff and customers, and, at least in Nigeria, acquiring half of the government's business. That the BBWA was concerned with this competition was reflected in the fact that it twice tried to make 'arrangements', both times declined, with the Colonial Bank. In 1917 it offered to exchange shares in BBWA for the Colonial Bank's West African business;[154] in 1934 essentially the same offer was made with the additional incentive of allowing Barclays Bank one or two directors on the board of BBWA.[155]

Despite the Colonial Bank's refusal to be co-opted, it seems that it was willing to enter into gentlemen's agreements to limit competition. Fry notes (unfortunately without providing dates), that

> [T]hey [the two banks] had agreed ... not to open or reopen branches in certain places without giving an agreed period of notice to the other bank. Understandings about maintaining the same rates for the principal transactions had existed in various areas, and a habit of discussing points of potential dispute had grown up.[156]

Newlyn and Rowan confirm Fry's data. Writing in 1954, and commenting on the very high rates charged for internal banking transactions in West Africa, they stated that although banks were reluctant to reveal their charges, 'There appears to be little inter-bank price competition and there are some signs of inter-bank collaboration.'[157] There was no real competition until, with independence impending in the 1950s, the banks became rivals in a race to open up new branches to cash in on the funds of the rising African elite.

Faced with the oligopolistic organisation of the British banks, African traders found it difficult, if not impossible, to avail themselves of the financial services they needed to enable them to compete in the import-export trade with Europeans. Moreover, it was evident that the two banks perceived their role primarily as one of servicing the expatriate community, not of providing the elementary facilities which would result in the development of the indigenous economy. Through interlocking directorships, the two banks had ties to some of the largest mining and trading firms in Ghana (such as Ashanti Goldfields and the African and Eastern Trade Corporation),[158] as well as to the major shipping line. It is not surprising, therefore, that the banks viewed their purpose as primarily to serve the expatriate community, both government and commercial. Their functions were to supply coin, to make advances for payment for the cocoa crop, and to repatriate profits for the cocoa-buying firms. Basically, they assisted the import-export trade. '[T]he seasonal purchase, transport and shipment of the [cocoa] beans absorbed a great deal of cash along the line, and this was for many years provided by bank advances.'[159] Large sums of money were made available every year to the expatriate trading firms in order that they might buy the goods produced by Ghanaians. This money was then disbursed by the firms to their producers, who spent it largely (although not completely) on imported goods. The money was thus rapidly recovered by the firms, who then returned it to the banks. Since there was no scope for investment in Ghana itself, at least in European eyes, the money was repatriated to England to be invested there.

Decisions as to who was to receive credit based upon profits from the import-export trade were made not in Ghana but at the banks' head offices in London.[160] Thus, firms such as the UAC, who had their own London office, were at an advantage compared both to the small European firms and the African trader. Moreover, the two banks engaged in the practice of giving preferential rates to certain favoured customers, so that the larger trading firms thus enjoyed financial advantages not only over Africans, but also over the smaller European firms. This system of 'most favoured mercantile customers'[161] was kept secret, the banks stating publicly that they charged the same rates to all.

Aside from supplying coin for the buying season and then repatriating it to London after the season was over, the two banks had few functions to perform in Ghana. Outside of the cocoa season, none of the expatriate firms borrowed to any extent from the BBWA or the Colonial Bank; they tended to be self-financing in their day-to-day needs. The idea of using the banks to expand credit in Ghana, to promote investment and production, and to generalise the use of modern financial services, was never entertained, either by the banks themselves or by the government. There was no obligation felt to provide services for the African community.

In their book on colonial banking written in 1954, Newlyn and Rowan argue that Africans were perceived as unreliable in their financial dealings, and it was for this reason that the banks were not eager for their patronage. Reasons for not giving loans to Africans included the following:

(a) The generally poor reputation of Africans for commercial and financial responsibility.
(b) The absence of organized accounts in most African businesses.
(c) The failure of many African businessmen to make full use of their banking accounts and their tendency to be secretive over business matters.
(d) The difficulties experienced by Africans in providing banks with suitable security.
(e) The lack of close personal relationships between European banking executives and their African customers, and the absence

of intermediaries.[162]

These perceptions of Africans were even more prevalent during the early twentieth century than they were during the pre-independence period of which Newlyn and Rowan write. To a certain extent, such impressions were accurate; it is the case that African businesses often failed, that illiterate traders could not keep modern accounts, that few Africans had the kind of collateral which the Europeans desired, and that some were corrupt. Within this framework, however, there were means which could have been used to provide banking facilities.

Indigenous traders who keep exact mental records of phenomenally large commercial empires are legendary in West African banking circles, for indeed, after independence the new African regimes obliged the expatriate banks to offer credit even to illiterates. Furthermore, after independence European banking officials were trained to be able to evaluate an African's worth even without written records, by visiting his premises and inspecting his business. Collateral, in these cases, was based on stock turnover.[163] Before the independence period, however, credit of this type was not normally given by the banks. The main avenue for credit for indigenous traders was to borrow from expatriate import-export firms; but in so doing African traders were 'tied', either as customers or as suppliers, to the firm with which they dealt. The firms could afford to give credit to traders because they could cut off a trader's supplies in the event of default on payment; banks had no such control. But the independence of African traders was severely constricted by this practice.

The banks hesitated to give any kind of credit without solid collateral. Unfortunately, the European view of collateral, at least for Africans, was immovable property such as land or housing. Ghanaians could not use land as a basis for credit as it was still largely communally owned and inalienable.[164] Nor were the productive capacities of the land of use to the banks, which were both forbidden from and uninterested in taking over farmland and plantations. Africans, then, were left with only two resources if they were to obtain credit: houses and gold trinkets. But there was a limit to the amount of credit which one could obtain in exchange for the 'family jewels', and Europeans were reluctant to take houses as collateral as they often found it difficult to foreclose mortgages, especially since borrowers could always claim that in fact the property involved belonged not to individuals but to entire families, and therefore could not be alienated.

It was commonplace for expatriates in Ghana to criticise wealthy Africans for investing their money in large family homes instead of in their trading or agricultural enterprises. But there is some indication that this much-abused practice was at least partially a result of a European policy which insisted on real property as collateral. One could speculate that money which might have been better invested in cocoa farms or in private roads to the farms had to be put into buildings because Europeans needed visible, tangible evidence of a man's wealth. No doubt had there been the 'close personal relationship' between African bank customers and European bank executives, which Newlyn and Rowan discuss, such a need for tangible proof of a man's assets might have been obviated. As it was, however, attitudes of racial prejudice overrode any chance for equality of treatment with European bank customers, even in cases in which Africans might be good credit risks. As long as Africans were denied equal treatment in commercial matters, their chances of competing successfully with Europeans were minimal; but as long as they were viewed as uncompetitive, they were denied equal treatment.

The government's policy of paternalism towards the 'natives' militated against equality in commercial transactions. Administrators tended to view Ghanaians either as cheats or as gullible fools; in the former case the capitalist world was to be protected against them, in the latter they were to be protected against modern capitalism. Close personal and formal contacts between business and government enabled the latter to influence the former in their decisions as to the financial reliability of Africans. The state even went so far as to give detrimental information on potential Ghanaian clients to non-British banks who were considering financing their enterprises, thus at one blow both limiting the competitiveness of Africans with European entrepreneurs and ensuring that non-British banks would not attempt to enter the colony.[165]

No doubt, on the whole, Africans, given their minor role in trade, their lack of capital assets, and their isolation from the European business community, were not as good commercial risks as Europeans. Banks interested primarily in their own profits were bound to be cautious about their African customers. But there is some indication that the banks were overly cautious; that in fact, they discriminated solely on the basis of race and denied even the most elementary, risk-free services to Africans. They were, naturally, willing to take African deposits although they did not actively seek them out; in 1910, £263,000 of the BBWA's £1,074,793 in deposits were owned by

140   Oligopolisation of the Ghanaian Economy

Africans.[166] In other services, it appears that banks were willing to cater to Africans only upon payment of a higher fee than Europeans were expected to pay. While banks are unusually secretive about their rates, there is one document extant, dating from 1905, which indicates that the BBWA discriminated even in its most basic services between Europeans and 'natives'. While Europeans paid three-quarter per cent commission for bank drafts, Africans paid 1 per cent; while Europeans could exchange notes for gold up to £10 free of charge, Africans paid 1 per cent commission; while the BBWA accepted Bank of England notes up to £50 free of charge from Europeans, it charged 1 per cent to Africans.[167]

For the African then, the monopoly of the colonial banking system by one bank up to 1916, and by two banks, in close agreement, after that date, resulted not only in a denial of banking services on the grounds that Africans were not as commercially sound as their European counterparts, but also in deliberate discrimination on the grounds of race. The two British banks had complete control over banking in Ghana, but they extended only limited services, and those at high costs, to Africans. Their function was not to help to extend credit to the commercial community as a whole, but rather to safeguard commerce for the expatriate import-export firms.

The banks, along with mercantile traders and the shipping lines, constructed an oligopolistic system. Expatriate firms in the three sectors interlocked and dominated the Ghanaian import-export economy almost completely. Capitalist competition even among Europeans might have resulted in net benefits for Ghanaians, lowering prices of imported consumer goods and raising prices paid for cash-crop exports, but this was precluded, and the range of opportunities available for Africans was, therefore, narrowed.

Notes

1. Research for this section was conducted prior to the publication of Frederick Pedler's *The Lion and the Unicorn in Africa: The United Africa Company 1787–1931* (Heinemann, London, 1974). Pedler's sources and my own are similar, although, of course, Pedler's history is far more extensive. However, my conclusions as to the function of the United Africa Company as a contributor to the overall development of Africa differ radically from Pedler's. See my review of his work in *Canadian Journal of African Studies*, Vol. 10, No. 1 (1976), pp. 191–3.
2. Freda Wolfson, 'British Relations with the Gold Coast, Nineteenth Century', University of London, unpublished PhD thesis, 1951, pp. ii, 106.
3. 'The Story of UAC in Ghana', *The Unicorn* (House Magazine of the United

Africa Company in Ghana), Vol. 16, No. 3 (May/June 1970), p. 22.
4. Rankin, *The History*, p. 60.
5. Ibid., p. 68.
6. Dumett, 'British', p. 334.
7. Rankin, *The History*, p. 87.
8. Ibid., p. 321.
9. Ibid., p. 90.
10. Ibid., p. 5.
11. Interview by Dr W.J. Reader with W.K. Findlay, former director of Lever Brothers and Chairman of the Niger Company, Liverpool, 4 March 1964. Included in P.N. Davies (ed.) *Trading in West Africa* (Croom Helm, London, 1976), pp. 149–50. I am grateful to Dr Davies for allowing me to use the original interview.
12. Rankin, *The History*, p. 108. By this point Lever Brothers had been renamed Unilever.
13. The *Financial News*, 17 December 1933, enclosed in GNA CSO 621/30.
14. Report contained in UAC Rankin file.
15. UAC: 'Agreement with Maypole Dairy Company'.
16. UAC Rankin file: report 38 on A&ETC holdings.
17. Ibid.
18. Cadbury's Quaker motives are questioned by Roger Southall, in his 'Cadbury on the Gold Coast, 1907–38: The Dilemma of the Model Firm in a Colonial Economy', unpublished PhD thesis, University of Birmingham, 1975. I am grateful to Dr Southall for having allowed me to read a draft of his dissertation in 1974.
19. Norman Edwards, *Cadbury on the Gold Coast* (Publications Department, Bournville, 1955), p. 4.
20. Ibid., p. 14.
21. Report by the Acting Director of Agriculture, 22 October 1937, on Cadbury Brothers, in GNA CSO 851/30.
22. Edwards, *Cadbury*, p. 22.
23. Ibid., pp. 29–31.
24. Cherry Gertzel, *Merchant Adventure* (John Holt and Company, Liverpool, 1951), p. 48. A 'factory' was a small trading station.
25. JH: Jacket no. 536(ii).
26. H.D. Cotterell, 'Reminiscences of One Connected with the West African Trade from 1863 to 1910', in Davies (ed.), *Trading*, p. 74.
27. *Stock Exchange Yearbook* (1939).
28. Interviews with office managers, Paterson Zochonis and Busi and Stephenson, Accra, July and August, 1974.
29. 'Your Company in Ghana', *The Horseman* (House Magazine of G.B. Ollivant (Nigeria) Limited), No. 7 (April 1964), p. 4.
30. 'G.B. Ollivant Ltd.: A History', *Link* (Magazine of the UAC Group in Nigeria), Vol. 4, No. 1 (March 1970), p. 1., and interview, G.B. Ollivant, Manchester, November 1974.
31. Interviews, SCOA and CFAO, Accra, February and March 1974.
32. Interview, Swiss African Trading Company, Accra, March 1974.
33. 'Memorandum: The Basel Mission Trading Company and the Commonwealth Trust' (Government Printing Office, Gold Coast, 1928) and GCLegCo, 25 October 1928.
34. This point is made by C.W. Newbury in 'The Tariff Factor in Anglo-French West African Partition', in Prosser Gifford and William R. Louis (eds.), *France and Britain in Africa: Imperial Rivalry and Colonial Rule* (Yale University Press, New Haven, 1971), p. 256.
35. Gold Coast Executive Council Minutes, 16 July 1932, CO 98/69.

36. LonCC, 22 June 1931.
37. Reported in ManCC, 15 March 1933.
38. ManCC, 18 January 1934.
39. ManCC, 1934–35. 'Greys' are bolts of raw cotton.
40. Statement in the GCLegCo by the Comptroller of Customs, 12 June 1934.
41. Importation of Textiles (Quotas) Ordinance 1934, in GNA Adm. 29/6/8.
42. Statement by the Acting Director of Public Works, in GCLegCo, 23 February 1931.
43. Memorandum from the Colonial Office to JWAC, 13 December 1929, reported in ManCC, 11 February 1930.
44. Letter dated 13 July 1933, from the Commonwealth Trust to the London Chamber of Commerce, in LonCC, 9 October 1933.
45. Statement in GCLegCo by Mr Korsah, 15 March 1937.
46. Statement in GCLegCo by Nana Ofori Atta, 23 March 1938.
47. Gold Coast Executive Council Minutes, 12 May 1938, CO 98/37.
48. Statement from the Provincial Council of Chiefs, Eastern Province, to the Commissioner for the Eastern Province, 1 June 1934. In GNA Adm. 29/6/8.
49. Rankin, *The History*, p. 90.
50. Nowell Commission, p. 49.
51. Rankin, *The History*, p. 148.
52. P.T. Bauer, *West African Trade: A Study of Competition, Oligopoly and Monopoly in a Changing Economy* (Routledge and Kegan Paul, London, 1963), pp. 66–7.
53. This author contacted a number of companies and institutions, but was unable to locate any documents of the Association of West African Merchants. One reply to a request for information stated that AWAM documentation had been destroyed by bombing during World War II; other replies denied any knowledge of the existence of the organisation. The only documentary evidence on AWAM which this author has been able to locate is a small file in the Ghana National Archives, GNA CSO 192/34, entitled 'AWAM'. The file contains AWAM's official address in 1934 and a list of members including, among others, UAC, SCOA, CFAO, G.B. Ollivant and John Holt.
54. '[T]he fall in the price of cocoa has been accompanied by a fall in the price of imported articles, many of which are sold by the UAC and other cocoa buyers.' Letter from Mr Jones, for the Colonial Secretary, to the Acting Commissioner, Central Province, 15 March 1933, in GNA CSO 168/33.
55. Letter from an official of UAC to the Colonial Secretary, Gold Coast, 3 March 1933, GNA CSO 229/33.
56. UAC Rankin file: reports 38 and 55 to Head Office, 1928, on state of affairs on the West Coast.
57. Rankin, *The History*, p. 131, and *Stock Exchange Yearbook* (1939).
58. *Stock Exchange Yearbook* (1939).
59. Bauer, *West African Trade*, pp. 131–2.
60. From a letter dated at Kumasi, 7 April 1939. Access to this letter was obtained privately through a former employee of one of the major expatriate firms in Ghana.
61. See Chapter 6, section 4.
62. GCLegCo, 4 December 1930.
63. Ibid.
64. Handwritten memorandum dated 12 January 1938, GNA Adm. 23/1/956, Cape Coast.
65. Memorandum dated 15 January 1938, GNA Adm. 23/1/956, Cape Coast.
66. Document dated 8 February 1938, GNA Adm. 11/1460.
67. Speech by Nana Ofori Atta in GCLegCo, 2 November 1918.

68. Question by Nana Ofori Atta in GCLegCo, 30 December 1920.
69. Speech by T. Hutton-Mills in GCLegCo, 2 November 1918.
70. Letter from the Provincial Council of Chiefs, Central Province, to the Secretary, Board of Directors, UAC Ltd., February 1933, in GNA CSO 168/33.
71. P.N. Davies, *The Trade Makers: Elder Dempster in West Africa, 1852–1972* (George Allen and Unwin, London, 1973), p. 62.
72. Ibid., pp. 41, 51, 62.
73. See section 3 below.
74. The history of the Woermann Line is taken from the booklet 'Deutsche Afrika-Linien: A Short History of the German Africa Lines' (Deutsche Afrika Linien, Hamburg, 1971).
75. Leubuscher, *West African Shipping*, p. 99. In 1904 Woermann signed an agreement with the Hamburg-America Line granting Woermann 75% and the other line 25% of German trade to West Africa. Woermann, however, retained control of management and the two companies shipped under the same name. 'Deutsche-Afrika Linien', p. 18.
76. 'Deutsche-Afrika Linien', p. 10.
77. Daniel Marx Junior, *International Shipping Cartels* (Princeton University Press, Princeton, 1953), p. 38.
78. Davies, *The Trade Makers*, p. 91.
79. Richard Fry, *Bankers in West Africa: The Story of the Bank of British West Africa Limited* (Hutchinson Benham, London, 1976), p. 33.
80. RCSR: Cmd. 4669, Part I, p. 1.
81. Ibid.
82. Davies, *The Trade Makers*, p. 110.
83. RCSR: Cd. 4670, Q.5378.
84. Ibid., testimony of J.A. Hutton, Q.13513.
85. Cmd. 1802 (1923).
86. RCSR: Cd. 4670, testimony of Sir Ralph Moor, Q.7009.
87. RCSR: Cd. 4668, p. 16.
88. Leubuscher, *West African Shipping*, p. 22.
89. RCSR: Cd. 4670, testimony of George Miller, Q.4797.
90. Ibid., testimony of G.B. Zochonis, Q.13391.
91. Ibid., Q. 13289.
92. RCSR: Cd. 4668, p. 26.
93. Davies, *The Trade Makers*, p. 173.
94. Ibid., p. 225–8.
95. *International Shipping*, p. 242.
96. *West African Shipping*, p. 18.
97. RCSR: Cd. 4670, testimony of Sir Ralph Moor, Q.7005.
98. Letter from the Board of Trade to the Colonial Office, 4 February 1903, quoting a despatch from the Gold Coast and complaints from Lagos. CO 96/411 des. 7392.
99. RCSR: Cd. 4670, testimony of James Batty, Q.6934.
100. Report on Swanzy's Lighterage Company to the Chairman, African and Eastern Trade Corporation, 19 December 1928. UAC Rankin file.
101. RCSR: Cd. 4668, p. 28.
102. Testimony of Mr Batty to RCSR, recorded as his view in LonCC, 13 February 1907.
103. Davies, *The Trade Makers*, p. 223.
104. UAC: document 559.
105. Leubuscher, *West African Shipping*, p. 18.
106. A statement by the government to this effect is found in GCLegCo, 16 October 1905.

107. Executive Council Paper 648/32, 31 October 1932, C.O. 98/69.
108. RCSR: Cmd. 4670, testimony of John Holt, Qs. 5041, 5043.
109. Davies, *The Trade Makers*, p. 150.
110. RCSR: Cd. 4670, testimony of Mr Batty, Qs.6715–22.
111. Leubuscher, *West African Shipping*, p. 40.
112. Ibid., p. 43.
113. Ibid., p. 51.
114. Davies, *The Trade Makers*, p. 221.
115. Ibid., p. 241.
116. Statement by Mr Whitfield, European unofficial representative for the shipping interests, to GCLegCo, 17 February 1930.
117. Leubuscher, *West African Shipping*, p. 52.
118. Marx, *International Shipping*, p. 28.
119. Ibid., p. 29.
120. In 1909, for instance, there was a 10% *ad valorem* duty on all foreign (non-British) silver imported into the colony. LonCC, 9 December 1909.
121. GCLegCo, 12 April 1889.
122. GCLegCo, 4 August 1908.
123. Letter from the Colonial Secretary, Accra, to LivCC, 6 June 1906, reprinted in LivCC, 2 July 1906.
124. GCLegCo, 23 February 1926.
125. GCLegCo, 2 March 1932.
126. GCLegCo, 17 March 1938.
127. CO 98/69, 22 June 1936, and CO 98/37, 4 February 1938.
128. It is not known why colonial officials were considering the introduction of units of currency of one-tenth pence; one-eighth pence, or half a farthing, might have been considered a more logical unit. Nevertheless, this is the unit which was discussed. Treasury to Colonial Office, 3 February 1910, despatch 3517 in CO 96/502, and Treasury to Colonial Office, 17 November 1911, despatch 37278, CO 96/512.
129. Interview between the Gold Coast Governor and Mr Samuel, a UAC Director, reported in GNA CSO 708/31.
130. 'Departmental Committee Appointed to Inquire into Matters Affecting the Currency of the British West African Colonies and Protectorates. Report, with a Despatch from the Secretary of State', Cd. 6426 (1912) (The Emmott Committee), p. 6.
131. Ibid., p. 5. Hereafter the West African Currency Board is referred to as WACB.
132. W.T. Newlyn and D.C. Rowan, *Money and Banking in British Colonial Africa* (Clarendon Press, Oxford, 1954), p. 50.
133. Letter from the Treasury to the Colonial Office, 15 August 1900, despatch 26641 in CO 96/369. This point is also mentioned in A.G. Hopkins, 'The Creation of a Colonial Monetary System: The Origins of the West African Currency Board', *African Historical Studies*, Vol. 3, No. 1 (1970), p. 125.
134. Newlyn and Rowan, *Money and Banking*, p. 36.
135. Kay, *Political Economy*, Table 24a, 'Government Revenue by Source, 1900–60', pp. 350–1.
136. Unsigned memo, 1915, in GNA Adm. 12/5/151.
137. GCLegCo, 17 November 1919.
138. ManCC, 12 May 1919.
139. GCLegCo, 31 December 1918.
140. Speech by Nana Ofori Atta in GCLegCo, 30 June 1919.
141. LonCC, 18 February and 18 April 1932.
142. Testimony of Mr Pickering of Pickering and Berthoud, Manchester, to the

Emmott Committee, Cd. 6427, Q.1927.
143. GCLegCo, 1 June 1912.
144. Amin, *Accumulation*, Vol. II, p. 438.
145. RCSR: Cd. 4670 (1909), testimony of Leslie Couper, Q.9118, part 14. Hereafter the Bank of British West Africa is referred to as BBWA.
146. UAC, document 588, 'Bank of British West Africa'.
147. Hopkins, 'The Creation', p. 113, fn.51.
148. RCSR: Cd. 4670, testimony of George Miller, Q.4406.
149. 'Agreement with the Bank of British West Africa, Limited, as to the Transaction of the Banking Business of the Government, (16 June 1896)', (Gold Coast, 1900).
150. RCSR: Cd. 4670, testimony of John Holt, Q.4600.
151. Davies, *Trade Makers*, p. 119.
152. Colonial Bank and Barclays Bank, DCO, *Reports*, for years mentioned.
153. Fry, *Bankers*, p. 91.
154. Ibid. pp. 92–3.
155. Ibid., p. 143.
156. Ibid., p. 146.
157. Newlyn and Rowan, *Money*, p. 84.
158. *Directory of Directors* (Great Britain), (1925, 1935).
159. Fry, *Bankers*, p. 31.
160. This description of banking services is taken from 1974 interviews with representatives of Standard Bank of Ghana (formerly the BBWA) and Barclays Bank of Ghana, as well as with representatives of several of the leading expatriate firms still in Ghana.
161. UAC, document 588, 'Bank of British West Africa'.
162. Newlyn and Rowan, *Money*, p. 81.
163. Interview with an African director of Barclays Bank of Ghana, Accra, May 1974.
164. Fry, *Bankers*, p. 63.
165. Alexander Baron Holmes IV, 'Economic and Political Organizations in the Gold Coast 1920–1945', University of Chicago, unpublished PhD thesis, 1972, pp. 113–14.
166. Hopkins, 'The Creation', p. 112.
167. Taken from a list of BBWA charges, dated 1 February 1905, in UAC: document 588, 'Bank of British West Africa'.

5 THE STATE AND PERIPHERAL CAPITALISM: THE ROLE OF THE COLONIAL GOVERNMENT IN UNDERDEVELOPING GHANA

Those changes which took place in Ghana's economic structure during the colonial period were contingent not only upon the impersonal forces of the world capitalist market, but also upon the actions of the colonial state. The state was a representative not of the Ghanaian people, nor even of a certain segment of the Ghanaian people, but rather of a foreign imperial power. As such, despite token representation on local decision-making organs by traditional African chiefs and members of the new petty bourgeoisie, the state was a dictatorial power.

In debates on the role of the state in independent capitalist economies, discussion often centres on the question of whether the state is, in Marxist terms, 'a committee for managing the common affairs of the whole bourgeoisie',[1] or whether it has an independent role. In the case of colonial Ghana, it is argued that the state acted on behalf of the metropolitan bourgeoisie insofar as the interests of that bourgeoisie did not conflict with the interests of the state itself. Colonial rule was imperial rule, and imperial interests were not always the same as the interests of the expatriate businessmen who had dealings with each individual colony. Although it is not within the purview of this book, it could be argued that at the level of the entire empire, the metropolitan state acted in the interests of the metropolitan bourgeoisie. But on the local colonial level, while access to governmental decision-making bodies was given to local expatriate businessmen, such access did not ensure congruity of interests between expatriate officials and expatriate entrepreneurs. The possibility for conflict between the two groups is clearly demonstrated in the colonial government's policies towards transportation, which, while they were geared overall towards facilitating the export-import trade, were also aimed at keeping up the government's revenues.

The section in this chapter on the financing of the state also reveals the constraints under which the colonial governments had to operate. Colonies were expected to be self-financing; they were not funded by the imperial state. Yet investment by private expatriate firms was extremely limited, and only certain types of taxation were feasible. African protests and refusals to pay had eliminated the possibility of direct taxes, of whatever nature. The state was therefore obliged to rely on indirect taxes, especially customs duties, but such taxes could only be imposed with the agreement of the expatriate traders. Because of their rights of consultation both with the colonial government and the home government (through the Colonial Office) members of the expatriate bourgeoisie had considerable input into financial decisions made by the colonial state. African input, by comparison, was almost irrelevant.

1. Relations between the State and the Expatriate Bourgeoisie

Although several formal means of communication between the British expatriate bourgeoisie and the colonial state were quickly established in Ghana, none of them might have had much import had it not been for the informal ties of nationality, race, and, to a certain extent, class, which bound the two communities together both at 'home' and on the coast. There were very few whites in Ghana during colonial times; what white men there were tended naturally to gravitate towards one another. Only in the larger centres such as Accra could they afford to be at all choosy about with which of their compatriots they would socialise. A European club in Accra was the focus of social events; no Africans were permitted into this club until independence in 1957.[2] Here decisions could be made over cocktails at sundown, later to be translated into government language for the benefit of the Africans whom both communities ostensibly served.

In Britain, too, there were informal ties between the more powerful of the businessmen and the men who made government policy. Members of Parliament from Liverpool and Manchester were often also members of major trading families. In London, there were close ties between the African Section of the London Chamber of Commerce and members in both the House of Lords and the House of Commons.

Informal contacts such as those described above were reinforced by the ease with which former members of the colonial service could enter the business world, where indeed their familiarity with the West African coast was most appreciated. Occasional protests reached the ears of the government about this practice, usually from groups which were not themselves recruiting such former administrators. In 1918 the Manchester Chamber of Commerce protested to the Colonial Office that former government men would possess confidential information about the competitors of their new employers.[3] In 1928 J.E. Casely Hayford, an African, raised a question in the Legislative

Council about the proposed directorship of a new diamond-mining firm, Alluvial Diamonds (Gold Coast) Limited, and the alleged presence on its board of two ex-governors and three ex-officials of Ghana.[4] In neither case did the state agree that there was any cause for concern over possible conflicts of interest.

Such informal contacts were further buttressed by the establishment of the Joint West Africa Committee,[5] a consultative organ composed of two members each from the London, Manchester and Liverpool Chambers of Commerce which was entitled to discuss matters of common interest to the three Chambers on a regular basis with the Colonial Office. The committee resulted from growing pressures, especially from Manchester and Liverpool, for consultation as military and administrative interests in the Gold Coast increased. In 1904, the machinery of the JWAC was instituted, with the proviso that only matters on which the three Chambers agreed were to be discussed with the Colonial Office. The committee's purpose was to serve as an 'informal means of communication between the Chambers of Commerce and the permanent staff of the Colonial Office in the preliminary discussion of commercial, shipping, mining and industrial questions relating to the West African Colonies and Protectorates.'[6] On top of the consultative privileges which it granted to the JWAC, the Colonial Office also accorded to the Chambers the right to correspond directly with the governors of all the colonies.[7] The only conditions were that copies of all correspondence between the Chambers and the governors were to be sent to the Colonial Office,[8] and that urgent matters could be acted upon by the government without consultation. This privilege of direct correspondence gave the governors a certain independence of the Colonial Office, and it also gave the Chambers more freedom to put pressure on individual administrators. Conferences with governors who came home on leave were frequent.

Added to their ability to influence the Colonial Office in Britain was the representation which was given to the members of the British business community as 'unofficial members' in the Gold Coast Legislative Council. Until 1934 the Council was authorised only to make decisions for the Gold Coast Colony; after that date it was also the decision-making body for Ashanti and the Northern Territories. However, its actual power was limited as it acted, except in a few cases, essentially as a 'rubber-stamp' for Colonial Office policies dictated from London. Merchants and miners were given representation on this Council, with its very limited functions, as early as 1886, when two European unofficial members and two African unofficial members were appointed. These four unofficials were the only legal representatives of their two communities until 1916, when the Council was expanded to include a third European unofficial and six Africans (three chiefs, one each from the Twi-, Fanti- and Adangme-speaking areas of the Colony, and three 'educated natives' to represent the Western, Eastern and Central Provinces). The third European unofficial was to be appointed specifically as a balance between the mining and the merchant communities of expatriates, two communities which often had serious differences of opinion especially regarding transport policy. The miners were preoccupied with building railways which could carry equipment into the mining areas, while the merchants wanted to invest in roads to facilitate the export of cocoa and other agricultural goods, and the import of consumer manufactured goods.

> In all probability, the new member will, in the first instance, be connected with the Bank of British West Africa; and he will be, to some extent, an impartial European member, who will be able to take an independent view as between, for example, the views held by merchants on certain questions in opposition to those held by the representatives of the Mining Interest.[9]

It was no coincidence that the new member would represent one of the then most powerful expatriate concerns in Ghana, the BBWA, and, along with it, the Elder Dempster shipping line.

From 1916 to 1925 the merchants pressed for more representation on the Council, because even though most policy was made in London, they hoped to have some say over decisions which might be left in the local government's hands. Whenever business interests might be seriously affected by legislation, 'extraordinary' members representing the business community were introduced into the Council.[10] But this extraordinary representation was still considered to be insufficient. At a meeting in London in 1919 in which Governor Guggisberg appealed for more revenue to carry out his development programme in Ghana, for example, the Chairman of the London Africa Committee implied that without more representation, merchants would not support his appeal for funds.[11] Partly as a result of such pressure, the Council was expanded again in 1926, to include five European unofficial members. One mercantile member was to be elected by a mercantile electoral committee, the members of which would be nominated by firms who were members of recognised Chambers of Commerce (in Ghana); one mining member was to be elected by the Gold Coast Chamber of Mines;

and three Europeans were to be chosen by the governor. 'It is probable that among these three European Unofficial Members one will represent the banking interests, another the shipping interests, and a third the mining interests.'[12]

There were no unofficial members of the Gold Coast Executive Council, the body of top administrators which implemented policy decisions handed down from London, and drafted and introduced legislation for the Legislative Council. Even at this level, however, British expatriates had better access than did Ghanaians to government. While the Executive Council did not permit Africans to appear before it, it occasionally called in European members of the business community to discuss pertinent issues.[13]

Despite this additional representation at the local level, the expatriate business community viewed its access to metropolitan decision-making bodies as far more important than its access to local ones. None of the commercial representatives on the coast, in any case, was an important member of his firm; indeed, the directors of many 'African' firms had never set foot in Africa.[14] The real powers, both commercial and administrative, confined their contacts with each other to London and such consultative organs as the JWAC.

To supplement their power on the JWAC, members of the business community were given a great deal of representation on the Royal Commissions which at various times investigated aspects of West African trade or development policy. The firms were given direct representation, for instance, on the Committee on Trade and Taxation (1921), the Private Enterprise Committee (1924),[15] and the West African Currency Board (which operated continuously from 1912). Whenever the Colonial Office informed the Chambers of Commerce that it welcomed their views and would like to hear from them, the Chambers replied that they wanted actual members on the Commissions on the grounds that they, the businessmen, were the most important people in the colony. The Colonial Office, asserting its own independence, did not always take kindly to this argument. In 1912, it denied the expatriate firms representation on the West African Lands Committee;[16] in 1936 it denied them representation on the Overseas Trade Development Council.[17] But even in cases in which they were denied representation the firms were at least given ample chance to speak and present their point of view. With the exception of the testimony by African chiefs and educated men before the Belfield Commission on land use, no such chance was given to Ghanaians. Although there were plenty of educated Ghanaians, and Ghanaians who were involved in trade and shipping, their views were never sought. *De facto*, a great deal of power accrued to the hands of the expatriate business community which, through its expertise and knowledge of West Africa, could often influence 'impartial' commissioners sitting on investigative bodies.

In pursuit of their goal of influencing policy, the British Chambers of Commerce which maintained constant contact with the Colonial Office, also encouraged the formation of local Chambers of Commerce within Ghana, which were recognised as legitimate spokesmen for the expatriate mercantile community.

> Chambers of Commerce have been formed in the principal commercial centres in all our West African Colonies. They are of comparatively recent date and arose out of informal meetings which used to be held by the Agents of the various companies in order to discuss matters of local interest, and to fix prices to be offered for produce for stated periods. These meetings developed into Chambers of Commerce, which have proved of considerable assistance to the Governments. The existence of these Chambers has enabled a more effective liaison between unofficials and officials to become established, and ensures a method whereby collective rather than merely individual views of the trading community can be put forward.[18]

By the early twentieth century the network of Chambers of Commerce in Ghana was already extensive. In 1892, a Chamber existed in Cape Coast, and in May 1895 one was formed in Accra.[19] By 1902 there was a Chamber at Sekondi,[20] and in 1911 a Chamber was formed in Tarkwa.[21] Several of the Gold Coast Chambers affiliated to the British Chambers and used them as their spokesmen in the Colonial Office. Their preoccupations, however, were often of a petty nature, concerned with minor changes of regulations in the colony, and they could not always count on the support of the parent Chambers in such cases.

The Chambers were predominantly European bodies. It was not their inclination to accept or encourage Africans in their midst. African enterprise was a separate entity with clearly defined limits, and it was generally acknowledged by Ghanaians that they simply were not allowed to join the European Chambers of Commerce, except as representatives of registered firms.[22] Although few records of the early Ghana Chambers of Commerce are now available, two government files on the Cape Coast and Winneba Chambers indicate that most members were Europeans, with a few Africans representing British firms and the odd African representing himself.[23] The need for election to Chambers of Commerce would exclude many Africans whose commercial behaviour did not meet with the approval of their European counterparts.

At least one attempt was made by Africans to set up their own Chamber of Commerce, not in opposition to the European Chambers but to complement them. In 1936 the Gold Coast Merchants' Association, as it was called, had about thirty members in Accra, and also had branches in Kumasi and the Western Province. Membership was open to 'Any African concern established and directly interested in the commerce and trade of the Gold Coast, [Ashanti?], Northern Territories and Mandated Territory of Togoland.'[24] Most of the members were merchants, although one or two were engaged in produce buying and some lawyers were attached to the organisation. The principal object of the Association was stated to be the 'protection of African commercial concerns',[25] and it was envisaged that by acting together the members would have more credibility as businessmen, would have access to information, and generally would be more influential. Both the European Chambers and the government looked on this venture with a benevolent paternal eye; but unlike the European Chambers, the Merchants' Association was neither considered a representative body nor consulted as to policy by the government.

Without the kind of access to government, either in the colony or in Britain, which the European business community enjoyed, the African elite was obliged to concentrate on its representation in the Legislative Council. Although as of 1916 Africans were allowed six representatives on the Council, three more than the British had by the 1916 Constitution and one more than the British unofficials after 1925, in practice this representation meant little. African opinion was simply not considered to be as valid, meaningful, or representative as British opinion.

In any case there was an official majority on the Council, and official members were obliged to vote for the policy put forward by the government; that is, by the Colonial Office; they could not vote independently.[26] In rare cases in which all the unofficial members were opposed to a measure, governors after the First World War would usually reconsider it. But what generally occurred was that the European unofficials joined the official members, while the African unofficials were in opposition. Time after time in the Legislative

Council Africans opposed a measure which all the Europeans approved.[27] In such cases, they had no power.

The patronising manner with which the administration regarded the African unofficial members is shown in the following quote from the governor in 1904 in his address on the Estimates.

> The Governor concluded by saying that this is the first occasion on which he has presented Annual Estimates to the Council, and he is glad to see that they have been comparatively little criticised, and that the unofficial members recognise the steps that are being taken for the development of the country.[28]

That the attitude did not change greatly in the ensuing years can be seen in the reply which one European unofficial made in Council in 1928 when J.E. Casely Hayford suggested that Africans be allowed even more unofficial representation than they already had.

> I would . . . tell the Honourable Municipal Member for Sekondi (Casely Hayford) that on the day on which an unofficial majority sits in the Council that will be the day when British, I might say European, capital will commence to leave this Colony . . .
> [T] he Honourable Member for Sekondi is, in my opinion, about one hundred years before his time in his desire for self-government.[29]

Whatever representative functions the Ghanaian unofficials did enjoy, moreover, were further jeopardised by the offhand way in which Legislative Council meetings were run. The unofficials were rarely given agendas to read before the meetings, and often were expected to make decisions on bills which they had never seen before. Rules were almost always waived by the Attorney-General so that the first, second and third readings of a bill could be held at the same meeting, thus not allowing any time for consultation or discussion. In any case, there were very few meetings of the Legislative Council: usually there were about three a year averaging one and one-half days each in length.

The types of complaints which Ghanaian unofficials made against the Legislative Council often bore marked similarities to the complaints made by the European unofficials. For, despite the fact that the lines drawn were usually racial, that is, African versus European, there was some conflict between the two European groups, the trading and the administrative, as well. The expatriate community in Ghana, while tight-knit, was by no means monolithic. Administrators were occasionally motivated by an idealism, or at least a sense of responsibility to the 'natives', which the commercial community lacked. After the First World War, once all of Ghana had been conquered or 'pacified', former military men were replaced by a group of people chosen to be ostensibly impartial administrators.[30] These new African colonial civil servants tended to come from the 'new poor' in Britain, the downwardly-mobile former landed gentry, or to be the younger sons of respectable families who often still maintained an attitude of looking down on trade. According to Robert Heussler, the laudatory historian of the colonial civil service, their chief characteristics were their honesty, gentlemanly conduct and devotion to duty.[31] Whether such praise was warranted or not, it was the case that the social origins and values of the administrators differed to some extent from those of the traders and also that, as training in administration, forestry and agriculture became more common among civil servants, their sense of responsibility to the colony (or at least their capacity to see beyond the present and consider Ghana as a resource to be preserved in the interests of the Empire as a whole) was often greater than that of the profit-seeking traders.

In 1908, the Chief Justice of the Gold Coast, Sir William Brandford Griffith, gave a speech in the Legislative Council which was an impassioned defense of the traders in the Colony.

> He says that to the traders the whole Colony, Native and Europeans, owe a debt of gratitude; that it is thanks to the traders that we now have this flourishing Colony; that when the Colony was struggling in its infancy it was the traders who pulled it through ... [W]hat would the Colony have been without the traders to depôt and to ship its produce? What would the Colony have done, what would the mines have done, without the shipping companies?[32]

Such outright praise of traders was rare from the mouth of an administrator, for despite the fact that, to the Ghanaian, the two groups appeared almost inseparable, there were often strains between them. The issue of land ownership created differences between them; so also did the increasing oligopolisation of Ghana's trade throughout the twentieth century. Individual members of the colonial government sometimes objected to the amount of monopolisation of the economy and the takeover by the UAC of so many smaller enterprises. One UAC Director complained that:

> There is a terror of what they call 'monopoly' in Government circles. For instance, this Company was going to link up with an existing cold storage company in the Gold Coast, for the sake of economy; yet we had to go to extraordinary pains to prove to officials that the proposition came from the smaller cold storage company, as it is always assumed that it is this company which is eating up all the others.[33]

The government also made a few attempts to protect Ghanaian cocoa farmers from the vagaries of the world market, attempts which were not appreciated by the firms and which were usually stifled after complaints had been made to the appropriate officials at the Colonial Office. In 1900, for example, the Liverpool Chamber of Commerce complained that government traders were interfering in the market place by buying cocoa at prices higher than the expatriate firms were offering.

> The Governor admitted that his Government had given, and still proposed to give, some assistance to native planters, who had been offered only nominal prices for their produce at the ports, rather than allow their plantations to perish from neglect, owing to their alleged unprofitableness.[34]

The governor was eventually obliged to agree, under Chamber pressure, that such government cocoa buying would be only a temporary measure.

In 1909, the Chambers again complained of government attempts to help African sellers, this time only by informing the cocoa producers of what the prices for cocoa were in Europe.

> [T]he Government Officials in the Gold Coast appeared to be habitually exhibiting to the native at Coomassie, Accra, and elsewhere, information respecting the prices obtained in the markets for produce, and ... such prices were exhibited to the disadvantage of the European merchants... [35]

The Secretary of State for the Colonies assured the Manchester Chamber, when it complained of this practice, that the governor would be warned to include information as to the dates of the prices, and the costs of freight to Europe, in these notices.[36] By 1922, when once again 'Consideration was given to the advisability of communicating current cocoa prices to farmers through the medium of Political Officers', it would seem that the somewhat idealistic civil servants had learned their lesson, as 'it was decided that the practice should be discontinued for the present.'[37]

The incidents illustrate the types of conflicts which existed between the two expatriate groups in the colony. Both traders and administrators were directly responsible to their principals at home and, in fact, had very little power on their own. Those officials who wished to assist Ghanaians, in whatever ways they could devise, were aware that the Colonial Office was in frequent consultation with the expatriate business community and almost always put its needs and desires (which were so often congruent with the needs and desires of 'the Empire') ahead of those of the people whom it was supposed to be 'civilising'. The reality of oligopolistic control, and the obligation on the government to consult with a very small number of people who had a great deal of power over the economy in Ghana (more so, no doubt, than the Colonial Office itself) meant that without constantly heeding the Chambers of Commerce and doing their bidding the Colonial Office could have found its operations in Ghana disrupted. Insofar as the government was concerned with other than business activities it still had to take the wishes of the expatriate firms into consideration. All government decisions were circumscribed by the wishes of this sector.

Moreover, the view of the home government was that business, trade and free enterprise were the key to the progress and wealth of the empire. Britain, by 1900, had lost its position as leader of the world system of capitalism; at most it was *primus inter pares* with Germany, the United States, and France. The empire was to provide resources to finance its industries at home, and markets for its products. Companies such as Miller and Swanzy, and later the UAC; banks such as the BBWA and shipping lines such as Elder Dempster were what kept this vast profit-seeking empire together. The function of the colonial governments was to mediate between the firms and the peoples of the colonies, to ensure the smooth operations of the whole. Under such circumstances, their primary function was to institute the types of structures which would facilitate trade.

2. The Financing of the State

In keeping with the state's primary aim of creating a structure which would facilitate Ghana's contribution to the economic health of the empire as a whole, the policy was that the colonial government should be as self-financing as possible. Colonial governments in the British empire were constantly constrained by an imperial policy which decreed that colonies must be self-supporting, that they should contribute to, but not take from, the imperial treasury. Without a large inflow of funds from the imperial state, the Ghana government had to look for alternative sources of financing. Private investment in the colony was limited because it had little to offer the European investor, except in the area of gold-mining. The import-export trade was a low-cost industry which required little in the way of funding. Railways, such as they were, were costly, and the few miles of track in Ghana were not a priority investment for the coupon-clippers of the Western world. Most of the financing of the Gold Coast colony was, in the end, done by its African inhabitants themselves through their (indirect) payment of import and export duties.

After 1900, the percentage of Ghana government revenue which came from grants from the imperial government was miniscule. It declined steadily from 13 per cent in 1900 to 1 per cent in 1907, and from 1908 to 1929 nothing at all was given to the colony in the form of direct grants. The Depression-exerted needs of the colony after 1929, combined with the new 'development' policy of the home government in the same period, as exemplified in the Colonial Development Act, resulted in small grants during the 1930s, reaching as high as 5 per cent of the colonial revenue in 1939.[38] But on the whole, a most conservative policy was espoused by the home government.

The policies of the Colonial Development Advisory Committee, responsible after 1929 for allocating funds for development projects to the colonies under the Colonial Development Act, reflected this conservatism. Although the Committee had been urged to 'Take risks. Take some initiative'[39] in distributing its resources, in practice it was limited to financing 'schemes likely to aid and develop agriculture and industry in the Colonies, Protectorate and Mandated Territories, and thereby [likely to] promote commerce with, or industry in, the United Kingdom.'[40] In a provision prescient of contemporary 'tied' foreign aid, all contracts financed under Colonial Development Act funds had to stipulate 'the placing of orders in the United Kingdom and the use of plant, machinery and materials of British manufacture': as well, they had to stipulate that all goods be carried on British ships and all insurance be provided by British companies.[41] Clearly, 'development' in the colonies was to be secondary to development in Britain. The Act allocated £1 million a year for development projects in 1929 (later reduced because of austerity budgets during the

Depression); it was estimated that these funds could stimulate £40 million worth of borrowing by the colonies in 'the city'.[42] Until 1939, Ghana received direct grants of £108,695 from the development fund (excluding grants which it shared with other colonies). The grants financed such projects as rinderpest immunisation, a water scheme in Tamale, the provision of electric lights in Cape Coast, and training for forestry officers;[43] that is, rather than being innovative and providing new directions in development, they simply provided additional revenues for the type of project in which the Ghana government was already investing its funds.

The imperial state hesitated to guarantee all but the safest of loans to the colony. Development was to be financed out of colonial revenues; since these revenues, as will be shown in tables 5.1 and 5.2, consisted primarily of import and export duties and railway revenues, the capacity for development fluctuated with the state of the import-export economy.

> The trustee was not to use his own money to make the ward's estate more productive. The most he might do was to use his own credit to guarantee a loan. Colonial revenues must be able to meet the service of any loans they were permitted to raise, and the salaries of any staff they were permitted to employ.[44]

The 'trustee' referred to in the above quote was the imperial government, while the ward was the colony.

In matters of development financing, even when the Colonial Office wished to invest funds, it was constrained by the demands of the Treasury. The attitude of the Treasury was that it should not invest any money in Ghana; anything it supplied was a loan, and repayment of loans had to take priority over development projects. In 1904, for example, the Treasury criticised the Colonial Office for allocating £300,000 to building a railway in the Gold Coast, instead of to repayment of its debts. 'The debts constitute a first charge on the colony.'[45] Since development could not be financed without loans, and as it was the Treasury which gave loans and backed credit, it had the upper hand. Any ambitious plans emanating from the Colonial Office could be checked by the Treasury's demands for debt repayment and a balanced budget.

The Ghana development policy, according to Peter Sederburg, also depended very much on the individual governor. Most governors were conservative in their policy and preferred to have a balanced budget or a surplus. Between 1901 and 1939, in Ghana, there were 15 years of deficit and 23 of surplus. '[T]he period as a whole ran a surplus of approximately £2,439,000 despite a world war and two trade depressions.'[46] Sederburg describes the general revenue and expenditure policy of the government in the following way.

> The Gold Coast Government appeared to be most interested in its own self-maintenance as an order-preserving framework within which the foreign firms could operate fairly free from restrictions. These operations were to be achieved at minimum cost to the British taxpayer ... This general goal was manifested through the pursuit of intermediate ends indicated by the expenditure data. Thus, state operations were kept simple; the colonial regimes' role in social and economic development was relatively circumscribed, as shown by a low rate of capital expenditure. There was practically no state involvement in directly productive activities, such as agriculture and industry.[47]

While the government received little by way of income from its imperial trustee, equally little came its way as a result of its dealings with the expatriate commercial classes, either through rents or royalties. Rents on government lands and buildings never constituted more than 1 per cent of the colonial revenue. A few thousand pounds, never more than £30,000 a year, was all that the rents amounted to in absolute terms. Similarly, royalties on mining and timber concessions, pegged at 5 per cent of profits, varied between only 1 and 4 per cent of government revenue.[48] The government was somewhat lax in collecting royalties; up to 1921, for example, it had not bothered to collect timber royalties although they were legally chargeable.[49] Moreover, it frequently, on an *ad hoc* basis, exempted imports by foreign firms, especially the mines, from duties on the grounds that the imports would contribute to the eventual overall development of the colony.

The expatriate firms might have tried to argue that their contribution to the colony as a whole, if not to the actual government, was far more significant than appeared at first glance, since their entrepreneurial activity within the territory had backward and forward linkages which stimulated growth. In fact, however, it seems that neither the mines nor import-export trade stimulated many other enterprises. Aside from providing a few opportunities for brokers, and for a group of small shopkeepers and agents who sold the goods which the Europeans imported, expatriate firms did little to stimulate the economy. No industrial production was needed to facilitate trade, nor was there any processing, either of goods to be exported or of goods imported, in which to engage.

Moreover, very little investment was required to maintain the European retailing establishments necessary to induce the African to buy cheap manufactured goods. The sole investments made by the trading firms (aside from investments by some of the firms in their own transport businesses) were in buying and selling stations ('mucky little stores'),[50] a few sheds for storage of cocoa along the docks and bungalows for their European staffs. While it is difficult to obtain accurate figures of total investments, there are some data available which give an indication of investments by a few large European firms in Ghana just prior to their amalgamation into the UAC. The total investment in all of Africa in 1928 by both Miller and Swanzy, the two oldest and largest European firms in Ghana, was only £628,729.[51] Similarly, in 1937 Cadbury, J.S. Fry and Rowntree had a total investment in the Coast of only about £175,000, consisting of living quarters, offices, stores, and necessary equipment, such as weighing scales.[52]

The only significant amounts of money invested in Ghana by expatriate businessmen were to be found in the gold mines. Even with regard to mines, however, it must be kept in mind that many existed in name only, or, even when their nominal capital seemed to be significant, their actual subscribed capital was a very small amount. Between 1880 and 1904, for example, some 476 companies were registered for mining and exploration in West Africa, especially Ghana and the Ivory Coast. Their nominal capital totalled some £43 million, but much of this capital was never subscribed. Despite the mining booms only thirteen companies reported any production in 1904, and only four of these had produced over £10,000 worth of gold. Nevertheless, mining was a substantial percentage of investment: Frankel estimated that of all the non-government capital issues in London for Africa as a whole between 1900 and 1936, capital issues from mining and exploration companies constituted 66 per cent. *In toto*, Frankel estimates that the amount of both public and private capital invested in Ghana between 1870 and 1936 was about £35 million.[53]

With the limited amount of capital which it was able to raise, the government was obliged to seek alternate sources of financing for its activities. Taxation was the answer, although direct taxation was not

Table 5.1: Import and Export Dues as Per Cent of Government Revenue, by Five-Year Averages, 1885–1939

Years	Average Government Revenues (£000s) (i)	Average Import Duties (£000s) (ii)	(ii) as % of (i) (iii)	Average Export Duties (£000s) (iv)	(iv) as % of (i) (v)	Total % (iii) + (v)
1885–89	130	111	85	–	–	85
1890–94	189	166	88	–	–	88
1895–99	286	221	77	–	–	77
1900–4	530	354	67	–	–	67
1905–9	702	417	59	–	–	59
1910–14	1197	712	59	–	–	59
1915–19	1773	881	50	198*	11	61
1920–24	3652	1573	43	533	15	58
1925–29	3983	2316	58	294	7	65
1930–34	2618	1343	51	359	14	65
1935–39	3670	2003	55	662	18	73

Source: 1885–99, Gold Coast, *Blue Books*; 1900–39, Kay, *Political Economy*, Table 24a, 'Government Revenue by Source, 1900–1960', pp. 348–9.
*Excludes 1915.

possible, as both Europeans and Africans opposed it. The only experiment in direct taxation which had ever been implemented in Ghana took place in 1852, when the governor, after consulting with the various paramount chiefs along the coast, imposed a head tax of one shilling on every man, woman and child in the Colony. It was hoped that this tax would finance British expenditures with as much as £20,000 per annum, but widespread indifference, supplemented by some active protest, precluded its payment. The highest figure ever raised was £7,567 in 1853, and the tax was abandoned in 1861.[54] The Sierra Leone hut tax rebellion of 1896 reinforced the government in its policy decision not to risk disruption by imposing any more taxes. A system of municipal taxation was introduced in the 1920s in the major towns of Cape Coast, Sekondi and Accra, and direct taxation was introduced in the Northern Territories in 1937,[55] but the country as a whole never suffered the burden of direct taxation.[56] Plans to introduce an income tax in the early 1930s were delayed because of opposition and 'agitation'.[57]

Without direct taxation as a means of financing its activities, the government had to turn to indirect taxation; primarily, to import and export duties. Table 5.1 presents total government revenues, total import duties, and total export duties for five-year averages from 1885 to 1939, stating import and export duties as a percentage of government revenue. For the first ten years, import duties alone constituted some 80 per cent or more of government revenue; later the percentage declined gradually to a little under 60 per cent until export duties were introduced as well in 1916, after which point their joint contribution to the colonial revenue rose to between 60 and 75 per cent in the late 1920s and 1930s. A substantial part of the government's funds, then, came from the import-export trade, and in this sense the colony was truly self-financing.

It should be noted that until 1916 there were no export duties in the colony, although it would have seemed administratively easier to tax the few large colonial exports than to tax the multitude of imports. One cause of this anomaly was that the British merchants repeatedly and insistently opposed any attempt by the government to impose an export tax. In fact, they opposed all taxes at the same time as they pressured for more development of infrastructure and transportation in the colony. Retrenchment in other expenditure, not taxation, was seen as the way to finance colonial development.

But given that they had to accept some form of taxation, the merchants preferred import duties. Their logic for this argument was that 'import duties, . . . affected more than one particular commodity, and the taxation was not a direct burden on the native.'[58] The merchants, in other words, saw the taxes as a burden not on themselves so much as on 'natives', i.e., they admitted that all customs duties, except for import duties on mining equipment, were passed on to the consumers. They feared the political consequences of imposing a high tax on the cocoa producer, as against spreading taxes among all the consumers of the colony. It would also seem that, given the very inexpensive cost price of many imported goods, a tax on these goods would still not raise the price beyond what the average Ghanaian could pay, whereas a tax on exported goods might reduce the buying price below that at which the average Ghanaian was willing to sell.

Because of this opposition, no cocoa export tax was imposed until World War I. When the British Chambers of Commerce acquiesced in the government's institution of the tax in 1916, they

The State and Peripheral Capitalism   163

insisted that it only be a wartime measure.[59] But a tax once imposed is difficult to remove, and in Ghana the export tax soon became a permanent feature of the economy. As one Colonial Office official had written in 1911, 'We must not allow the principle of Govt. [sic] by Chambers of Commerce to be carried too far, esp. re their "principle" that no taxation should be enforced which directly affects the merchants.'[60] Once the government had managed to impose duties despite commercial opposition, it was not prepared to relinquish its income from them.

Implicit, and sometimes explicit, in all the debates about whether taxes should be imposed, removed, raised or lowered, was the awareness that it was the Ghanaian consumer or producer who bore the burden of the import and export duties; that it was the Ghanaians themselves, in fact, who financed what development of their country occurred through the payment of indirect taxes. If import duties were raised, the cost of imported goods was raised commensurately; while if export duties were imposed or raised, the price paid to the African producer for his crops was lowered. But the converse was not always the case; when import duties were removed prices did not go down, nor were African farmers necessarily paid more when the export duties were lowered (as they were by the governor in 1924 *on condition* that farmer's prices be raised).[61]

The government, the educated African community, and the expatriate business community all, at various times, indicated their awareness and acknowledgement of the fact that in the end, it was the Africans who paid the import and export duties of Ghana. As early as 1893, with regard to a petition presented by the principal merchants of the Gold Coast against a 10 per cent import tax, the then governor reported:

> [W]ith regard to the ... 'grievous tax upon trade' I have been informed by a gentleman ... that at one of the meetings convened by Messrs. Swanzy with the object of obtaining signatures to the Complaint, one of the persons present refused to sign it, stating that there was not a merchant in the Colony who had not added more than ten per cent to his prices and was consequently making more money by it, and if anyone objected it should be the consumer.
>
> [A 'native gentleman' said] ... if the ten per cent duty was taken off it would not lessen the cost of goods ... to the consumers, but would go into the pockets of the trading community

just as the old four per cent duty [abolished as of 1887] did when it was discontinued.[62]

Complaints by Africans that they did not benefit from reductions of duties were a constant refrain throughout the colonial period. As late as 1938, Nana Ofori Atta argued, 'I think I can say that certain commodities which were sold at lesser prices have been increased in price with the removal of duty or sold at the same price.'[63] The business community, certainly, never denied that it passed the full burden of the duties on to Ghanaians; its sole concern was that if the burden became too high, Africans would stop buying or selling. The Sekondi Chamber of Commerce argued in 1921 that

> with the existing [export] tax, large quantities of Cocoa in the country would never be brought to the market, as owing to the cost of cartage, the amount the producer would get for his produce would not pay him for the cost of labour. The repeal of the present tax would just make the difference between a profitable and non-profitable industry.[64]

Similarly, Mr Batty, head of the A&ETC, argued in 1921 before the Committee on Trade and Taxation in West Africa that

> If the Government are going to derive their revenue by direct taxation on production, there is a great danger — it may not be before us today — but there is a very great danger that we may find ourselves in a position of the native refusing to produce because we cannot pay him a price sufficient to induce him to do so.[65]

Yet, although both government and business realised that the burden of indirect taxation was borne by the Ghanaian, such a burden was considered legitimate and there was no suggestion that someone else, perhaps the firms themselves, perhaps the European consumers of the exported produce, should bear the full or even partial weight of the tax. A committee which investigated and accepted the proposal for export tax in 1916 justified the tax on the grounds that money made by Ghanaians was clear profit.

> The Committee fully realized that the direct effect of this tax would be felt by the cocoa planter inasmuch as he would receive

so much less per [head] load ($^1/_3$) than he would otherwise receive, but it must be borne in mind that in this Colony the cocoa industry is wholly in the hands of natives. They have not such items as shareholders' dividends or the cost of European supervision to bear, and, outside the actual cost of headload transport from the farms to the railway, the money they receive for their crop is a clear profit.[66]

Seemingly the costs of labour, organisation and enterprise (plus the cost of waiting five years for the cocoa crop to mature) were legitimate costs only for Europeans, not Ghanaians, to claim.

By assuming the burden of paying import and export taxes, Ghanaians themselves financed a large part of state revenues. There is no guarantee, however, that these revenues would be converted into state investments which would benefit the African community. The long-term goal of the state was to invest in infrastructure which would facilitate trade in the interests of the empire; within this framework, its investments favoured expatriate traders over the indigenous community. Moreover, the state suffered financial constraints, which affected even its modest attempts at development.

3. State Policy and the Creation of Infrastructure: Transportation

The development of transportation in Ghana is a clear illustration of two points as regards overall state policy towards investment in the colony; first, that investments were geared towards the interests of the expatriate bourgeoisie so long as these did not conflict with the interests of the state itself, and second, that Africans in Ghana bore the major expenses of such investment. The state's policy towards transportation was to create an infrastructure which would expedite the mining industry and the import-export trade, while at the same time using the transportation system, especially the railways, as a source of revenue. African interests in trade routes and African investments in transportation were secondary to these two aims.

Even without pressure from European commercial concerns, no doubt the Colonial Office in London would have regarded it as its business to build railroads and roads in Ghana. Among other reasons, it was obliged by the terms of the Berlin Treaty to build railways in the territories which were allocated to Britain.[67] Moreover, the colony had to be self-supporting, and in order to support itself it needed revenues which could only be generated by trade. But the contact which the British business interests had with the government in Ghana helped to generate transport policy, to determine the types of transportation which were to be constructed and where they were to be constructed.

The earliest intention of the colonial government was to build railways which would facilitate the development of the mining industry by allowing the importation of sophisticated technology. As long as the only form of transportation inland to the mines was by headloading, all machinery had to be broken up into pieces weighing not more than 60 pounds. During the first 'gold rush' of the 1890s, when hundreds of small companies were floated to exploit the gold resources of Ashanti, it became obvious that such a form of transport was inefficient. The Colonial Office began to experience a great deal of pressure to develop railways.[68] The first railway line in Ghana was built in the late 1890s and early 1900s, from the port of Sekondi to the gold mining area of Prestea-Tarkwa, and thence to Obuasi, the centre of Ashanti Goldfields.[69] Preferential rates were charged for mining equipment, which was seen as an investment conducive to development.[70] Railway construction was financed by the government from its own revenues, or through the floating of loans. The state did not view Ghana as a good location for private investment in railway construction, as the land was not properly surveyed, and there were problems with climate, labour and supplies which private investors could not handle. It discouraged the idea of private investment in railway construction although it let out contracts for construction to private individuals (including Africans)[71] and allowed mines to construct their own railways when the government lines did not fulfil their needs. Between 1902 and 1913, the British government granted three loans totalling £3,163,000 to the Gold Coast government for railway and harbour construction.[72] Additional financing was obtained by the floating of loans on the London market.[73]

But private interests, although they acknowledged the difficulties of building railways in a tropical country, were often dissatisfied with government policies and argued that a system of private investment and construction would be better. Petitions were frequently sent to the Colonial Office urging both private construction of railways and the taking over of already constructed railways by private firms on the grounds that government administration was inefficient.[74] The government did in fact make several ventures into the contract system on a large scale; for example, in 1909 it agreed to give a contract to the firm of W.H. Murphy, in Dublin, to build the Accra-Mangoase line.[75] On the whole, however, it found that the contract system, although it might provide good opportunities for profit (or graft) to private firms, was not satisfactory.

The argument as to who was to construct railways, government or private enterprise, went on until 1923 when the question was investigated by the Private Enterprise Committee.[76] This Committee argued that the early railways built by contract had been too costly because the government had had no control over spending; complete construction by government was a better system.[77]

> [W]e feel assured that at the present stage of development no wholly private company would be tempted to embark upon railway projects without special inducements in the form of land concessions, mineral rights, or a guarantee of interest at a rate which would render construction by the State itself a more economical alternative . . .
>
> [I]t is not to be anticipated that private enterprise will be found willing to finance, construct and operate railways unaided by Government in the present stage of development in Tropical Africa.[78]

By 1923, however, the railway infrastructure necessary for investors in Ghanaian trade had already been created, so that the question of who was to finance it was no longer a live issue. Moreover, the government by that time had long had a policy that mining companies could build their own railway lines connecting to the government railway lines when necessary, as long as they charged reasonable rates to the general public.[79] To encourage such private construction the Private Enterprise Railways Construction Bill was passed in 1907, stipulating that 'the provisions of the Public Lands Ordinance shall apply to lands required for such a railway, and the Government are thereby empowered to acquire such lands on behalf of the licensee.'[80] This Bill confirmed an earlier Bill passed in 1905 which retroactively gave the Prestea Railway Limited the right to compulsory purchase of land on which it had already built its railway.[81] African members of the Legislative Council were against this Bill, arguing that it was yet another infringement of indigenous property rights.

> [S]ome of the lands proposed to be compulsorily purchased by the Company for this Railway are Stool property. If the Company is allowed to purchase land absolutely, other Companies will come and ask for a similar privilege and the precedent now laid down

may be followed. The result of this will be that in the course of time the Chiefs may be compelled to alienate all their ancestral property.[82]

Merchants, cocoa-buyers and general traders also opposed the extension of the railway system, but for a different reason. They felt that road-building suffered at the expense of railway (and later, harbour) construction. They argued that the gold-mining companies had extra access to and pull with the Colonial Office. This view was especially reinforced in 1903, when it was discovered by accident that in 1901 the government had made an agreement with Ashanti Goldfields that the Sekondi-Kumasi railway would go through the Ashanti Goldfields headquarters in Obuasi. In 1900, the Ashanti Goldfields Corporation had approached the government 'with an offer of a guarantee of interest upon the capital which would be required if the Government undertook to extend the railway from Tarquah to Coomasie . . .'[83] The agreement eventually settled upon included the following terms:

> That the Government have the right to convey troops and all stores over the whole line at 'cost of conveyance'.
> That if in any year the excess of gross receipts over working expenses is less then £30,000, the Corporation shall pay to the Government a sum equal to the difference, but not exceeding £30,000.
> That while in the case of a deficit the Corporation are liable to the extent of £30,000 per annum, on the other hand, if in any year the receipts shew an excess of over 4½% on the outlay, the Corporation are to receive a fifth of such net profits.[84]

Both the traders and other mining companies, once they heard of this agreement, protested vigorously, over a period of several years, against it. Under the provisions of the agreement for low freight charges for government, the traders felt that they would be subsidising the transport needs of Ashanti and the Northern Territories. Further, they felt that 'Ashanti Goldfields . . . would practically fix the rates'[85] so that high charges for imported manufactured goods and for cocoa, palm oil and other exports would subsidise low charges for mining equipment. With all of its other advantages, it was the last straw that Ashanti Goldfields was entitled to a share of the railroad's profits in return for accepting responsibility for a deficit which never, in fact, occurred.

> [T]he liability of the Ashanti Goldfields Corporation under the Agreement to recoup any deficits on the Railway to the extent of £30,000 per annum, ha[s] not come into operation owing mainly to the high rates for traffic which the various Companies ha[ve] paid upon the goods forwarded by them over the railway.[86]

The opposition from both the traders and rival mining firms to this agreement was so intense that the government was eventually obliged to cancel it. Negotiations took place over a period of several months to settle upon a lump sum which Ashanti Goldfields should pay the government in return for having had the railway built through Obuasi; eventually, however, the agreement was cancelled without any payment at all by the firm. As soon as the agreement was cancelled, the government revised the rates on the Sekondi-Tarkwa railway.[87]

That such an agreement as the one referred to above could have been made in the first place was merely a reflection of the government's overriding concern, in the early colonial period, to facilitate the development of mining and of railways, controlled by government, which would provide it with revenue. Table 5.2 indicates the percentage of government revenue which came from railways. Between 1904, when

Table 5.2: Government Revenue from Railways by Five-Year Averages, 1900–39

Years	Average Government Revenue (£000s) (i)	Average Revenue From Railway (£000s) (ii)	(ii) as % of (i)
1900–4	530	42	8
1905–9	702	160	23
1910–14	1197	322	27
1915–19	1773	513	29
1920–24	3562	902	25
1925–29	3983	506	13
1930–34	2618	0	0
1935–39	3670	5	0

Source: Raw figures from Kay, *Political Economy*, Table 24a, 'Government Revenue by Source, 1900–60', pp. 348–55.

the Sekondi-Kumasi line was completed, and 1925, when competition from road transport began to undercut railway carriage, railway revenue averaged about 26 per cent of total government revenue. By increasing or decreasing railway rates on various products, the government could control development as well as increase or decrease its own income.

Given the government concentration on railways, road construction often seemed like a neglected step-sister. A Department of Roads was created in Ghana in 1894; in 1901 this became the Department of Transport. But it would seem that for the first two decades of its existence the Transport Department's function was not to build roads so much as it was to find labourers to act as government carriers or to work on government railways.[88] Such neglect of actual construction occurred despite much pressure from the Manchester and Liverpool business communities, who, because they were so involved in import-export trade, were anxious for roads to be built to the cocoa-farming areas of the colony so that farmers could get their produce out, and so that traders with imported goods for sale could go deeper and deeper into the 'bush'. Yet as late as 1926 the policy as regards road building was still to give priority to roads feeding the railways, then to roads serving other useful trade purposes, and finally to roads built for administrative purposes.[89] The primary purpose of roads was to act as feeders to railways even when railways were not conveniently located for trade purposes.

Until 1918 the government could argue that wide roads were not a necessity, since the most predominant forms of road use were head-carriage and cask-rolling. For either of these activities, narrow paths were preferable to wide roads which could not provide adequate shade for the African labourers engaged in carrying or rolling. There was no transport by beasts of burden, whose susceptibility to the tse-tse fly rendered them useless. After 1918, however, European firms, and also the government, began to import light lorries in large numbers, and the demand for good roads increased. Traders began to oppose other forms of investment in transport, especially the Central Province Railway which was constructed in 1923, on the grounds that more roads should be built first. '[I]n the Western Provinces there [is] . . . a large area of available land suitable for the cultivation of cocoa, where there [are] . . . neither adequate roads, nor adequate transportation facilities . . .'[90]

Much of the construction of roads which took place was not a result of government initiative, but rather of African initiative.

So great was the enthusiasm for road-building that in Ashanti, for example, it was not unusual for villagers to give road engineers a free hand to demolish houses or cut their way through cocoa farms, provided the road passed through or near the village.[91]

Villages even went so far as to give contracts to European firms to build roads for them.[92] For example, in 1925 the General Manager of Railways reported that the inhabitants of the village of Obomen had engaged a local contractor to build an 800 foot high road up the Kwahu Scarp, at the cost of £6,000, in order to get their produce out to market.[93] The government grew to rely on such African enterprise for the upkeep of roads. Early transport policy was that all villages were to contribute compulsory quarterly labour on the roads in return for a small payment; later the government came to expect that villages would also finance road construction. Indeed, whenever the issue of land concessions was raised the government argued that concessions rents obtained by the various tribes should be invested in roads, which no doubt would benefit the Africans concerned but which would also benefit the European traders. Ghanaian initiative removed much of the burden of financing local transportation routes from the shoulders of the government.

Despite the fact that government investment policies concentrated more on railways than on roads, a considerable network of roads was built up in Ghana during the colonial period. On the whole, the network had a north-south orientation, since both roads and railways were geared for the export trade. The railways were built to promote the southerly flow of goods and the rates charged reflected the directional flow; low rates on agricultural produce going to, and on imported goods coming from, the ports. The railway system as it eventually was established consisted of a line from Kumasi to Sekondi, a line from Kumasi to Accra via the cocoa producing Eastern Region, and a line along the coast from Accra to Sekondi and Takoradi. Neither railways nor roads adequately criss-crossed the country in an east-west direction.

Table 5.3 presents figures for railway traffic in percentages for the years 1900–39. This, of course, is not a completely accurate reflection of trade patterns of the colony, since many goods were transported by roads. Nevertheless, it does present some idea of the trade patterns. Except for the years 1911 to 1922, the proportion of local traffic carried on the railways was low; generally between 10 and 20 per cent. Much of this carriage consisted of internal trade among different markets, and also of the supplying of food to the mines.[94] With the exception of the years 1911 and 1918 (in the latter year a quota on cocoa exports was imposed by the imperial government in order to save wartime shipping space) over 50 per cent of the railway carriage was of imported or exported goods in all years. In the 1900s, before roads were built, the percentage was very high, being 95 per cent between 1905 and 1909. It dropped in the 1910s but rose again in the 1920s and 1930s to between 70 and 85 per cent. However, much of the export tonnage in the latter two decades consisted of manganese from the mine at Nsuta. Between 1910 and 1939, cocoa averaged about 20 per cent of the tonnage. Imported goods declined as a per cent of railway carriage between 1900 and 1939 although the absolute amount of imported goods carried rose fairly consistently. In the 1900s a large percentage of the imported goods was mining equipment; railway cars brought in mining equipment and left the mining areas empty for lack of exportable goods, until a system of feeder roads was developed. Later, the composition of the imported goods became more varied; but at the same time lorry traffic began to compete with rail traffic for the carriage of goods to market places which might not be on the main railway lines, so that the total percentage of imported goods on the railways fell.

The development of a fairly complete north-south system of roads,

Table 5.3: Uses of the Railway by Different Sectors of the Economy, Percentages by Five-Year Averages (Main Products Only) 1900–39

Years	Local Goods % (i)	Cocoa % (ii)	Exports % (iii)	Imports % (iv)	Total % Imported and Exported Goods (iii) + (iv)
1900–4*	n.d.	n.d.	n.d.	n.d.	n.d.
1905–9	5	2	17	78	95
1910–14	33	10	12	55	67
1915–19	46	24	31	24	55
1920–24	25	28	50	20	70
1925–29	15	18	68	17	85
1930–34	19	21	65	14**	79
1935–39	13	16	63	22**	85

Source: Based on raw figures from Kay, *Political Economy*, Table 32a, 'Railway freight traffic (excluding livestock), 1900–60', pp. 388–9.

*1900–04, no data.
**No data for imports 1932 and 1939. Percentages total more than 100 as cocoa is included twice, under 'cocoa' and under 'exports'.

The State and Peripheral Capitalism 173

both as feeders to the railways and as independent routes to the coast, provided opportunities for the setting up of transport companies both by the large European firms and by independent Ghanaians. Large firms such as CFAO and the UAC ran their own fleets of lorries. '[The UAC] carries on extensive road motor transport services, chiefly for its own use, for the carriage and distribution of merchandise and native produce between main centres and points not served by sea, river, or railway.'[95] Elder Dempster also ran a road transport company with garages and workshops at Nsawam.[96]

African transport firms could not, of course, compete with the European firms either in size or in scope. Often an African entrepreneur had just one lorry which he ran on a shoestring budget making the down payment on the lorry to a European firm and keeping on hand enough money for running expenses only. The government argued that 'shoestring competition' by Africans was unfair; that the railways suffered because Africans offered poor quality services at low prices.

> [I]n certain places, it is possible to obtain a 30 cwt. lorry on first payment of probably £20. That £20 is the only capital the purchaser possesses. We also know that there is a very large trade in one-gallon tins of petrol. The reason is the lorry-owner is only able to produce, when he starts the day's work, sufficient money to buy one gallon; he then proceeds with that gallon in the hope that he will collect a few shillings in fares to purchase a further supply; if he does not, he remains on the road until his brothers come and help him . . . no organised system of transport, whether it be road or rail, can possibly compete successfully with motor transport as it is run to-day in the Gold Coast . . . the competition between road and rail is unfair.[97]

The 'unfair' competition to the railways from African lorry drivers, combined with the presumably slightly fairer competition from European firms, was great enough to cause the government considerable concern in the late 1920s and 1930s. The amount of government revenue supplied by the railways fell from 26 per cent in 1926 to 3¼ per cent in 1927; from 1928 to 1938 the government received no revenue at all from the railways. While presumably at least part of this drastic decline in resources was caused by the Depression of the 1930s, evidently it was also caused by a drop in the percentage of goods, specifically of cocoa, which was carried by the railway. Table

174 *The State and Peripheral Capitalism*

5.4 presents statistics on the percentage of cocoa exports carried by rail and by other forms of transport (after 1918 'other' was presumably almost exclusively by lorry). A decline in the percentage of cocoa carried by rail after 1930 coincides with the decline in railway revenues from cocoa.

Table 5.4: Cocoa Exported by Road and Rail, Percentages by Five-Year Averages, 1900–39

Year	Cocoa Exported by Rail (%)	Cocoa Exported by Other Means (Roads) (%)
1900–4	n.d.	n.d.
1905–9	7	93
1910–14	45	55
1915–19*	78	23
1920–24	80	20
1925–29	66	34
1930–34	56	44
1935–39	54	46

Source: Based on raw figures from Kay, *Political Economy*, Table 21b, 'Volumes of Major Exports, 1900–60', pp. 336–7 (col. i) and Table 32c, 'Railway freight traffic (excluding livestock) 1900–60', pp. 388–9 (col. ii). NB n.d. = no data.
*1915–19 excludes 1918 when a shipping quota was imposed and cocoa was stored at port.

Because of the declining railway revenues, the government moved in the 1920s and 30s to take measures to guarantee traffic to the railways at the expense of road traffic. Its aim was to curb competition on roads competitive with railways, such as the road between Nsawam and Accra. In the early 1920s the government tried reducing charges for various goods travelling on the railway; however, since one of the goods for which rates were reduced was petrol, competition continued as before. In 1927, the government changed its policy and raised the duty on petrol by 100 per cent,[98] in order to raise the costs of lorry transport firms. Parallel to this it decided to stop making repairs on certain major roads, so that lorries could no longer travel on them.

> Government is at present incurring a large expenditure in establishing motor transport routes in parts of the country where the railway

does not exist, and therefore it does not appear that it would be justifiable for us to maintain alongside the railway a major road for the convenience of private interests strictly limited to a small area in the whole country.[99]

At the same time, the government instituted a 'road-gap' policy, designed to deliberately leave gaps in major roads to force exporters and importers to ship by rail. This policy was formally abandoned in 1929,[100] but as late as 1936 several of the gaps still existed, for instance, the gaps between Anyinam and Wiresei on the Accra-Kumasi road, between Agona and Simpa on the Takoradi-Tarkwa road, and between Brofoyedru and Fomena on the Cape Coast-Kumasi road.[101] In 1936, the governor decided to definitely fill in the gaps, but only on condition that a new policy of 'scheduled' roads be instituted.[102] This policy provided that on new roads, the government could, if it wished, prohibit the carriage of imported goods inland from the coast, and the carriage of exportable goods, especially cocoa, south to the coast. The 'scheduled roads' policy was not rescinded until 1945 and resulted in considerable hardship not only for the independent lorry transporter, whether African or European, but also for the cocoa farmer.

> [T]ake a man who has a large estate between Nkawkaw and Anyinam; if he wants to go to Koforidua to replenish his stocks of say soap, rice and other commodities, and sell his cocoa, he would have, according to this Bill, to take his cocoa up north to a Railway Station: he cannot bring it down to Anyinam; he must take it to Nkawkaw or the nearest station up. On getting there, as the passenger train will not take his cocoa, he has got to wait for the goods train, which may not travel that day, to bring the cocoa down to Koforidua, and as he is not allowed to travel on the goods train, he has to wait until the next passenger train; all this means delay. At Koforidua he sells his cocoa, makes his purchases of goods. These he cannot take by lorry, so he has to wait until there is a goods train going, by which he will consign the goods, after which he takes the passenger train himself, whereas by a lorry he could accompany his products and do it all in one day . . . And, at the same time, although the lorry industry is principally not in the hands of the Africans, yet those who do run these lorries pay licenses and after all is said and done, if they earn money it is not a loss to the country, because it is in the country.[103]

176   *The State and Peripheral Capitalism*

The institution of the road-gap and scheduled road policies indicates clearly that in the matter of transportation, although on the whole the government was concerned to build a transportation infrastructure which would facilitate trade, yet in matters of detail it was willing to sacrifice the needs of the expatriate commercial community and of indigenous African entrepreneurs to its own revenue needs. Although the business community had considerable powers of consultation with government, acceptance of its views was not automatic. Its wishes could be superseded by the needs of the colony as a whole, as represented by government policy. Nevertheless, in the largest sense of policy, government and business were usually in accord and the mechanisms of consultation provided for the emergence of consensus, within certain bounds, as to the directions colonial development, or lack of development, should take. Once the basic infrastructure for trade had been established, little else was done for the economy of Ghana. By facilitating development of the gold mining industry as well as the import-export trade, the state was both fulfilling its own needs for revenue and encouraging imperial needs for trade and commerce.
The provision of roles for Africans in the peripheral structure which arose from the fulfilling of such needs was a secondary consideration.

Notes

1. Karl Marx and Friedrich Engels, 'Manifesto of the Communist Party', in Lewis S. Feuer (ed.), *Marx and Engels: Basic Writings on Politics and Philosophy* (Anchor Books, Garden City, New York, 1959), p. 9.
2. Interview with an African director of Barclays Bank of Ghana, Accra, May 1974.
3. ManCC, 12 March 1918.
4. GCLegCo, 1 March 1928.
5. Hereafter referred to as the JWAC. The JWAC existed until at least 1956; the author was able to locate its Minutes for 1905 to 1919, but the Minutes for 1919 to 1939 appear to have been lost.
6. LivCC, 31 January 1905.
7. LivCC, 24 March 1903.
8. LonCC, *Twenty-Second Annual Report* (1903), p. 62.
9. Speech by the Governor, GCLegCo, 8 August 1916.
10. For example, for the meeting of 24 and 28 August 1912, in which the question of concessions was discussed, the President of the Accra Chamber of Commerce, and representatives of Millers Limited, the BBWA, and Prestea Block A Limited (a gold mine) were appointed. GCLegCo, 24 and 28 August 1912.
11. LonCC, 12 September 1919.
12. Speech by the Governor, GCLegCo, 22 February 1926.
13. On 11 June 1921, for example, Messrs Rosenthal and Crombie Steedman appeared before the Executive Council to discuss the cocoa export tax. CO 98/43.
14. '[S]ome reference was made to the difficulties which occurred owing to the

restriction of authority in the case of commercial representatives on the Coast. The opinion was expressed that the Government had a real grievance because these representatives were not fully authorised to speak for the home concerns. It had on more than one occasion been suggested that Principals should themselves make regular visits to the Coast.' ManCC, 22 October 1928.
15. Cmd. 1600 (1921) and Cmd. 2016 (1924), respectively.
16. ManCC, 8 July 1912.
17. LonCC, 31 January 1936.
18. 'Report by the Hon. W.G.A. Ormsby-Gore M.P. (Parliamentary Under-Secretary of State for the Colonies) on his visit to West Africa during the year 1926' (His Majesty's Stationery Office, London, 1926), p. 168.
19. LivCC, *Forty-Sixth Annual Report* (1896), p. 89.
20. LivCC, 15 September 1902.
21. LivCC, 19 June 1911.
22. At a conference between African leaders and European businessmen on 16 December 1930, Nana Ofori Atta asked a question about the admittance of Africans to Chambers of Commerce. The reply from the Accra Chamber was 'the Constitution of the Chamber contained no colour bar and . . . all were open to election provided that they represented registered firms.' GNA Adm. 11/1070.
23. The author made extensive inquiries as to the whereabouts of such records and could locate only one file each on the Cape Coast and Winneba Chambers, recorded respectively as GNA Adm. 23/1/255, Cape Coast and GNA Adm. 23/1/277, Cape Coast.
24. Gold Coast Merchants' Association, *Constitution*. Information on the Gold Coast Merchants' Association was provided by Mr N.T. Clerk of Accra, April 1974. Mr Clerk was himself a photographer and trader with connections in Europe; he and his cousin were the guiding lights behind the organisation. The GCMA existed until 1957, when it merged with the European organisations to form the Ghana National Chamber of Commerce. I am indebted to Mr Clerk for providing me with a copy of the GCMA Constitution and Rules.
25. Ibid.
26. Statement by the Governor, GCLegCo, 26 November 1914.
27. One of the few occasions when a bill was withdrawn was in 1930 when the cocoa cess (tax) bill, designed to impose an additional seven per cent tax on cocoa exports to finance a cocoa marketing scheme, was introduced. African opposition to this scheme was reinforced by opposition from the home Chambers of Commerce, hence, the Governor withdrew the cess. GCLegCo, 4 December 1930.
28. GCLegCo, 27 September 1904.
29. Statement by Mr Youngman, GCLegCo, 9 March 1928.
30. Robert Heussler, *Yesterday's Rulers: The Making of the British Colonial Service* (Syracuse University Press, Syracuse, 1963), p. 25.
31. Ibid., p. 43. Heussler's view, however, should be contrasted with that of H.D. Perraton, in 'The Man on the Spot: British Officials in Late Nineteenth Century Africa', in *The Theory of Imperialism and the European Partition of Africa* (Centre of African Studies, University of Edinburgh, Edinburgh, 1967), pp. 146–7. Perraton views the civil servants, at least of this earlier era, as social, financial, professional and personal failures, often possessed of a touch of sadism and a desire to dominate.
32. GCLegCo, 26 October 1908.
33. Notes of Mr Muir's (a UAC Director) and Mr Mellor's (a UAC official) conversation with Mr Lunn, undated. UAC Rankin file.
34. LivCC, *Fiftieth Annual Report* (1900), p. 181.
35. ManCC, 3 May 1909.
36. Letter from the Earl of Crewe to ManCC, 27 May 1909, included in ManCC,

14 June 1909.
37. Gold Coast Executive Council, 30 January 1922, CO 98/43.
38. Based on raw figures from Kay, *Political Economy*, Table 24a, 'Government Revenue by Source (1900–1960)', pp. 348–55.
39. Speech by Mr J.H. Thompson, Lord Privy Seal, to the Colonial Development Advisory Committee, 1 August 1929, CO 970/1.
40. Quoted by Mr Boyd, member of Colonial Development Advisory Committee, 1 August 1929, CO 970/1.
41. Minutes of the Colonial Development Advisory Committee, 9 October 1929, CO 970/1.
42. Minutes of the Colonial Development Advisory Committee, 6 November 1929, CO 970/1.
43. Minutes of the Colonial Development Advisory Committee, 9 April 1930, 24 July 1930, 28 September 1932. CO 970/1 and 970/2.
44. Kenneth Robinson, *The Dilemmas of Trusteeship: Aspects of British Colonial Policy Between the Wars* (Oxford University Press, London, 1965), p. 26.
45. Treasury to Colonial Office, 18 June 1904, despatch 21782 in CO 96/421.
46. Peter C. Sederberg, 'The Gold Coast under Colonial Rule: An Expenditure Analysis', *African Studies Review*, Vol. 14 (1971), p. 192.
47. Ibid., p. 200.
48. Based on raw figures from Kay, *Political Economy*, Table 24a.
49. Gold Coast Executive Council, *Minutes*, 2 July 1921, CO 98/43.
50. These words were used by a former European cocoa buyer when describing his company's premises in an interview. Accra, August 1974.
51. UAC Rankin file: Reports. It is possible that the properties were overvalued as the purpose of the valuation was to indicate the worth of the African and Eastern Trade Corporation upon its amalgamation with the Niger Company in 1929.
52. Cad:288/74.
53. Information on mining investments is taken from Frankel pp. 161, 181, 158.
54. McPhee, *Economic Revolution*, p. 210.
55. Announcement made by Governor in GCLegCo, 15 March 1937.
56. Details of the taxation system are taken from McPhee, *Economic Revolution*, p. 207 ff.
57. Gold Coast Executive Council, *Minutes*, 9 November 1931, CO 98/56.
58. ManCC, 11 February 1930.
59. LivCC, 15 May 1916.
60. Unsigned minute dated 19 May 1911, in despatch 16738, CO 96/512.
61. Governor to GCLegCo, 26 March 1924. The governor reduced the cocoa export tax to 1s 8d from 1s 4d per pound because at a conference at the Colonial Office in 1923, Mr Batty, head of the A&ETC, had promised that 'any further reduction of the duty on cocoa would at once go to the price paid to the native.'
62. Gold Coast, 'Despatch from Governor Griffith' (1893), (Photocopy, Balme Library, Legon, Chana), p. 49.
63. Speech in GCLegCo, 15 September 1938.
64. Reported in LivCC, 6 June 1921.
65. Committee on Trade and Taxation, Cmd. 1600, Minutes of Evidence, Q.648.
66. Speech by the Treasurer in GCLegCo, 26 September 1916.
67. Despatch 2198 no. 41, in CO 879/40.
68. As early as 1891 the Liverpool Chamber of Commerce was pressuring the Colonial Office, on behalf of the Gie Appantoo Mining Company, to build railways. The Company presented the Chamber with a memorial 'on the subject of improvements in the way of access to their properties, desired by the Gold Mining

Companies of the Gold Coast.' LivCC, *Forty-First Annual Report* (1891), p. 90.
69. Details as to the dates of construction of roads and railways in Ghana can be found in Peter R. Gould, *The Development of the Transportation Pattern in Ghana* (Northwestern University Press, Evanston, Illinois, 1960).
70. Dumett, 'British', p. 287.
71. McPhee, *Economic Revolution*, p. 113.
72. D.K. Greenstreet, 'The Transport Department – the First Two Decades (1901–20)', *The Economic Bulletin of Ghana*, Vol. 10, No. 3 (1966), p. 35.
73. McPhee, *Economic Revolution*, p. 114.
74. In 1911 the London Chamber suggested leasing the Nsawam-Accra railway to a private concern on the grounds that it would be better run. LonCC, 12 January 1911.
75. Reported in the JWAC, 17 February 1909.
76. 'Report of the Committee appointed to consider and report whether, and if so what, measures could be taken to encourage Private Enterprise in the Development of the British Dependencies in East and West Tropical Africa, with special Reference to Existing and Projected Schemes of Transportation.' Cmd. 2016 (1924).
77. Ibid., p. 6.
78. Ibid., pp. 18 and 21.
79. JWAC, 25 July 1906.
80. GCLegCo, 30 December 1907.
81. Statement by Mr Hunt, a European unofficial member, in GCLegCo, 23 November 1905.
82. Statement by Mr Brown, an African unofficial member, in GCLegCo, 23 November 1905.
83. Letter to the London Chamber of Commerce from R.L. Antrobus of the Colonial Office, in LonCC, 21 March 1904.
84. LonCC, 11 July 1904.
85. Ibid.
86. Report of a subcommittee of the London Chamber of Commerce on the Ashanti Goldfields Agreement, LonCC, 15 November 1904.
87. Statement by the governor in GCLegCo, 6 February 1905.
88. Greenstreet, '*The Transport Department*'.
89. Statement by the governor to GCLegCo, 22 February 1926.
90. LonCC, 11 January 1923.
91. K.B. Dickson, 'The Development of Road Transport in Southern Ghana and Ashanti since about 1850', *Transactions of the Historical Society of Ghana*, No. 5 (1961), p. 38.
92. See the statement of the governor describing the employment of Italian contractors in the Akwapim hills, GCLegCo, 23 October 1916. '[T]he natives of some of the now flourishing towns situated on the summit of the Akwapim range of hills, recently employed an Italian contractor, at their own charges, to construct a motor-road, 10 miles in length and costing £800 per mile, leading down to and forming a junction with the PWD's road from Adawso to Mangoase.' But the governor went on to say 'This work, it should be noted, was designed, not to serve any immediate commercial purpose, but to enable the wealthy cocoa farmers of this division to spend as much time as possible with their families in the hills.'
93. Memorandum by the General Manager of Railways, 1925, in CO 96/663.
94. Gould, *Development*, p. 2.
95. UAC Rankin file: 'Notes on the History of the United Africa Company', p. 3.
96. The Elder Transport Company is mentioned in a speech by the governor in

GCLegCo, 3 February 1925.
97. Speech by the Secretary for Native Affairs in GCLegCo, 8 March 1932.
98. Reported in LonCC, 20 September 1927.
99. Governor to GCLegCo, 22 February 1926.
100. Governor to GCLegCo, 26 September 1929.
101. Governor to GCLegCo, 19 March 1935 and 20 February 1936.
102. GCLegCo, 31 July 1936.
103. Speech by Mr Christian, an African unofficial member, in GCLegCo, 31 July 1936.

6 THE PERIPHERAL ECONOMY AND CLASS FORMATION

In this chapter it is not intended to discuss all aspects of class formation in Ghana during the colonial period, a formidable task for which the data presented in this book is inadequate. Clearly, the configuration of social classes which existed in Ghana in 1939 was not a result simply of developments during the colonial period, but was also highly dependent on the pre-colonial social, economic and political structure. Similarly, aspects of colonial rule other than the economic also affected class structure; the role of missions and the colonial education system, for example, was extremely important.

Nevertheless, it is worthwhile to examine the effects on class structure of the specific economic framework, and to document the processes by which certain changes in class formation took place. In this respect, we can look particularly at three social class developments; the creation of a petty bourgeoisie (along with the underdevelopment of the bourgeoisie as a result of competition with expatriate entrepreneurs); the evolution of a more highly stratified rural society as a result of the switchover to cash-crop (cocoa) production; and the beginnings of the development of a proletariat, as a result of the need for workers in the mines and on government projects, as well as the need for migrant cocoa labourers.

The formation of social classes in Ghana was reflected throughout the period in various manifestations of class conscious actions, some of them as simple as the various protests by representatives of the petty bourgeoisie in the Legislative Council which have been noted in this book. Others were specifically economic, especially the frequent actions which were attempted against expatriate control of marketing in both the import and export sectors. While, again, it is not within the scope of this book to present a complete history of class-conscious activities (which would, for example, necessarily have to include actions taken by chiefs to protect their traditional rights) one incident is examined in detail. This is a protest, made by the various classes which were formed by the very creation of the peripheral economy, against expatriate control of that economy, in 1937/38. The cocoa boycott of 1937/38 provides a rather dramatic finale to the period of classic colonial control of the Ghanaian economy.

1. The Underdevelopment of Commerce and the Ghanaian Petty Bourgeoisie

For purposes of this discussion, the petty bourgeoisie is considered to be the class of small property owners and small traders, whose aspirations to enter the bourgeoisie are constantly thwarted, at the same time as they are constantly threatened by the possibility of losing their tenuous hold on property and descending into the ranks of the poor peasantry or the proletariat. A complete class analysis of Ghana would need to consider the question of whether essentially propertyless strata such as professionals, clerks and civil servants should also be considered petty bourgeois, or whether their interests, indeed their political 'consciousness', would clearly be separated from those of small traders and entrepreneurs.[1] However, this discussion is concerned only with the latter category which was more directly influenced by Ghana's oligopolistic, expatriate-controlled peripheral economy.

The process of institutionalisation of colonial rule in Ghana resulted in the progressive disintegration of the class of Ghanaian traders and entrepreneurs which had evolved in the course of the slave trade and the 'free' legitimate trade of the nineteenth century. As more and more Europeans entered the West African trade, their competitive advantages pushed out their African rivals. Ghanaians suffered from the process of establishment of oligopolistic control of trade, both in the sense that independent African entrepreneurs were eliminated through competition, and in the sense that new roles for Africans were limited to dependent commercial activities such as commission agenting and brokerage.

There is considerable evidence to suggest that competition between Ghanaian and European merchants was conducted on a fairly balanced basis until about the mid-nineteenth century. On an economic level, and moreover on a political level, Africans and Europeans regarded each other more as equals than they were to do in the twentieth century. The Europeans did not at first consider themselves as a superior race dealing with an inferior race; in fact, as Margaret Priestley demonstrates in her book, *West African Trade and Coast Society*, a number of intermarriages took place between the original European traders in Ghana and aristocratic African families. '[T]here were few resident traders, lacking white female company, who did not enter into a more settled relationship with a local woman.'[2]

Well into the nineteenth century, until with better health facilities it was possible for more Europeans to live in Ghana, and especially for

white women to accompany their husbands, European traders were
only too willing to socialise with their Ghanaian counterparts; the gulf
was not between white and black but between educated and uneducated
in the coastal towns.[3] Africans and Europeans belonged to the same
trade organisations and the same Chambers of Commerce until the 1870s.[4]
Together, the two groups of educated traders ran the forts and
administered justice in the areas under British control. It was not unusual
for Africans to hold administrative positions in the British hierarchy,
although the highest ever held was by James Bannerman as temporary
Lieutenant-Governor in 1850.[5]

Just as there was relative equality between black and white in the
social and political systems in the early nineteenth century, so there was
equality of black and white traders. Trade was still small-scale and high
risk. 'Trust', the willingness to trust one's trading partners, was one of
its most important aspects, and as Edward Reynolds points out, the
willingness of Africans to trust Europeans was as important as the
Europeans' willingness to trust Africans.

> The granting of credit had been a feature of Gold Coast trade from
> at least the seventeenth century with both Africans and Europeans
> offering credit terms. Africans frequently offered the European
> trader staple exports on credit when the goods he wanted were
> not immediately on hand. The European trader likewise offered
> the African trader goods on credit to be paid for with the produce
> of the country when it was available.[6]

Many Africans traded independently, while many others worked as
commission agents for European houses. Although, Reynolds contends,
there was not enough room in the trade to accommodate all the Africans
who wished to enter it, on the other hand it was possible for some
Ghanaian traders to import as much as £20,000 to £30,000 worth of
goods each year on credit.[7] Especially after 1853, when steamship
lines were introduced in the West African trade and regular crossing
enabled small independent entrepreneurs to ship their small consign-
ments with a security of arrival dates which had been unknown to them
before, many opportunities arose for African competition with the large
European firms.

But by the end of the nineteenth century the tenuous system of
equal trading relations had collapsed. No longer was it true, to quote
J.E. Casely Hayford, that 'The run of Europeans who came out to the
Gold Coast were quite a superior class of men, [who] ... mixed freely

with the intelligent sons of the soil, and helped to lay the foundations of a new civilisation.'[8] Rather, the European firms were reorganising in such a way as to minimise the need to use African traders. Direct shipments to European employees on the coast were being substituted for shipments consigned on credit to African trading partners.[9] The change to direct shipping was in part a deliberate attempt to remove African competition; Andrew Swanzy, a partner in F. and A. Swanzy, maintained that indigenous merchants 'drove the European merchants from the trade by ruinous competition.'[10] But by this time the European merchants were also arguing that too much credit was being extended to Africans who did not repay their debts.[11]

At least part of the reason, however, for the inability of African merchants to repay their debts was the fact that Africans were consistently charged more than Europeans for the same trade goods. Reynolds points out that 'As early as 1826 it had been reported that trade goods were sold to Europeans on the coast at cost price, to mulattoes at a higher price and to blacks at a still higher price.'[12] In 1856 an African trader by the name of Joseph Smith, in debt to the firm of Forster and Smith for £18,000, discovered that Forster and Smith had consistently, over a period of 15 years, been charging him between 20 and 50 per cent more than it charged white traders for the same goods. He therefore claimed that Forster and Smith had made £27,000 extra profits in their dealings with him, and far from his owing them £18,000, they owed him £9,000. Smith's claim was not acknowledged, however, and he died a bankrupt.[13] Such treatment of African traders seems to belie the notion that blacks and whites were trading as equals; although it could be argued that whether or not racism pervaded the commercial atmosphere, Africans were higher risk trading partners than Europeans because of their underdeveloped banking system, as well as the underdeveloped legal structure of trade (for instance, a lack of laws concerning bankruptcy).

Indeed, of the fifteen large Ghanaian businessmen of the nineteenth century whom Susan Kaplow, in her 'African Merchants of the Nineteenth Century Gold Coast' investigated in detail, only five escaped bankruptcy or serious financial difficulty.[14] Ghanaians simply could no longer compete with Europeans who held numerous advantages along with increasingly oligopolistic control. For example, whereas Africans had to transport their goods down the inland waterways to the coast by canoe, Europeans possessed steam launches. Africans found it difficult to obtain enough British specie to pay customs duties, whereas British traders had enough specie not only to pay duties, but also to pay cash for agricultural produce; thus pushing African traders, who were obliged to barter for such products, out of the market. Europeans consistently undercut Africans in sales, while overpricing them in purchasing.[15] One Ghanaian trader complained in 1889:

> But now our African markets are failed and the only business we can transact is commission business, because lot of Europeans firms has been established here who sell their goods invoicely and also give 10% commission to all buyers who buy from one pound upwards, so there is no profit at all in our works here when we order [sic].[16]

As a result of the unequal terms of competition and of technological developments whose costs to Ghanaians were prohibitive, many scions of indigenous trading families began, in the mid- to late-nineteenth century, to move out of trade and into professional life. Many mulatto Ghanaians, formerly able to compete in trade because of the advantage of their partial European ancestry, began to move into professions such as trading agents, teaching, evangelism and the ministry.[17] Law was also a favourite recourse for the son of a trader who had lost his fortune. Professional Africans, with degrees from British universities, began to replace traders in positions of power in the British administrative structure. After 1904, of all the Ghanaians who sat as unofficial representatives on the Gold Coast Legislative Council, only one was a trader.[18] Of the 26 men who were included in the biographical work, *Gold Coast Men of Affairs*,[19] only one or two engaged in any sort of trade.

The decline of African traders as a significant economic force was accompanied by their decline in other spheres as well. Not only did the Gold Coast Chambers of Commerce systematically exclude Ghanaians by the turn of the century,[20] but they were also excluded from government, as the administration initiated a policy of putting power into the hands of the 'traditional' chiefs who seemed more likely to support British rule (those who did not were easily replaced); and from social intercourse with the whites, who now had a large enough community of trade and government personnel, including wives, to enable them to be socially exclusive. The introduction of direct colonial rule, with its consequent steering of educated Ghanaians into the professions and away from competitive trading, facilitated the eventually complete economic takeover of the import-export sector by foreign, predominantly British, firms.

Part of this process of consolidation of all trade in European hands entailed a continued circumscription of options for Ghanaian participation in the economic life of the country. During the early twentieth century, a number of new mechanisms were employed by the European firms to exclude even a minimal amount of indigenous Ghanaian competition. Africans who tried to engage in trade on their own could be, and were, easily undercut by their European competitors, with the occasional direct help of the expatriate government. For example, as early as 1887 legislation was passed which made it difficult for the small African entrepreneur to trade. This legislation imposed a licence fee of five pounds on all retailers and wholesalers in the Gold Coast Colony; a licence of five pounds, while almost irrelevant to a European wholesaler, could break an African retailer.[21]

But such legislative enactments were relatively infrequent in Ghana, as there were many purely commercial means of forcing out independent Africans from trade, such as undercutting their prices.

> The [African] traders here would buy and sell from the European companies, some even imported on their own. But you could not get very big. There were no restrictions, but these monopoly companies could break you if you did well. Especially if you brought in a new line, which would compete with something they were selling. They had so many reserves, they could reduce their prices and show losses, until they forced you out of business. We could not do that because we did not have the reserves.[22]

Another method to undercut Ghanaian competition was to offer the independent African a position as an agent for a European firm, with a guarantee of more custom than he could obtain on his own.

> Around 1900, the early part of the century, there were so many merchants, especially in Cape Coast . . . But then UAC and the other big firms would give them positions as agents if they were competing. If they were selling something cheaper than the European firms, the firms would offer to give them jobs as their agents. And then the European firm would tell its customers that they had to go to this particular agent rather than direct . . . The firm absorbed Africans because it was well-established in Europe. It would write Europe that it wanted to take on a particular man as an agent. And then it would name the man as distributor and tell its customers they must apply through the distributor for goods, instead of directly. UAC would have a catalogue, and they

would have to order through the commissioned agents.[23]

Africans could also be tied to European firms through the 'passbook' system. Under this system, African traders obtained passbooks which entitled them to make wholesale purchases on a credit basis from certain European stores. The amount of credit which each African could obtain depended upon his record with the particular expatriate firm, but also upon the particular European official with whom he or she dealt. Thus, often, the figure was arbitrary, and could be changed overnight if an official were replaced. The African trader was also tied to the creditor firm for his source of supplies, since the granting of credit was contingent upon his spending his money in the store that granted it. The system continued even after the establishment of a banking system in Ghana, as the European banks did not give credit to Africans. Moreover, the passbook system contained some abuses. 'These included ... illicit behind the counter sales, cash sales by chits of essential goods, also making the sale of scarce goods conditional upon the purchase of stagnant lines.'[24] Thus, the commercial system in Ghana quickly became one in which Africans were tied, as agents or distributors, to individual European firms. They might be 'independent' in the sense that they did not work on salary, but they were no longer independent importers and exporters as many had been in the precolonial period.

A poignant example of such undercutting of indigenous traders, forcing them to become dependent on an expatriate firm, is to be found in the National Archives of Ghana in a file entitled 'Trade in Salt Fish by the United Africa Co. Ltd. at Dunkwa — Petition by the Women Fish Sellers Against.'[25] In 1930, an official of the UAC had informed the fishwomen at Dunkwa that from then on, there was no need for them to go to the coast to buy fish. The UAC would buy the fish wholesale, and then sell it to the market women, who would remain the retailers. But the market women feared that they would become dependent on the UAC for supplies; and also that the UAC would start selling fish retail in its stores. '[E]ven presently we are being competed with by Messrs. United Africa Company Limited as they are selling some of the fishes we are selling at their stores ...'[26] Already, the women complained, the union of the old European firms into the UAC had made their husbands redundant as workers; now the wives' livelihoods were to be removed as well.

> We were brought here more or less by our husbands who are employees of the Combine and other European establishments and our working on fish has helped enhance the Companies' operations in this district. These husbands of ours have been thrown off from their work because of the Union made [i.e. formation of UAC] and our husbands who are now workless depend upon us for their daily maintenance, etc.
>
> That since the advent of Europeans into this Colony before we ever stepped into this interior, we have not seen any European Company undertaking to oust women of their little vocation as is presently bringing to bear in Dunkwa and we resent this absolutely.
>
> That in as much as we have been convinced of the United Africa Company trying by all means to oust us from our living we strongly protest against such procedure by the United Africa Company. We know of Europeans buying and holding monopolies for certain goods which are not allowed to be sold to any other firms save themselves and we on this coast and more especially in Dunkwa will never allow such throwing off again to affect us in the same way as it affected our husbands who not from their own faults have been distressed and have become heavy burdens on our shoulders.
>
> That we have no alternative, but that if United Africa Company means to compete with us then their salesmen or saleswomen should come to the market shed and do any work in fish as the exclusive sale of fish in the United Africa Company's store shall very much militate against our trade ... [27]

The fishwomen's protest was sent to the governor, who on being informed by the UAC that they could obtain fish cheaper than could the market women, refused to take any action. In any case, as one official pointed out in a memorandum, the process of increasing dependence on a few large firms was inevitable.

> This would seem to be a matter in which Government cannot interfere even if it would; at the worst it is only a repetition of what has happened so frequently during the last thirty years in England — small traders being ousted by the big limited liability company. Moreover an example of the system of which the women now complain, is to be seen in respect of other commodities — Manchester cloths, cigarettes and so on — in every market in the Colony the women buy these (on credit) from the 'European' stores, generally within a stone's throw from the market itself,

and proceed to retail them at their stalls. That is all that is proposed
in connection with the 'stink fish' trade at Dunkwa.[28]

This incident indicates graphically the process by which independent
African traders became dependent on expatriate firms. Often, independer
Ghanaians, having been pushed out of business, became storekeepers for
Europeans, working on a commission basis or simply on salary. (This
type of job was of course available for men only.) The job of storekeeper
was not easy, and required a fair degree of education and a practical turn
of mind on the part of the man occupying the position. One African
agent in 1902 had the following tasks. 'This gentleman was entirely in
charge of the store, attended to the shipping of any palm oil or palm
kernels and took delivery of any goods arriving by Cargo boats from
England or the continent and kept proper books and accounts.'[29] The
storekeeper was responsible for hundreds of different articles of trade.

> [The] small stores in surrounding villages [were] all kept by mission
> educated natives, sales sheets had to be made out every day, cash
> paid in every week, stocks were taken at the end of every month
> and although there were hundreds of lines each article had to be
> accounted for . . . [30]

Although he was held responsible for any losses his store might incur,
the storekeeper was given very little responsibility in buying and selling,
and even less in financial matters. He could not, for instance, write
cheques.[31] To ensure his financial responsibility, he often had to post
bonds of from £200 to £500, or to mortgage his house to the
expatriate company, before he could be employed. In addition, the
company would withhold his first several hundred pounds commission
(if he worked on commission basis), paying perhaps 5 per cent interest,
as a guarantee against his absconding.[32]

Very strict regulations of employment (applying to European as
well as African storekeepers) were enforced to ensure that employees
could not go into trade on their own or change companies, taking
'trade secrets' with them (and, in the case of Europeans who were
allowed to grant credit, often taking African customers with them as
well). Storekeepers had to sign contracts stating that they would not
give away trade secrets or divulge the names of a company's manufacturers or agents.[33] These regulations were perceived by Ghanaians
as being in restraint of trade, but there was little they could do about
them.

With such conditions laid upon their employment, many Ghanaians working for expatriate firms found that their individual enterprise was stifled, not rewarded. Africans, moreover, were not promoted within the expatriate firms; although they were competent, the idea of using Africans for senior positions was unattractive to European businessmen. When, for example, all the white employees of Alexander Miller died in Ghana in the 1880s, the company was forced into the position of 'devolving the care of the firm's interests on the African staff, a condition of affairs which had never existed before and which Mr Alexander Miller contemplated with much disquietude.'[34] Rather than trust Africans with the business, the office was temporarily closed.

At the end of our period, in 1938, the UAC claimed that it was willing and eager to promote Africans in its establishment.

> Let it not be thought . . . that the Company regards the African simply as a hewer of wood and drawer of water. The whole of the clerical service is open to the educated African . . . No purely clerical work is performed by Europeans, but all by Africans . . . There are Africans holding executive positions as important as that of District Manager.[35]

In reality, in 1939 the entire UAC (not solely the company in Ghana) had only 39 African managers.[36]

Africans who held the same jobs as Europeans were consistently treated less well and paid less. While records of Africans in employment are difficult to obtain, a report written by a Sierra Leonian agent by the name of Coker, on the occasion of his retirement from the firm of John Holt in Nigeria, can be taken as indicative of the general European policy towards African employees.

> One of the irritating things in Nigeria and which helps to hinder the progress of trade at a station occupied by a blackman is the tendency on the part of some of the authorities to give more credence to what a European of another firm tells them to that of a blackman working for them. Take a station at which white and black are in charge of the factories and there be an agreed rule between the firms as to prices and dashes in nine cases out of ten, the European will break the rule in order to get more than his share of the produce, if your blackman were to report or do the same in order to get for you your full share of the trade no

credence will be given to his report, and he will be told stop; As a wire was once sent to a certain blackman 'Stop buying produce with soap dashes else I remove you from charge'. In very truth the white man who reported him was giving out 10 times more soap and tobacco dashes . . .

[I]n some cases where you will see the European with all things necessary for his comforts you will see the Africans without even a chair, a table or a bed although both are working for the same firm. . .[37]

Within the context of the import-export trade, there were, of course, also some roles for African middlemen to play as brokers; that is, as persons buying cocoa on behalf of the exporting firms. According to a census taken in Ghana in 1931, there were at that time 1,500 cocoa brokers and 37,000 subbrokers in the country.[38] The 1,500 brokers were obviously the more powerful of these two groups; they were the ones who had direct dealing with the European firms and who were able to receive credit from the firms in the form of cash advances. Credit was given to the brokers so that they could go into the 'bush' and buy crops from the farmers in advance of the actual harvest; the aim was to obtain the cocoa at a lower price than would be charged once the harvest was in. The sub-brokers, on the other hand, were agents for the brokers who might simply be working on a few pounds advance, with little wealth of their own.

In the face of European oligopoly, Ghanaians were ingenious, untiring, and inventive in their attempts to become traders in their own right. Many moved into more than one line of business, engaging, for example, in cocoa farming, brokerage, timber exporting and shipping. One of the most successful Ghanaian entrepreneurs was Nii Kwabena Bonne III, a Ga chief from Accra. During his youth, before being installed as chief, Nii Bonne worked as a clerk, a contractor, a builder and a merchant. He became actively engaged in the import-export trade and in that capacity travelled all over the world, at one point making a journey overland from Europe to Japan in order to reclaim a debt from some Japanese customers. Nii Bonne formed various companies, none of which lasted for any significant amount of time, and all of which were plagued by various forms of swindling by both his British and his African colleagues. He also, at one point, tried to ship gold, but was arrested and fined for allegedly trying to illegally export diamonds as well.[39]

Nii Bonne's activities as a contractor included building drains, houses and 'factories' for Europeans, as well as building the Dodowa market on contract to the government. Activities such as these, by Nii Bonne and others, indicate that Africans were not content simply to try the traditional means of enterprise in Ghana, the import-export trade, but that they were also interested in developing industry. Ghanaian farmers, for example, not only built their own roads and bridges in order to facilitate the export of their cocoa, but they also used their construction skills to help build railroads and mines. 'In the case of each Railway much of the work was done by minor contracts entered into with the natives. Contracts of this sort ranged in value from £1 to £30 and even more.'[40]

Various other attempts were made by Africans to enter manufacturing or processing, but all met with discouragement either from government or the expatriate firms. Far from granting help to indigenous manufacture, the government from as early as 1887 imposed duties on all goods manufactured in the colony,[41] yet at the same time it allowed goods which were necessary for European industrial development, especially mining plant, to be imported free of duty.

Ghanaians could not, of course, compete with European-made products and so indigenous industry declined in the face of imports. African processes of manufacture were too simple and expensive to compete with Europeans. In 1891, for example, Prince Edward Aggrey of Cape Coast tried to interest the Liverpool Chamber of Commerce in an indigenous process of manufacturing dyes from barks. The Chamber dismissed his attempt, noting that 'such dyes, etc., could be produced here in greater quantities from superior materials and at less cost than in Africa.'[42]

Thus, it was not because of lack of initiative on their part but rather because their undeveloped economy could not compete with developed European capitalism that Africans were obliged, if they were at all enterprising, to enter trade as the only way in which they could make large sums of money. Many of the most prominent of Ghanaians were active in trade as either their primary or their secondary occupation. But most of the companies which African entrepreneurs set up failed; they could not compete with Europeans who had more knowledge, financing and resources. The roles left over for Ghanaians in the economic system were suitable only for the development of a petty bourgeoisie dependent on the metropolitan bourgeoisie for its existence. Attempts by Ghanaians to join the 'big' bourgeoisie failed; it was obvious that they were not to be permitted independent economic activity. Although objectively they, like the metropolitan bourgeoisie, exploited the producers and consumers of Ghanaian society, their possibilities for advancement as a class were blocked. As a class, therefore, as will be demonstrated in section 4 of this chapter, it was in their interests to unite with other sectors of Ghanaian society, especially the rural cash-crop producers, against the interests of the Europeans.

2. Rural Class Formation

The formation of new social classes in rural areas of Ghana can be explained by its increasing dependence on cash-crop agricultural production for the world market, especially its heavy dependence on cocoa exports. The spread of production for exchange instead of for use resulted in changing concepts of wealth, and the division of producers into rich and poor. Land, although it remained communal property, took on a new value, and those who controlled the most land became the wealthiest people. While land itself did not become private property, and thus could not easily be converted into other forms of wealth, the usufruct of the land was privately controlled and cash-crops produced on the land could be bought and sold.

The introduction of private production of cash-crops for the world market resulted, according to Samir Amin, in the 'Kulakisation' of the economy, that is, 'the constitution of a class of indigenous planters of rural origin, the virtually exclusive appropriation of the land by these planters, and the employment of paid labour.'[43] This Kulak class in fact constituted a rural petty bourgeoisie which was characterised by possession of more than one farm, the employment of labour, and engagement in other activities such as money-lending, brokerage and trade. These farmers were 'petty' bourgeois in the sense that although they were producing cash-crops for the market through the use of hired labour, they were not engaged in the creation of surplus value through the actual process of exploitation of labour power, nor did they actually own the means of production (although one could argue that, through the spreading prevalence of 'usufruct-mortgage', they controlled the means of production).

The rural petty bourgeoisie was the wealthiest of four groups which emerged in the countryside. The second group was a middle peasantry comprised of families who worked only one farm, using only their own labour, but who were not in debt. These were followed by an indebted peasantry which had to borrow money from the rural petty bourgeoisie and often in order to pay its debts, had either to engage in share-cropping arrangements with the creditors or give up usufruct entirely. It would seem that by the 1920s and 30s the division between the rural bourgeoisie and the indebted peasantry was becoming more and more clear cut, although the indebted peasants were never completely dispossessed of access to land, the actual physical ownership of which could not be alienated from the tribe. Finally, there was a class of landless migrant labourers from the Northern Territories and the French colonies, who worked for the petty bourgeoisie.

A number of individuals who first availed themselves of the new opportunities for cash-crop farming (that is, farming specifically for the external market) were chiefs. Already wealthier than the average tribal member because of their control of stool lands and their receipt of dues, fines and tributes, some chiefs became wealthier still through the sale of concessions to Europeans. Chiefs who negotiated concessions on behalf of their tribes were occasionally tempted to misappropriate the funds received, or to grant special rates to the Europeans in return for secret bribes.[44] It was common for Europeans to overcome chiefs' scruples as regards concessions by the distribution of what was charitably known as 'consideration money'. Consideration money was granted over and above the public 'gifts' which a European might give to a chief and his elders. With such additions to the already considerable advantages they had over ordinary farmers, chiefs could easily invest in cocoa farms. They were also permitted, by customary law, to commandeer labour to work on their farms, although, as their subjects became more tied themselves to the external market, they became less and less willing to devote their labour to the chief's farms.

It was not necessary, however, for an individual to be a chief or to have some initial advantage in order to become a wealthy farmer. Each family in a tribe was entitled to a section of the tribal land to cultivate as it wished, and the products of this land, after payment of tribute, were its own. Cocoa trees or palm trees grown on tribal land were the property not of the tribe but of the individual who cultivated the land. Those who wanted more land for cultivation could, upon application to the chief, be granted more. Land was a free good, not an object of property, at least within each tribe. Those Ghanaians who came originally from areas in which the land was not suitable for cash-crops, especially cocoa, migrated to other areas where they could buy or rent usufruct of land from the indigenous tribe. Their payments to the chief were, of course, greater than the payments made by the indigenous people; but the principle of instalment payment was well recognised and land could be paid off gradually from the profits from selling cocoa.[45]

The Peripheral Economy and Class Formation 195

Polly Hill lays great stress on the notion that African cash-crop producers were entrepreneurs; innovative and risk-taking and at the same time characterised by rational investment and planning. She argued that producers were characterised not only by their willingness to invest but also by their willingness to expand, to increase their areas of production and delegate responsibility to relatives or hired labourers. A farmer might barely oversee his land, leaving responsibility for day-to-day cultivation and decisions in the hands of his employees. As he accumulated wealth, he might try to expand into different activities; trade being often blocked beyond the middleman's role by the European distribution system, a frequent new role to adopt was that of money-lender.[46]

For while some farmers were able to become rich through cash-crop production, others found themselves going under. If they had a bad crop or if the international price for cocoa was low, they might not recover their investment in their farms. Moreover, they were often tied into the consumer network so much that they could not wait for the sale of their crop in February or March in order to buy the goods they needed; hence, they took out loans on the security of their future crops in September. With the growth of production for the external market, there was much more occasion for farmers to borrow and indebt themselves.

Three different types of people engaged in money-lending in the countryside. Rich farmers practiced money-lending as a means of investment; debts were often paid off in cocoa crops or in usufruct of the debtor's land, enabling the rich farmer to increase his own saleable product. The rich farmer was often a farmer-*cum*-chief, or even a farmer-*cum*-chief-*cum*-broker. His object might be to control as much cocoa as possible in order to sell to the Europeans. Cocoa brokers pure and simple also engaged in money-lending; it was their objective to 'corner' as much of the cocoa supply as possible at the beginning of the season, at the lowest possible prices, hoping to reap substantial gains from the cocoa on its sale to European firms at the end of the season.

There was much resentment among farmers at the high rates of interest which borrowers had to pay for loans. One African borrower complained in 1912 that

> Richmen are very barbarous cruel and inhumanity [sic] in loan; charging unreasonable interest ten shillings (10s) on a pound sterling (£1) charge sheeps before loan. Sale of money for double

interest weekly. Pledge of cacao farms for a period of five years in hands of debtors; who neither has nothing to do to pay the debt nor against his daily bread.[47]

By his last accusation, that the debtor had 'nothing to do', the writer of this sad letter was complaining against the prevalent practice of creditor's completely taking over farms. The creditor was unlikely to invest in the farm or even to keep it in good order; as the following report demonstrates, his only interest was the crop.

> The District Commissioner, Akwapim, recently informed me that noticing the neglected condition of the farms along the Aburi Nsawam road he made enquiries as to the cause and learned that they had become the property of money lenders, not necessarily cacao brokers, owing to the original owners being unable to repay the loans obtained at exorbitant rates of interest. The money lenders . . . content themselves with plucking the cacao but pay no attention to the farms which they hope that the real owners will ultimately reclaim.[48]

But even when they were allowed to stay on their farms, peasants who had pledged the entire crop, regardless of its size, were unlikely to work to increase the crop; any increase would simply go to the creditor. Entire crops were often pledged simply as interest, not as principle, for a loan. In 1936, C.T. Shephard wrote of this system, which was then at its most prevalent because of the world economic depression (although it had started well before the depression)

> In most cases, the lender takes possession of the farm, and reaps the crops, until the debt is liquidated. The crop is usually regarded as interest. The crop of a low-yielding farm is sometimes regarded as a mere perquisite of the lender and the borrower is required to meet his obligations from other sources. The crop of a high-yielding farm may be considered sufficient return to liquidate both the capital and interest in an agreed number of years. In other cases, the borrower remains in possession of the farm. He may give the lender two thirds of the crop — one third being for repayment of capital, and the other third being for interest — and retain the remaining one third as consideration for his labour.[49]

Interest rates generally varied anywhere between 25 and 100 per cent, or even higher. One report from the Western Province of the Colony in 1934 mentioned one loan on which a total of almost 300 per cent interest had been paid.[50] Shephard sampled, in his investigations, 93 farmers who had borrowed, between them, £2,015; they had already paid a total of £465 in cash for their debts and supplied their creditors with 2,495 loads of cocoa, nevertheless, they still owed some £2,379.[51] In 1933/34 he estimated that some 75 per cent of all farmers in Ghana had pledged part of their crop to money-lenders; moreover 30 per cent of the farmers had pledged one or more farms and 5 per cent had pledged all their farms.[52]

The cocoa broker with his advances, and the rich farmers with his loans, were figures of no little power in the rural Ghanaian community. By lending money to poor peasants in return for a pledge of their crops, they could keep them in perpetual debt. Rural society began rapidly to differentiate between a petty bourgeoisie and ordinary peasants, both groups tied into the system of cash-crop production for the external market but the former successful both in production of its own crop and in the expropriation of the crop from others, while the latter often succumbed to debt and poverty.

While the market provided opportunities for large profits to successful farmers, its vagaries were all too often an important factor in bankrupting producers as well. Those who became wealthy and expanded their investments in production ran high risks of losing those investments if the cocoa price declined, as it periodically did, on the world market. As one chief reported in 1934, while discussing the practice of 'pledging', or mortgaging, farms:

> It is considered that many have been obliged to resort to such practices as a result of disappointment of the Cacao industry. They have become prosperous almost too suddenly and had been tempted, both men and women, to engage labourers, and also the greed in the acquisition of extensive forest lands, or in the hope of high prices, but quite unexpectedly Cacao has let many people down at a time when they had invested their savings in large forest lands and cacao plantations, the cost of which, in most cases, not fully paid.[53]

The problems of both small and large cocoa producers, with their frequent indebtedness and bankruptcies, were an important motive in government moves to establish cocoa co-operatives in the late 1920s and early 1930s. In an attempt to safeguard 'traditional' society against the effects of Ghana's incorporation into the world market, and, as well, to guard against what were perceived as unscrupulous activities by entrepreneurial Africans, the colonial administration tried to persuade farmers to join co-operative marketing societies. The societies were to be allowed to give credit to their members, but it soon became obvious that such credit would not be able to serve the purpose, as some members had hoped, of paying off their pledges. 'Experience during the past two years of loans from Societies to their members shows that relief from mortgage-debt is beyond the powers of most of our Societies, at any rate in their present stage of capitalisation.'[54] The state's feeble attempts to organise structures which would thwart the development of new social formations were bound to fail; although individual rich farmers might rapidly, in times of crisis, become poor peasants, the structure which permitted the emergence of these stratified social groups had solidified, and the social classes themselves could not be eliminated.

The characteristics which distinguished the rural petty bourgeoisie from the middle and poor peasants were not only their greater wealth and their ability to participate in activities such as money-lending, but also the fact that the former employed labour while the latter did not; peasant agriculture was confined to the use of family labour. The retention of tribal structures and especially of the custom of family obligations in the wider kinship network guaranteed some support to the peasant; moreover, although he could lose the produce and even the usufruct of his land, the peasant always retained ultimate possession of the farm since the system of private ownership of land had not developed to the stage at which it could be completely alienated to a creditor.

Thus, in Ghana, it was never the case that a class of landless labourers emerged from those who had originally had access to land. A class of labourers in the cocoa areas existed, but these were migrants from the Northern Territories and from the surrounding French colonies, who might have been landless in Ashanti or the Colony but who retained access to land in their homelands. These migrant labourers travelled to the Colony and Ashanti in order to work on the cocoa farms, for the mines, and on government construction projects. The terms of payment for migrant labourers varied, although in general, by the late 1930s, a labourer in the cocoa industry would receive about eight pounds a season.

There were three basic methods of payment. One was to give the labourer a third of the crop at the end of the season; this was his sole reward for his season's work and it was up to him to market the cocoa

The Peripheral Economy and Class Formation

as best he could. Another was to grant him a piece of land which he could farm as his own, so that he could sell the produce from that land, or live on it himself. Finally, he might be paid in cash at the end of the season. The labourer generally had to wait out the entire season before he was paid, and his total payment depended, except in the few cases in which a lump sum was agreed upon beforehand, very much on the state of the cocoa crop and the amount which his employer could obtain for the cocoa.

> With regard to the terms of the labour contracts entered into, systems differ in various native states. All that can be definitely said to be common to all, is their general vagueness since the reward to be paid is not fixed in advance but left subject to certain eventualities. In Krobo country it is customary for the farmer to supply the labourer with a certain amount of food during the season, and to give him a sum of money at the end. In Akim it is common to pay the labourer in cocoa leaving him to conduct his own sales . . . But the most general practice, and that which appears likely to become in time universal, is to pay the labourer at the end of the season a percentage of the actual money received from the sales; the sum varies from 1s 6d to 2s for every 10s obtained by the farmer for his cocoa.[55]

Despite the vagaries of these methods of payment, most migrants preferred cocoa farm labour to the other opportunities available to them, working for the mines or for government. As will be shown in the next section, it was only with the greatest of difficulty that either expatriate miners or the government were able to create even the small proletariat which they needed for their own productive purposes.

3. The Beginnings of Proletarianisation

In the preceding section the development of a wage-earning (or partially wage-earning) class without direct access to the means of production was discussed in relation to the production of cocoa. In the cash-crop areas, migrant labourers were hired by the rural petty bourgeoisie to work the land. These labourers occupied an intermediate status; they were a class in formation. While they maintained their rights to land in their traditional pre-capitalist social structures, in the areas in which they worked they were landless. They were moving between two modes of production, one pre-capitalist and communal, one itself still in transition but moving in the direction of capitalism.

'Migratory workers do not form a new social class but rather fall into a transitional category. We assign a special place to this group because migratory workers reflect the transformation of traditional structures into emerging modern ones.'[56]

This class in formation, the incipient proletariat of Ghana, was not confined to the cocoa areas. In fact, there were three sources of the proletariat; cash-crop farming, mining, and government labour. The last two were more clearly areas of proletarianisation; while labourers on cocoa farms might have access to plots of land or shares of the crop, labourers in mines were paid only in wages for their industrial production; for government works projects, as well, the payment was clearly in wages. Thus, while all migrants had access to agricultural land in the areas from which they migrated, some were more proletarianised than others; those who were dependent strictly on wages were differentiated from those who were allotted plots of land or who were paid by shares of the crop.

The introduction of wage labour for mining and government works was a process fraught with some difficulty, and one which took some decades to fully implement. Both government and business were confronted with the problem of persuading members of a pre-capitalist society, all of whom had rights of access to land, to abandon that land in favour of wage labour. From the time of the earliest colonisation through the 1920s (and even, to some extent, in the 1930s) there was a continual shortage of individuals willing to work for wages. As a result, despite principled opposition to such a policy, the state resorted to various methods of coercion to supply its own labour needs, as well as the needs of the expatriate mining community.[57]

The extent of coercion varied both with the needs of the two sectors for workers, and with the political input of liberals in Britain who preferred not to countenance forced labour. At all times, coercion was applied solely to tribesmen in the Northern Territories, not to workers elsewhere. Whereas it was accepted that the inhabitants of Ashanti and the Gold Coast would engage in independent cash-crop cultivation for the market, it was equally accepted that the Northern Territories would be a labour reservoir. The North was not developed as a cash-crop producing area.

The basic problem in the Northern Territories, from the point of view of the Europeans, was that able-bodied men were reluctant to leave their homes for work in mines (especially underground work) and for the government, when such employment would mean neglecting their own subsistence farms. Chiefs, as well, did not relish sending able-bodied men south when they themselves were dependent on tribute from what would be unworked farms. They complained that recruitment for the south left them only with old men and children to perform the vital tasks of cultivation.[58] Those young men who did voluntarily go south, moreover, preferred to hire themselves out for the more independent (and at times more profitable) work of looking after cocoa farms.

Thus, throughout the colonial period there were various proposals with regards to the best means of obtaining a labour supply. The proposals ranged from imitations of labour legislation in South Africa and Rhodesia,[59] to the simple payment of head money as incentives to the chiefs, to the imposition of a 'traditional' system of compulsory communal labour in tribal structures which, in fact, had not such traditional communal labour.[60] Whatever the official policy was regarding the forms of persuasion to be used in order to obtain labour, local political officers put consistent pressure on the chiefs to provide it. In at least one case this pressure included shooting people who refused to work.

> The Assistant Commissioner informed me that the chief of Bengbi had refused to come and report himself to allow his people to work for the Government. It became necessary to send out some constabulary who were attacked and in reply they killed one man who was behind a tree . . . The next day the chief came in and has been in with his people to work ever since. The effect of this regrettable shooting affair has therefore borne excellent results, and I cannot consider that any blame can be attached to anyone for it except the people themselves.

> Some chiefs said they wanted to satisfy the British but 'their people would not listen to them'. I showed them the headman of Bengbi (the one whose subject had been shot) who was present and told them to tell their people what the result of his disobedience had been.[61]

Such direct coercion, however, was rare. The more normal practice was to pay the chief 'head money' for each individual he recruited, and, as well, to use the moral authority of government officials to persuade the chiefs to release individuals for private enterprise.

The recruitment of labour in the Northern Territories was characterised by disputes as to which sector of the economy was most entitled to the scarce labour supply. The major dispute was between the mining sector and government. There were two points to this dispute; first that some government officials thought that it was detrimental to Africans to work in the mines at all, and second that the government was unwilling to allocate labour to the mines if it meant shortchanging its own construction plans. Thus, while at some times political officers in the North tried to persuade chiefs to send 'boys' down to the mines (and, as Roger Thomas points out, such persuasion had the force of command[62]), at others, officials in Accra opposed any such assistance. Governor Guggisberg, in particular, considered wage labour in the mines to be an activity detrimental to the health and morale of his African charges.

> The ... evil effects of the mining industry are apparent to anyone who goes through the mining areas of this country. In these areas agricultural production, except for the local supplies of food, has been almost entirely neglected. The inhabitants of the mining villages form a cosmopolitan crowd of hired labourers, whose moral development compares very unfavourably with that of the rest of the country. It may safely be assumed that they are, generally speaking, the scallywags of West Africa.[63]

The other reason for opposition to mine recruitment of labour was that it interfered with government construction plans, not only in the Colony and Ashanti, but also in the North itself. Just as Northern chiefs were often reluctant to send young men south as it meant reduced agricultural output, so Northern administrators began to find that they could not get supplies of labour to build roads and public works. The competition from the south for labour was too severe. As one district commissioner wrote in 1919:

> Labour is now here plentiful and cheap — artificially so it is true — but it will not be in a few years ... before the war [an] increasing number of youths left the Province every year for the South. In future if the conditions are as favourable, they will not stay up here, and work for nothing in preference to seeking ... munificent remuneration elsewhere ... With regard to the remuneration paid to labour etc. here, it has of course been quite impossible to pay anything like the rates recognised even for the N.T.'s. The method followed has been that of getting gangs from various chiefs, these work in the station from 10 to 14 days. The method of payment

is that every few days they are provided with Peto [a fermented drink]. They bring their own food in with them.[64]

Both government and mines, moreover, faced further competition from the much more lucrative and attractive (from the labourer's point of view) work available in southern Ghana on cocoa farms. Here labourers could work independently and at their own pace, often receiving plots of land to farm at the same time as they cultivated the cocoa, and sometimes with a chance of becoming cocoa farmers themselves. It was estimated that some 5 per cent of the migrants stayed in the Colony every year, many to establish their own permanent farms, instead of returning home.[65] The peak period on the cocoa farms coincided with the dry season in the North, when the labourers did not need to cultivate at home. Thus, they could easily mix their traditional mode of production with their new roles in the south. The mining industry in fact complained that cocoa was draining it of labour. In 1916, for example, the West African Chamber of Mines complained to the Colonial Office:

> [We] call your attention to the serious position of the Mining Companies operating in the Gold Coast Colony West Africa due to the shortage of native labour . . . normal shortage has been still further accentuated by the rapid growth of the cocoa industry . . .[66]

But the state was reluctant to make any attempts to reduce the flow of labour to cocoa farms in order to accommodate the mines, since by this time it was already well aware that a large percentage of its revenues came from the cocoa industry.[67]

At times, however, the shortage of labour, especially relatively disciplined, skilled labour for the mines, was so severe that various attempts were made to recruit foreigners. Most of these attempts were to increase the supply of Kru from Liberia and Mende from Sierra Leone,[68] but at one time even Chinese labourers were imported, and a debate then ensued as to whether 'Coolies' were suitable immigrants for the Gold Coast. In 1914 it was confirmed that the Abontiakoon mines had in their employ 26 Chinese, who had been in Ghana between three months and three years.[69] It was considered that while the Chinese would make good skilled labourers, their wages would be prohibitive, and they would not, obviously, make good foremen over African workers.[70] In 1915 it was decided that 'no person not of European or West African origin or descent . . . shall be permitted to land in the Colony without the written consent of the Governor.'[71]

Yet although the demands for Kru, Mende and Chinese labour might indicate a lack of skilled labourers in Ghana, in fact it seems the opposite was sometimes the case. It is difficult to understand why Gold Coast administrators felt a need to import labour when by West African standards, Ghana was possessed of a highly skilled labour force, and expatriate firms from other European colonies often attempted to draw on Ghanaian skilled labour. Such attempts were made by requesting the Executive Council of the Gold Coast to approve the export of workers. Generally speaking, the Executive Council turned down all requests for export outside of West Africa, for instance to the West Indies or Central America, but it often approved requests for other West African colonies. In 1897/98, for example, it granted permission for the export of 22 boatmen to the Ivory Coast, of 30 labourers for the Congo Railway, of 300 labourers to the Sierra Leone government, and of five bricklayers for the Basel Mission in South West Africa.[72] Such occasional exports of skilled labourers continued for over two decades. In 1918, among other cases, the Executive Council approved the export of four coopers to the Ivory Coast for CFAO and another five for SCOA, as well as ten coopers to the Congo for Lever Brothers.[73] The practice continued until the early 1920s when the flow of requests for skilled labourers from Ghana slowed down.

Such requests for skilled labour from Ghana seem to indicate that despite complaints that it was difficult to obtain an adequate supply of unskilled labourers for roads, railways and mines, in actual fact the labour supply was quite sophisticated, at least in comparison with other European colonies in West Africa. This sophistication reflected the eagerness of Ghanaians to avail themselves of educational and training opportunities. While a class of skilled artisans thus developed spontaneously, it was difficult to develop an actual proletariat. Ghanaians preferred, if they could, to be independent farmers, or even quasi-independent farm labourers. Southern Ghanaians became clerks, minor bureaucrats or company agents; when they engaged in manual labour, it was either as independent cash-crop cultivators or as skilled workers. Northerners, although they had access to fewer opportunities, tried to imitate this pattern. When they did contract to work as unskilled labourers, they preferred to work only a few months at a time, so that they could return to their land when necessary. When they were coerced into longer contracts, usually one year, by the combined action of government officials and their chiefs, they often ran away.

Even when Northerners were willing to work for wages, the working and living conditions, especially in the mines, were often impossible to endure. Conditions resembled those presently imposed upon migrant mine labourers in South Africa. Miners lived in compounds separated off from the communities in which the mines were located; they had to eat unfamiliar food, they were not allowed to bring their wives and families with them, and they had to endure the exigencies of underground labour (which southern Ghanaians refused to perform).[74] In addition, there were the risks of industrial accident and disease, which were further exacerbated by the fact that often the poorest physical specimens were recruited in the first place, since Northern chiefs, faced with government demands for labour, tried to keep the healthiest men at home to work on the farms and sent the weakest south.[75] In 1924 forced recruitment of labour was stopped when a government report concluded that conditions in the mines were too appalling to oblige anyone to work there.[76]

Under such arduous conditions, complaints about the lack of discipline of Northern workers must be considered carefully. A continual criticism was that Africans, unlike European workers, were undisciplined, and had not, indeed, accepted the 'work ethic'; they did not realise that they must, while in the employ of their masters, try to produce as much as possible and work as hard as they could. In a report on labour conditions in Ghana in 1926, Mr Holmes, the Secretary for Mines, indicated that some improvements had finally been made in this regard. Whereas formerly miners had been 'work-shy' and willing to depend for food on their womenfolk, who were engaged in trade, now the idea of not working carried some stigma; and playing on this stigma, the mines were beginning to hand out 'loafer's' cards.

> The presentation of a 'loafer' ticket to a boy [labourer] is beginning to bear not only the loss of a day's pay, which did not matter, but a stigma, which does. The happy complacency of the habitual loafer is beginning to be disturbed by jeers and even contempt and to this gradual growth of public opinion we can look to an increase in the available man power independent of an increase in the actual population.[77]

Given poor working conditions, including a high incidence of disease, given the fact that many labourers were forcibly recruited in the first place, and given poor pay incentives, it is not surprising that the process of socialisation of the incipient proletariat into work patterns which were generally accepted as normal in Europe should have been arduous and time-consuming. Most important of all, as long as there was a high demand for their services on cocoa farms (a demand which was only stemmed by the inflow of migrants from the French colonies, who were obliged to work in order to pay taxes, unlike the untaxed Ghanaians), and as long as they had the option of returning to their own lands in the north, there was little reason for workers to accept the new capitalist work ethic. Northern labourers were not completely proletarianised precisely because they were not completely cut off from the means of production; as migrants, they still had access to the means of production in their pre-capitalist homelands. As Stavenhagen indicates, migrant labourers of this type are a proletariat in formation, not an actual proletariat.[78] The very fact that migrant labourers had access to their traditional agricultural communities was a boon to the mines and to government in the sense that they could underpay the workers, who relied for subsistence partly upon their home resources. As one District Commissioner wrote in 1914:

> I have at the present time some 120 labourers working on the roads and stations at 6d per diem but I would not have obtained them at this figure unless some slight pressure had been put onto the chiefs, as the price of food has been steadily rising owing to the shortage of rain and only local boys fed from their own villages will work at this rate.[79]

But the price of cheap labour was inefficient labour. Workers not fully alienated from their pre-capitalist mode of production, not fully separated from the means of production, could not be fully proletarianised. For capitalism to emerge, 'It is not sufficient that there be a mass of impoverished and propertyless individuals . . . What is required is that the mass of the direct producers are themselves propertyless, that is, without effective property in means of production.'[80] Until this occurred, a full proletariat would not develop in Ghana.

4. African Resistance to Expatriate Economic Control: The 1937/38 Cocoa Boycott

Despite the fact that new social classes were emerging in Ghana during the colonial period with different relations to the mode of production,

The Peripheral Economy and Class Formation 207

all of the new groups remained subordinate to the political power of
the British state and the economic power of the European expatriate
firms. Political action, therefore, consisted not of class struggle but of
nationalist struggle, and in matters of economic protests, as the
following section will demonstrate, all indigenous social classes
attempted to unite against a common enemy.

In late 1937 a large pink poster appeared in the streets of Dunkwa,
in the Central Region of the Gold Coast Colony. In bold characters,
it read:

The Farmer's 'D' Slogan of Cocoa Crisis
1. Down with Pool firms.
2. Drown Pool Firms in their Pool Waters.
3. Dry Pool Waters with Cocoa Conflagration.
4. Doom Cocoa buying agreement.
5. Drag away plutocrats.
6. Drill the unscrupulous capitalists.
7. Disband cocoa trade monopolies.
8. Do hold-up absolutely and persistently.
9. Dictate your price.
10. Dignify your position and that of posterity.[82]

This poster symbolised the 1937/38 cocoa boycott, an act of economic
and political opposition by Ghanaians against European cocoa buying
firms which had 'pooled' to control prices paid to cocoa producers.

The boycott lasted from October 1937 to April 1938; its avowed
purpose was to break the hold which expatriate firms had on the
marketing of cocoa overseas. Tactics of the movement included not
only the boycotting of cocoa buyers, but also the boycott of all but
the most essential European-produced imported goods (whether sold
in European or African shops), sympathy strikes by market mammies,
lorry drivers and surf-boat workers, and, ultimately, the burning of
some 400 tons of cocoa. The boycott covered the Eastern Province
(the original cocoa-producing area), Ashanti, and even the northern
part of the Central Province, where cocoa was an important product.
There was also some minimal participation in the boycott in the
cocoa growing areas of the British Mandated Territory (Togoland).

The boycott was a success insofar as it resulted in the appointment
of the Nowell Commission, which arrived in Ghana in February 1938
and eventually recommended changes which the Africans had demanded,
but it was a failure insofar as the end result was the institution of a

Cocoa Marketing Board which, by using expatriate firms as its buying agent, perpetuated the system which the Africans had been protesting.

The control of marketing of raw materials produced in Ghana was, of course, an essential part of the economic grip maintained by the British colonisers. The 1937/38 boycott was not an isolated attempt by Ghanaians to break through this system; rather it was the culmination of a long history of boycotts. Such boycotts, usually concentrated in the more productive cocoa areas, are recorded at least as early as 1915; two larger boycotts took place in 1924 and 1930/31.[83]

The boycotts were organised against a system of selling which took the cocoa through many hands. The system of sub-brokerage and brokerage of cocoa, prior to its actual arrival at the point of export, combined with the systems of hedging and advanced pricing encouraged by the Cocoa Exchanges established in London and New York in the mid-1920s, resulted in a situation in which there was much room for profit-making by big business even when the Ghanaian producer received very little for his crop. Even during the 1930s, when the price of cocoa paid to the producer was low, some expatriate firms were paying heavy dividends.[84]

Immediately prior to the 1937 boycott, this situation was exacerbated by the formation, under the guidance of the UAC, of a 'Cocoa Pool'. This was, in effect, an agreement in restraint of trade; 13 major European firms controlling between them 98 per cent of the Ghana cocoa crop agreed to set prices for cocoa.[85] They also agreed on new policies which would curb the activities of middlemen Ghanaian cocoa brokers. At the same time, evidence came to light that prices of goods sold to consumers were also being fixed. Whatever the arguments made by the Europeans about the world economic crisis of the 1930s and the need to stabilise the situation, Ghanaians interpreted this type of activity as a direct and deliberate attempt to make more profits for the European firms at the expense of indigenous cocoa producers.

African protest movements have been studied as symptoms of reaction to colonial rule, but often without attempting to define who exactly in the African community was responsible for organising and precipitating the movement, and who would benefit from it. In Ghana, however, a number of files are available in the National Archives which allow the researcher to compile a detailed picture of the 1937/38 boycott. From the documents in these files, it would seem that it was the concerted effort of a small group of Ghanaian businessmen and rural petty bourgeois, who wanted to engage in the type of commerce dominated by Europeans, which was the precipitation of the boycott.

This group of wealthy farmers and coastal tradesmen, who wanted to be able to ship cocoa direct to the European and American markets without going through European middlemen, was backed by the middle peasantry who hoped, by boycotting, to have the price paid to them for cocoa raised. These peasants, moreover, ensured as much as they could that the poorer peasants and the migrant labourers from the Northern Territories would also boycott the European firms. Considering the sacrifices that such a boycott entailed, especially for the migrant labourers who were paid in cocoa which they then sold on their own account to the Europeans, the boycott was phenomenally successful. Although breaks in the boycott occasioned by the inability of the poor peasants and migrant labourers to sustain themselves without their regular cocoa income did occur, on the whole the boycott was almost complete in Ashanti and the Gold Coast Colony, up until the time that, through the Nowell Commission, the government reached a compromise with the Pool firms.

There were, then, three basic groups who were crucial to the success of the boycotts; the urban and rural petty bourgeoisie, cocoa brokers, who were affected by specific provisions of the agreement designed to push them out of trade, and peasants and migrant labourers. It was only because these three groups were able to co-operate, and because, through efficient organisation and propaganda, the leaders were able to inspire the poorer elements to adhere to the boycott even when their funds had run out, that it achieved the level of success it did.

Chiefs were willing to use their traditional powers of sanction to encourage the boycott. The Nowell Commission reported, for example, that not only were they swearing oaths and beating gong-gong in support of the boycott, but also they were denying their people the traditional functions of the chiefs, threatening to withdraw funeral rites and refusing claims to adultery fees in cases in which their subjects persisted in selling cocoa.[86] But chiefs were not only chiefs; they were also large farmers in their own right, sometimes money lenders or cocoa brokers on a large scale, and also entrepreneurs who were interested in buying up the stocks of cocoa which accumulated during the boycott at cheap prices and selling and/or shipping them at a profit. The Europeans, failing sometimes to recognise the multiple interests of the chiefs, especially in Ashanti, assumed that they were being coerced by educated entrepreneuers from the Gold Coast Colony into taking positions of support for the boycott. At other times, however, recognising these multiple aims, the Europeans attempted through charges of corruption to interfere with the chiefs' position *qua* chief. In one instance, it was alleged that Nana Ofori Atta, one of the most articulate spokesmen for the cocoa producers during the boycott, had been a target for bribes from the UAC in his capacity as a large cocoa farmer and would-be shipper. Accusations were made against Ofori Atta that he, as well as other chiefs, was deliberately ordering the boycott because he had wanted his tribespeople to give him a 'rake-off', or commission, for each load of cocoa which they sold, and they had refused to do so.[87]

An accusation such as the above is difficult to substantiate; it might easily have been made by a jealous farmer. In any case, cocoa was not sold until the end of February, despite any such bribes as may have been offered to Ofori Atta by the UAC. No cocoa was sold, that is, until the Nowell Commission had negotiated a truce based upon the fact that an investigation was underway and that an equitable solution should shortly be reached. But the accusation indicates a degree of suspicion of the powerful chiefs of the colony, even of those who, like Nana Ofori Atta, were verbally very supportive of the movement.

A great deal of debate took place among the Europeans as to whether it was simply the chiefs, or also the peasantry, who were behind the boycott. The UAC preferred to believe that it was simply the chiefs who were the instigators, but the Nowell Commission found otherwise, that the ordinary peasants were 'throughout' in sympathy with the boycott.[88] And indeed it is difficult to see how it could be otherwise. Peasants recognised that the chiefs were also concerned with their potential profits as large farmers and possibly shippers in the event of a complete boycott: nevertheless, they preferred African entrepreneurs to the Europeans, who they knew had a history of actively collaborating to keep down prices.

It was well known that leaders of the boycott were engaged in attempts not only to circumvent the monopolising European buyers, but also to circumvent the European shippers. Many contacts were made with outside businessmen, mostly Americans, who were willing to ship cocoa on contract for the striking producers. The government tried to cast doubts on the honesty of these interloping Europeans, but it would seem that at least some were sincere businessmen. It would also seem from what little evidence is available, that the large American chocolate manufacturing company, Hershey, was behind some of the independent attempts to ship cocoa.[89] One Mr Canalizo, whose name often cropped up as an adviser to African entrepreneurs, was rumoured to be an agent for Hershey, but try as they might, government officials were unable to ascertain proof of this alleged relationship. But it is definite that certain persons in America were urging the Ghanaians to continue their hold-up of cocoa in 1938. 'The meeting was informed of possible agreement with persons in America to buy their cocoa and that these persons ask the farmers to continue their Hold-Up until arrangements are completed.'[90] After the boycott was over, a buyer from Hershey arrived in the Gold Coast, apparently to buy up the cheap held-over cocoa.[91]

The purpose of the Hershey visit was seemingly innocuous, but the possibility remains that Africans were encouraged through Hershey representatives to try direct shipping schemes which would boycott the British middlemen and shipping lines. Nevertheless, although the aims of all the various organisations connected with the boycotts included the desire to make direct shipments to cocoa,[92] in fact no large shipments ever came off. The Africans were at the mercy of the Europeans with whom they were dealing. Although Ghanaian entrepreneurs 'created a never ceasing string of limited liability companies to break into trade in a big way [t]hese schemes were almost uniformly unsuccessful because of insufficient capital and skills.'[93]

Anthony Hopkins has traced the career of one Ghanaian entrepreneur, Winifried Tete-Ansa, who was prominently involved in many of the various shipping schemes put forward during the 1930s. Tete-Ansa, having been trained in business methods in England and America, advocated limited liability companies as a means of mobilising African savings on a group basis. But in a situation in which there was little capital in the first place, in which entrepreneurs were not united, and in which, moreover, there were hints of corruption about Tete-Ansa himself, there was little hope that Ghanaians could compete with the better organised Europeans.[94]

The chiefs, then, along with certain rich farmers (or in their own capacity as rich farmers) and the urban traders, had an interest in supporting the boycott in order to corner the distributive network for their own gain. Such an aim, however, was unattainable, except in the short run for very small amounts of cocoa. Neither capital nor time was available to arrange for large-scale organisation of independent African shippers.

Ostensibly, moreover, the aims of the boycott were to raise the prices paid for cocoa and lower the prices paid for imported goods. Implicit in this was a demand for a new mode of distribution which would profit chiefs, rich farmers and the urban traders. But any new mode of distribution which might be set up would impinge upon the already existing Ghanaian broker class. The brokers were aware that certain chiefs and entrepreneurs were trying to usurp their position, but the 1937 cocoa-buying agreement contained such a clear threat that for their own sake they were obliged to uphold the boycott. The agreement was constantly justified by the Europeans as a means of eliminating 'abuses' of the brokerage system and of therefore providing more payments to the farmers. The argument most repetitiously made was that vast sums of money were being wasted by the middleman system, by which Ghanaian brokers bought cocoa from peasants and then sold it to the coastal firms. Commissions, gifts and various perquisites given to brokers by the expatriates in exchange for their valued services, constituted 'abuses' and ate up funds which, the firms argued, would otherwise go direct to the farmers. These perquisites included such payments as the following: rent allowances to brokers or buyers for stores, repair allowances, weighing machine and tarpaulin allowances, labour allowances for clerks, watchmen, etc., the loan of bags, free transportation, the payment of an 'over-riding commission' on tonnage above a certain amount; and outright gifts to brokers, the most well known gift being a motor-cycle.[95] Nevertheless, although these abuses were constantly denounced in public, there is no mention of the problem of such abuses in the actual pooling agreement itself.

One of the abuses most stringently objected to was the practice of delaying declarations of stocks. The price of cocoa changed from day to day on the international markets, and as it changed, new prices to be paid for cocoa were wired out from London to the firms' Accra agents, who then informed their various agents in the other stations of Ghana. Brokers were usually given a few days to bring in their cocoa at the old price, as the agents were not able to inform them of the new price immediately. The brokers, however, often took advantage of this practice; if they heard that the price of cocoa had risen they would declare cocoa which they had actually bought at the old, lower price at the new higher price; if they heard that the price had fallen they would buy at the new price and then declare that they had bought at the old, higher price. This practice was ubiquitous and a source of rankle to all the European agents, yet to keep their brokers the firms had had to put up with the practice.[96] A provision of the new agreement was to be that the brokers would have only 48 hours to declare their stocks, to cut out their chances for over- or under-declarations. In order, however, that their brokers could not, in a pique, leave the firms when denied these opportunities, provision was also made that no firm would hire a broker previously employed by another firm participating in the agreement.[97]

The European firms tried to persuade the chiefs that the brokers' support of the boycott was based entirely on their desire for the 'unwarranted' profits obtainable through false declarations of stocks and through the various abuses listed above. They argued that the large farmers would obtain more for their cocoa if only they would join the firms in eliminating, or putting under control, the brokers.[98] The chiefs, however, were not convinced by this argument, partly because some of them were themselves engaged in brokerage activities, and partly because they were aware that brokerage was a risky business and that fortunes could be lost as easily as they could be made.

> [T]he merchants have given evidence before the Cocoa Enquiry Commissions and accused the brokers for being the cause of low price of cocoa therefore they entered into agreement so as to exclude them and deal with the farmers direct. This being their defence for the formation of the pool the chiefs have got to support the brokers who are sons of this country and keep fighting.[99]

Indeed, the firms were as aware as the farmers and chiefs that brokerage was a precarious business; so aware, in fact, that they argued to the Nowell Commission that the chief reason for the opposition of the brokers to the agreement was that the brokers had overpaid advances for the 1937/38 season, thinking that the season would be as prosperous as 1936/37. They were in no position to buy the cocoa crop at the prices that they had promised; therefore, they were encouraging the boycott to delay payment of their debts. Further, the firms argued that many of the chiefs who were enforcing the boycott among their people were actually acting in defence of their interests as cocoa brokers.[100] Thus the firms, by pointing out the money lending activities of brokers, professed interest in the welfare of the ordinary peasant who was in debt because of the nefarious system of advances on cocoa crops. The firms advocated, they claimed, a system of direct producer-to-shipper selling, so that the producer might earn the maximum possible. Their propaganda, throughout the course of the boycott, was directed towards this argument and was accepted at face value by the Nowell Commission.

In the light of such professed concern, it is interesting to note that one firm, when confronted with the actual possibility of eliminating the broker from the distributive network, rejected the idea. In a letter

to the John Holt Ltd. headquarters in Liverpool in early 1937, their
Accra agent argued that it would be possible to buy cocoa on credit
direct from farmers, thus eliminating the 'abuses' of brokerage. Rather
than adopting this suggestion, however, the Holt headquarters replied
that if brokers were eliminated, the Europeans would no longer have
control over the cocoa market. If they were not tied through credit
to the Europeans, the Ghanaians would be able to ship cocoa on their
own. By tying their customers, the expatriates could buy cocoa at
lower prices than they would have to pay if they were competing
on the open market with African shippers. The point of having
Europeans on the coast was to build up the cocoa trade on a credit
basis and make sure that it was sanely conducted.[101]

By such sane conduct of the credit trade, no doubt Holt was
referring to the conduct of the trade in such a way as to keep the
brokers, and through them the producer, tied to the European
firms at a minimum cost to those firms. His fear was that the
producers might be able to turn to independent banks to finance
their crops, and in so doing obtain enough finance to hypothecate
through the banks and sell on their own. It was imperative that
whatever cash the banks brought to Ghana should be channelled
through the firms, not given direct to the producers or to Ghanaian
traders. No clearer statement could be made of the absolute
necessity of keeping all Africans, down to the lowliest producer,
firmly in the debt of the expatriate companies. It was because the
brokers were fully aware of this means of perpetuating their indebtedness to the Europeans that they were willing to support the boycott,
although they knew that those who would profit the most from a
successful boycott would be not they, but the independent African
shippers and dealers with direct contacts overseas. Nevertheless, the
threat of losses of commission and perquisites, combined with the
real controls implicit in agreements among the firms as to hiring
brokers (who had hitherto been able to play one firm off against
another) induced the brokers to support the chiefs, rich farmers and
urban traders.

More surprising in terms of the expected support for such a boycott was the strength and organisation of the poor peasants and
migrant labourers from the cocoa areas of Ghana. The lowliest
producers, indeed, were well aware of the exploitation inherent in
the cocoa distribution system, but they were constrained in their
ability to boycott by the hard necessities of life. In debt as they
already were to cocoa brokers, who had advanced them money before

the season began, few peasants had capital to sustain themselves over the long four month hold-up. That they were able to conduct the boycott at all is an indication of the fact that they were not entirely dependent on the world capitalist market for their livelihood; they could, at least partially, retreat into a subsistence mode of agriculture in a crisis.

But the leaders of the boycott realised that middle and poor peasants could be self-sufficient only within certain limits; for example, it was always clearly stated that boycotts of European goods were not meant to include such basic necessities as sugar, kerosene, matches or tobacco. The market mammies who upheld the boycott were thus able to sustain themselves by the continued sale of these basic commodities. At the same time, the mammies supported the boycott not simply out of sympathy with the peasantry, but because it was in their own interests. They were tied to the European firms through systems of credit similar to those granted to the brokers; in order to finance themselves they borrowed from the European firms, who in return had guaranteed customers for their supplies. But those same firms who sold goods to the mammies also competed with them in their large 'department store' retail establishments in the coastal cities and regional centres, and in the lorry-loads of goods which they transported to the bush. As one organiser urging the mammies to continue boycotting argued,

> [Y]ou [the mammies] take certain articles so as to take them up-country to retail at some little profit but before you get to the up-country a lorry belonging to the same firms loaded full, with the same articles would have gone ahead of you and disposed of them at the same prices and sometimes a little cheaper.[102]

Mammies were especially urged to boycott the West African prints which were manufactured in England and then exported to Ghana, at prices inflated by the imperial protection which had denied to Ghana, since 1934, cheap Japanese cottons. That the boycott of these cloths had no little effect is evidenced by a report of the sufferings of the Lancashire cotton trade.

> Lancashire is having a bad time with cotton goods for West African trade. A considerable number of firms in the cotton trade have shipped nothing to West Africa for a long time and Lancashire people are blaming the price of cocoa for it . . . it is

supposed too that the West African native is boycotting British goods, particularly Lancashire cotton goods.[103]

Many of the mammies who boycotted the foreign firms were married to lorry drivers who also engaged in the boycott. Again, it was not sheer altruism in support of their peasant brothers which induced the lorry drivers to boycott; rather, they had specific grievances of their own. They were afraid that if the Europeans got control of the internal marketing of cocoa, there would be less transport work available for them. They were also afraid that the Pool would result in a permanent reduction of cocoa prices, affecting freight rates. They were already suffering moreover from the policy of 'scheduled roads' which denied to them cocoa traffic which legitimately could be considered theirs. Finally, they were generally in debt to the firms for the lorries themselves. In fact, although they were militant in their stand in support of the hold-up and boycott and although chief drivers made it their business to ensure that all their men participated in the strike, the lorry drivers were not as able to stand firm as other groups and were obliged by early 1938 to renew their licences for lorries and continue their labours.[104] A similar sympathy strike by the surf-boat men of Accra did not last long.[105] There was also a short strike by the workers who were engaged to supply palm fruit to the UAC Palm Oil Mill at Sese, near Takoradi.[106]

The general boycott and strike against Europeans from all sectors of the community no doubt encouraged poor peasants, who might otherwise have been tempted to give in to the firms, to hold out longer than they had originally intended. For indeed, the boycott was a strain on such peasants, and it was they, along with the hired labourers from the North who worked on the richer farms, who were the first to let out small trickles of cocoa in sales to the Europeans. During the 1930/31 boycott, there had been fairly frequent complaints against the richer producers by the poorer ones, who felt that the boycott was a plot to facilitate the acquisition of large stocks of cocoa for shipment rather than a genuine attempt to alleviate the lot of all producers. Although such claims were less frequent during the 1937/38 boycott, the suspicions still existed. But peasants were on the whole more willing to take militant action, and indeed began, in February 1938, to burn small lots of cocoa in support of their claims. Although only an estimated total of about 400 tons was burned,[107] the incidence of such protests was sufficient to panic the government administrators, who were instructed to keep a close watch on all burnings.

The Peripheral Economy and Class Formation 217

Some small lots of cocoa were sold during the 1937/38 boycott, presumably not only by the poor peasants, but also by the migrant labourers. Since the migrants were generally paid one-third of the cocoa crop at the end of the season, which they then marketed on their own in return for cash, if they could not sell their cocoa, they received no reward for their work. The labourers were not convinced of the value to them of the boycott. They knew that the price of cocoa was low, but living as they did on a season-to-season basis, and required, as those from the French territories were, to pay taxes, it was more important to them to acquire whatever cash they could. When, in 1937/38, they were not paid, many 'stole' cocoa (which was actually theirs, since normal payment for a season's work was one-third of the produce) and sold it to the buyers.[108]

The leaders of the boycott tried to exhort the migrant labourers not to sell, but with limited success. When one wealthy farmer tried to persuade them to discontinue their selling at Asamankese in February 1938, he was shouted down with cries of 'belly trouble too much to wait any longer'.[109] The labourers had no traditional authorities to constrain them, as their chiefs remained at home in the north and their local Zongo headmen were as dependent on cocoa revenue as they were. Further, they came from tribes which, if not actually despised by the Ashanti and other southerners, were not regarded as genuine parts of the Gold Coast community. Thus social pressure had little effect on them. While the wealthy cocoa farmers expressed concern for, and made arrangements for, their fellow tribesmen who encountered difficulties, on the whole there was little sympathy among them for the stranger labourers. For example, at a meeting in Suhum in April 1938, the question of Zabarima 'strangers' was discussed. The Chief Farmer advised:

It appears that some of the farmers who employed those Zabramas [sic] as labourers pay them by cash and some also by loads of cocoa, and these led the labourers to possess cocoa, which may be those that came to the market.

He then suggested to them that it will be better if a farmer who employed any of these labourers will turn them out from his village.

This advice was taken by the farmers.[110]

Nevertheless, despite such callous indifference to the plight of the migrant labourers, on the whole very little cocoa was actually sold to the firms during the boycott. The wealthy farmers, chiefs and brokers managed to control those who wished to break the hold-up. Between 26 November 1937 and 17 February 1938 only a little over 2,500 tons of cocoa was sold.[111]

In the end, the boycott was not successful in breaking up the collusion among the major European firms, nor was it successful in raising the price of cocoa. But it was successful in abolishing the actual cocoa agreement, and in obliging the government to reconsider the method of marketing the crop in Ghana. The Nowell Commission negotiated a truce between Africans and Europeans in February 1938. With the outbreak of war in 1939 a government marketing scheme was perforce introduced, a scheme which was refined into the Cocoa Marketing Board established in the late forties.

The 1937/38 cocoa boycott in Ghana indicates clearly two facets of the development of its cocoa production: the exemplary unity of so many Ghanaians in the face of organised oligopolistic control of the cocoa market by expatriate firms, and at the same time the divisions within the cocoa-producing community. Labourers from the north, while not landless in their own home, were nevertheless highly dependent on revenues from sale of their payment in kind (cocoa) in order to survive. Despite tribal differences with the actual cocoa producers, however, they did try to support the boycott. Poor producers had a less easy time than rich producers in holding out on sales, yet they were almost unanimous in their support. Rich farmers had the incentive not only of higher prices for their cocoa, but also of the possibility of entering the very lucrative trading and marketing end of the cocoa business. Even persons unconnected with actual cocoa production, such as market mammies and lorry drivers, willingly supported both the cocoa boycott and the companion boycott against imported European goods, in order to break what was perceived as a concerted European monopoly of all aspects of Ghanaian trade. And the cocoa brokers, who in their role as money lenders had many differences with the peasantry, perceived that unity with the producers was imperative in the light of the Europeans' propagandistic attacks upon their middlemen's profits.

Thus, it is evident that the monocultural dependence of Ghana's import-export economy had given birth to disparate groups all of whom, at the same time that they made their livings from such dependence, nevertheless perceived the relationship as essentially exploitative. It is not merely coincidence that the conflict between Ghanaians and Europeans should have found its expression in economic boycotts as well as in political struggles. The colony had been established essentially for economic reasons, and almost all Ghanaians had been affected by their country's peripheral role in the world economy.

Notes

1. For a discussion of the concept of the petty bourgeoisie in Africa, see Gavin Williams, 'There is no Theory of Petty-Bourgeois Politics', *Review of African Political Economy*, No. 6 (May–August 1976).
2. Margaret Priestley, *West African Trade and Coast Society* (Oxford University Press, London, 1969), p. 106.
3. Susan Beth Kaplow, 'African Merchants of the Nineteenth Century Gold Coast', unpublished PhD thesis, Columbia University, 1971, p. 170.
4. Ibid., p. 184.
5. Kimble, *A Political History*, p. 65.
6. Edward Reynolds, 'The Rise and Fall of an African Merchant Class on the Gold Coast, 1830–1874', paper presented to the International Congress of Africanists, 3rd Session (Addis Ababa, December 9–19, 1973), p. 89.
7. Reynolds, 'Trade', pp. 226 and 257.
8. J.E. Casely Hayford, *Gold Coast*, p. 95.
9. C.W. Newbury, 'Credit in Nineteenth Century West African Trade', *Journal of African History*, Vol. 13, No. 1 (1972), p. 91.
10. 'Select Committee of the House of Commons to Consider the State of the British Settlements on the Western Coast of Africa', 1865 (412) V. 1. Minutes of Evidence, testimony of A. Swanzy, Q.4673.
11. Reynolds, 'Trade', pp. 380ff.
12. Ibid., p. 387.
13. Kaplow, 'African Merchants', pp. 69–71. The incident is also recounted in Reynolds, 'Trade', pp. 387–8.
14. Kaplow, 'African Merchants', p. 62.
15. Ibid., pp. 114, 120, 121.
16. I.H. Caesar to Edward Challinor and Company, quoted in ibid., p. 117.
17. Reynolds, 'The Rise', pp. 14–15.
18. Kaplow, 'African Merchants', p. 232.
19. M.J. Sampson, *Gold Coast*.
20. Kaplow, 'African Merchants', pp. 183ff.
21. Speech by Mr Waters in GCLegCo, 28 September 1897. The licence Bill was passed on 19 December 1887.
22. Interview with a retired African employee of UAC, also formerly an independent businessman, Accra, June 1974.
23. Interview with a retired African employee of Union Trading Company, Cape Coast, June 1974.
24. Nii Kwabena Bonne III, *Milestones in the History of the Gold Coast* (Wodderspoon and Company, Middlesex, 1953), p. 65.
25. GNA CSO 1918/30.
26. Petition sent by over forty market women to the Governor, 17 October 1930, in GNA CSO 1918/30.
27. Letter to the Governor from two market women, Adwua Kwedwina and Ekua Anesiwa, and others, 30 October 1930, in GNA CSO 1918/30.
28. Memorandum to the Colonial Secretary, signature illegible, dated 11

November 1930, in GNA CSO 1918/30.
29. Harry Martin, 'Reminiscences as a member of the trading firm of Swanzy in the Gold Coast from 1902', typewritten Ms., 1965 (Rhodes House, Oxford), p. 2.
30. Ibid., p. 11.
31. Interview with a retired African employee of Union Trading Company.
32. Examples of such agreements can be found in UAC files entitled 'Pickering and Berthoud Native Storekeepers Agreements', and 'John Walkden and Company'.
33. Ibid.
34. Rankin, *The History*, p. 66.
35. Ibid., p. 145.
36. United Africa Company, *Your Company* (United Africa Company, London, 1959), p. 60.
37. Report by Coker to John Holt and Co., 28 March 1921. Included in Davies, *Trading*, pp. 165–6. I am grateful to Dr Davies for allowing me to use the original manuscript. ('Dashes' were gifts, or bonuses, given to customers to encourage their patronage.)
38. UAC, 'What Cocoa Means', p. 11.
39. Nii Bonne's fascinating career is recounted in his autobiography, *Milestones*.
40. McPhee, *Economic Revolution*, p. 113.
41. GCLegCo, 25 May 1887.
42. LivCC, 41st *Annual Report*, p. 91.
43. Amin, 'Underdevelopment', p. 116.
44. Belfield Report, p. 9.
45. Polly Hill, 'Some Characteristics of Indigenous West African Economic Enterprise', *Nigerian Institute of Social and Economic Research: Conference Proceedings* (1962), p. 116.
46. Ibid.
47. Letter to R. Beaver, Commissioner, Eastern Province, from Theodore Asiedu, of Tinkong, dated 17 May 1912, in GNA Adm. 11/1/411.
48. Report (unsigned) to Colonial Secretary, 26 June 1933, in GNA CSO 460/33.
49. Shephard, 'Report', p. 41.
50. Report on the Western Province of the Gold Coast for the year 1933/34, in GNA CSO 460/33.
51. Shephard, p. 127.
52. Ibid., p. 41.
53. Statement by Ofori Kuma II, Omanhene of Akwapim, 28 October 1934, in GNA CSO 460/33.
54. Director of Agriculture to Colonial Secretary, 6 April 1934, in GNA CSO 460/33.
55. This information is taken from a report by M.Y. Hewson, Acting District Commissioner, Koforidua, dated 25 April 1938, entitled 'Memorandum on Northern Territories and French Sudan Labour on the Cocoa Farms of the Eastern Province', in GNA Adm. 29/6/14.
56. Stavenhagen, *Social Classes*, p. 77.
57. Roger G. Thomas, 'Forced Labour in British West Africa: the Case of the Northern Territories of the Gold Coast 1906–1927', *Journal of African History*, Vol. 14, No. 3 (1973).
58. Ibid., p. 31.
59. The proposal to imitate South African legislation was made by Giles Hunt, a barrister in Accra, in 1909. See Thomas 'Forced Labour', p. 85. The Executive Council of the Gold Coast considered imitating Northern Rhodesian legislation as late as 1937. See CO 98/77, 7 September 1937.
60. Thomas, 'Forced Labour', p. 95.

61. Letter from the Commissioner, North-West Division, to Acting Chief Commissioner Northern Territories, Gambaga, 25 and 26 February 1907, in GNA Adm. 56/1/50.
62. Thomas, 'Forced Labour', p. 80.
63. Governor's comments on memorandum by the Secretary for Mines on the occasion of Ormsby-Gore's visit, 1926, in CO 96/662.
64. District Commissioner's Office, Tumu, to Provincial Commissioner North-West Province, Wa, 8 April 1919, GNA Adm. 56/1/84.
65. 'Annual Invasion of the Gold Coast by French and Northern Territories Subjects in Search of Labour', report filed as GNA Adm. 11/1076.
66. West African Chamber of Mines to Colonial Office, 2 September 1916, in GNA Acc. No. 2798/58.
67. Thomas, 'Forced Labour', p. 88. See also Table 5.1, re. export duties.
68. There are occasional references to these attempts in the minutes of the Executive Council of the Gold Coast. See for example CO 98/8, 28 September 1895.
69. Commissioner of the Western Province to the Colonial Secretary, 14 October 1914, GNA Acc. No. 2746/58.
70. Secretary of Mines to Colonial Secretary, 23 November 1914, GNA Acc. No. 2746/58.
71. 'Immigration of Labourers Restriction Ordinance', GNA Acc. No. 2746/58.
72. CO 98/8.
73. CO 98/22.
74. Mr Bryan, Colonial Secretary, to Giles Hunt, 5 October 1909, in GNA Adm. 56/1/84.
75. Thomas, 'Forced Labour', p. 101.
76. Ibid., p. 101.
77. Report by Mr Holmes on labour in the Gold Coast, CO 96/662.
78. *Social Classes*, p. 77.
79. District Commissioner Yeji to Acting Commissioner Southern Province, Tamale, 21 October 1914, GNA Adm. 56/1/84.
80. Hindess and Hirst, *Pre-Capitalist Modes*, p. 291.
81. This section is a slightly revised version of the author's 'Differential Class Participation in an African Protest Movement: the Ghana Cocoa Boycott of 1937–38', *Canadian Journal of African Studies*, Vol. 10, No. 3 (1976).
82. This poster can be found in GNA Adm. 23/1/798, Cape Coast.
83. On the 1930/31 boycott, see Sam Rhodie, 'The Gold Coast Cocoa Hold-Up of 1930–31', *Transactions of the Historical Society of Ghana*, Vol. IX (1968).
84. In 1936/37 the United Africa Company paid a dividend of 11%. *Stock Exchange Yearbook* (London, 1939).
85. JH:536 (ii), Gold Coast Cocoa Pool, 24 February 1938 – December 1939.
86. Nowell Commission Report, p. 67.
87. Extract from the Confidential Diary of the District Commissioner, Keta, 16 January 1938. In GNA Adm. 29/6/14.
88. Nowell Commission Report, p. 68.
89. D.C. Dunkwa to D.C. Cape Coast 10 July 1938. GNA Adm. 23/1/798. '[There had been] ... several meetings (Accra) ... about the monetary assistance offered by an American firm on the condition that a certain amount of cocoa should be sent to them to be kept in store pending the time when good price would be offered ... '
90. Report by the Superintendent of the Eastern Province Police, of a meeting at Mampong, 3 February 1938. In GNA Adm. 29/6/14.
91. Report by the Superintendent of the Gold Coast Police, Koforidua, 11 May 1938, in GNA Adm. 29/6/14.

92. The Rules of the Gold Coast and Ashanti Cocoa Federation, 1930, included the aim of acting as a 'Bureau' for the selling of cocoa. GNA Adm. 11/1640.
93. Holmes, 'Economic and Political Organisations', p. 72.
94. A.G. Hopkins, 'Economic Aspects of Political Movements in the Gold Coast and Nigeria 1918–1939', *Journal of African History*, Vol. 7, No. 1 (1965/66).
95. Cad: 288/65.
96. The author was informed of this practice in several interviews with former cocoa buyers, both African and European.
97. Nowell Commission Report, p. 209.
98. Extract from the *Gold Coast News*, dated 14 December 1937. In GNA Adm. 29/6/9.
99. Statement by Nana Akuamoa Akyeampong (Omanhene of Kwahu State), at a meeting in Winneba, 1 April 1938. In GNA Adm. 29/6/14.
100. An anonymous memorandum on the reason for the Pool, JH:536(ii), Gold Coast Cocoa Pool 24 February 1938 – December 1939.
101. This exchange of letters can be found in JH: Jacket no. 92. Letter from the Accra D.A. to Holt and Co. dated 11 February 1937, reply from John Holt dated 17 March 1937.
102. Speech by Mr Moore at a meeting in Cape Coast, 15 February 1938. GNA Adm. 23/1/798.
103. Cad: 289/325.
104. Information on the lorry drivers' strike is taken from GNA Adm. 11/1656 (Lorry Driver's Strike) and Adm. 29/6/13 (Cocoa holdup and Lorry Strike Police Reports).
105. GNA Adm. 11/1640. Document dated 27 November 1937. 'Whitfield of the Lighterage informed me in the evening that the boat crews at Saltpond had agreed to return to work.'
106. GNA Adm. 11/1640. Report from Western Province 13 December 1937.
107. Nowell Commission Report, p. 62.
108. On 29 January 1938 the Assistant D.C. of Cape Coast wrote that he had had to try a labourer accused by a farmer of stealing his produce. When it was discovered that he had stolen only his actual $1/3$ share the case was dismissed. The D.C. 'expressed the hope that the farmers would see that their labourers did not suffer while they held up their cocoa.' GNA Adm. 23/1/798.
109. Report dated 10 February 1938, Cad: 289/63.
110. Report dated 21 April 1938. GNA Adm. 29/6/14.
111. Report dated 26 February 1938. GNA Adm. 11/1640.

POSTSCRIPT: THE COLONIAL HERITAGE OF CONTEMPORARY GHANA

Although Ghana attained its independence some twenty years ago, in 1957, its development continues to reflect the structural inequalities of its former colonial relationship with the world capitalist system. The patterns of economic relationships which were established by 1915, according to Ghana a role as a producer of raw materials for the core capitalist economies, have been little altered. Inheriting a colonially-imposed state with little economic independence, the four political regimes which have ruled Ghana since 1957 (the Nkrumah regime to 1966; the military National Liberation Council to 1969; the civilian rule of Dr Busia to 1972; and the military rule of the National Redemption Council/Supreme Military Council to the present) have all resorted, with varous 'left' and 'right' modifications, to the same basic economic strategy; that of state intervention in the economy, in an attempt to effect some structural changes in the direction of agricultural and industrial independence within the framework of continued core capitalist domination. The net result of such twenty years of intervention has been the strengthening both of metropolitan control and of the comprador bourgeoisie at the expense of the declining peasantry and the growing proletariat.

State intervention has been directed from the top; it is superstructural intervention without a firm class base. On the one hand, the state's leading economic role, especially its participation in joint state-private agreements with foreign firms, has retarded the emergence of an independent bourgeoisie. On the other hand, the state, while 'developmentalist', is far from socialist; its continued economic cooperation with foreign capitalist governments and private expatriate firms necessitates repression of class conscious activities such as strikes.[1] As a superstructural excrescence, the state creates its own instability.

Contemporary Ghana remains a peripheral capitalist economy highly dependent upon the export of minerals and agricultural goods to the world market. In 1973, the latest year for which figures were available for Ghana's 1975–80 Development Plan, cocoa exports accounted for 58 per cent of its foreign exchange earnings, timber (the export of which has increased significantly since independence) for 19 per cent, gold for 10 per cent, and manganese, diamonds and bauxite for a mere 1 per cent, 2 per cent and 0.4 per cent, respectively. On the import side, the state's industrialisation policies are reflected in a composition with marked differences from the colonial period's heavy importation of consumer goods. Some 76 per cent of imports were listed in 1973 as non-consumer goods. Of this, twenty per cent consisted of capital equipment, while 40 per cent consisted of industrial raw materials, and another 16 per cent of fuels and lubricants.

Figures for Ghana's domestic output also indicate its continued peripheral status. Overall, productive activity is still dominated by the agricultural and extractive sectors. While manufacturing was responsible (by possibly inflated government estimates) for only 13 per cent of Ghana's Gross Domestic Product in 1973 (raised to 20 per cent if electricity and construction are included), 45 per cent of the Gross Domestic Product could be attributed to agriculture and extractive industries (including food production and livestock raising, cocoa cultivation, forestry, fishing and mining); while services, including government services, were responsible for 35 per cent.[2]

The development of capitalism in agriculture is proceeding at a rapid rate, especially in the former Northern Territories (now the Upper Region and the Northern Region) where, according to the five-year plan 'the Government is empowered to acquire any land for development. It is therefore possible under existing laws, to acquire land and lease to individuals and institutions interested in undertaking large-scale farming.'[3] (Such laws are a result of the colonial government's failure to guarantee indigenous rights to land in the Northern Territories as it had done in the Gold Coast and Ashanti.) The north has thus become a major area of state investment in food production, whereas in the south, where various tribal systems of land tenure still exist, the state is finding difficulties in facilitating 'the acquisition of land . . . for large-scale commercial farming.'[4] That the intent of the current regime is specifically to facilitate capitalist agriculture is evident in the manner in which it is leasing land. While small-scale peasant producers in the north are now experiencing land shortages, absentee owners from the business community, the civil service and the military are profiting from their state-sponsored farms.[5]

But it would seem that the National Redemption Council/Supreme Military Council's attempt, under its 'Operation Feed Yourself' campaign, to make Ghana self-sufficient in food through new capitalist agricultural production has failed miserably. In 1977, there were severe shortages not only of imported foods such as sugar and milk, but also, for the first time, of staple foods including maize, rice, gari, cassava and plantain.[6] By early 1977 the minimum wage per day of an Accra worker was barely enough to buy half a pound of meat or half a pound of tomatoes.[7] While the military government attributed the near-famine in many parts of Ghana to drought, capitalist speculation in food pricing, middlemen trading and hoarding, encouraged by the state's policy of granting land to absentee landlords at the expense of the indigenous peasants of the north, also contributed to the food shortage. Rather than overcoming its twin colonial inheritance of over-reliance on imported food and inadequate transportation routes for internal trade, the state has permitted the new absentee farmers to capitalise on these very weaknesses.

In industry as in agriculture, over-reliance on capitalism has meant ineffective use of resources. The 1975—80 Plan reflects the skewed nature of Ghana's economy, especially its truncated industrial structure. The Valco aluminium project at Tema does not yet process Ghanaian bauxite,[8] yet plans are being made for a steel mill in Kumasi, presumably relying on the two newly identified iron deposits.[9] (According to Judith Marshall, the German firm of Krupp is expected to be an investor in the steel mill.[10]) On the consumer side, the state is investing in cottage or craft industries, presumably in an attempt to keep local economies buoyant and stem migration to the cities. It is also investing in light industries and import substitution, in which up to the present inadequate use has been made of local raw materials. In 1974, for example, there was a serious shortage of soap in Accra, despite the fact that Ghana produces its essential ingredient, palm oil. In this case, the shortage was attributed both to smuggling and to the refusal of Lever Brothers, a subsidiary of Unilever, to produce soap without a greater state subsidy; the latter explanation reflects the irrationality of co-operation between the state and the multinational private sector in a case in which Ghanaians have the capacity to produce on their own, without expatriate participation. Similarly, the five-year plan notes that 3.6 per cent of Ghana's foreign exchange must be spent on fish, yet there is an indigenous fishing industry,[11] and the creation of the artificial Volta Lake in 1966 was supposed to have increased Ghana's fishing capacity.[12]

Ghana's long-term development aims will not be fully implementable as long as it continues to rely on state co-operation with multinational corporations, including both new investors and the newly diversified firms which have controlled much of Ghana's economy since colonial times, such as UAC, SCOA, CFAO, Cadbury, Paterson Zochonis and John Holt Bartholemew. Even during the period in which Ghana under Nkrumah adopted a 'left' strategy of development,[13] it would seem that no real attempts were made either to socialise or to nationalise the means of production in such a way as to remove expatriate control.[14]

There has, however, been some change in the pattern of control of the Ghanaian economy by expatriates. Prior to decolonisation, it has been argued, the method of extraction of the surplus from Ghana was primarily mercantilist; that is to say that it was an extraction of the surplus product created by pre-capitalist peasant cash-crop producers. Mercantile firms, with the aid of the financial sector, bought this product and exported it to Europe; in return they imported consumer goods. In the post-colonial period such mercantilist extraction has been partially reduced by state takeovers of some mercantilist-type activities. In the field of primary commodity production, the state is now the monopsonistic buyer of cocoa, as it has been since the original Cocoa Marketing Board was established by the British after World War II. In controlling the sale of cocoa to the world market the state has become a direct extractor of the cocoa surplus; such 'state sponsored extortion'[15] has incurred the hostility of cocoa producers, as most directly evidenced in the Ashanti cocoa farmers' hostility to Nkrumah in the mid-1960s.[16] In the field of retail and wholesale trade, the Nkrumah regime established the Ghana National Trading Corporation, reducing the role of expatriate firms in this sector but also alienating a large section of the Ghanaian petty bourgeoisie.[17] The present government has also obliged the largest expatriate trading firms such as UAC to transfer 40 per cent of their assets to Ghanaians; such transfer is a further encouragement to the contemporary development of a comprador capitalist class.[18] In the area of mining, the state took over complete control of the Tarkwa mines in 1961; however, this takeover was effected to save jobs in mines which had become unprofitable. Very recently, the state has acquired 55 per cent ownership of Ashanti Goldfields, leaving the other 45 per cent in the hands of Lonrho.[19]

As a result of the state's interference in the mercantilist and mining sectors, the former colonial trading companies began to diversify into the assembling of imported goods and the manufacture of light goods such as cutlasses. Unilever now makes soap inside Ghana, while Cadbury packages tea and produces a malt chocolate drink. Since the establishment of the Ghana Commercial Bank and the Bank of Ghana, as well as of independent Ghanaian insurance companies, the financial sector is no longer completely controlled by expatriates, and new types of investment are being financed, while loans are readily made available to Ghanaian businessmen, including bureaucrats and members of the military. Shipping has also been partially put under state control, with the creation of the Black Star Line which as early as 1966 controlled 17 per cent of Ghana's sea commerce.[20]

Such intervention by the state, however, has been made within the constraints imposed by the world capitalist system, without an attempt to withdraw from it. Despite recent very high prices for cocoa, Ghana's ability to accrue foreign exchange is on the whole ever more limited by the widening gap between commodity and industrial prices on the world market (as well as by the recent increase in the world price of oil). Similarly, its ability to re-orient the economy continues to be limited by its reliance on multinational investors. The Valco aluminium project is the most obvious example of the difficulty of such reliance. In order to obtain American loans for this project, the Nkrumah regime 'had to agree that the US-owned smelter might use imported alumina at least initially rather than develop Ghana's own deposits';[21] after eleven years, Ghana's deposits are still not being developed. A second example of extreme concessions to multinationals has been the National Liberation Council's turning over of all state rubber plantations and processing mills to Firestone.[22] The state's tendency to give more privileges to expatriate than to indigenous entrepreneurs is also reflected in the decision in mid-1977 to remove import controls for a number of key industrial firms, of which the majority were expatriate. Thus regardless of differences in their professed ideologies, all four regimes which have governed Ghana since independence have suffered similar economic constraints and have made similar concessions to the metropolitan bourgeoisie.

Such an analysis is not meant to imply that the class structure of Ghana is stagnant, nor that the capitalist class in the indigenous population is not expanding. Rather, it would seem that either the petty bourgeoisie, including manufacturers, traders, wealthy farmers, professionals and bureaucrats, directly controls state power, or the military rules on its behalf. (In this context the conflict between the Supreme Military Council and the professional groups, such as doctors, lawyers, architects and engineers, in early 1977 can be seen as the latter's protests against the former's inability to safeguard the economy against the world recession of the 1970s.) But the state must also be responsive to world economic forces; thus insofar as the petty bourgeois strata attempt to engage in large-scale extraction or production, they are continually confronted by the combined control of the state and expatriate investors. Thus, their only choice is to operate in the interstices of the state-expatriate union, in the small-scale production of locally-produced goods in which the expatriate firms are no longer interested.

One significant difference between colonial and post-colonial Ghana, as regards class formation, is that it is no longer the case that there is a shortage of workers for government or private capitalist activities. Rather, rural-urban migration has created a large proletariat and an equally large lumpenproletariat. Official figures state that the level of unemployment in Ghana is somewhat less than 9 per cent,[23] but these figures, it would seem, disregard the rural underemployed, as well as urban groups occupied in petty, transitory enterprises, street-corner trading and various illegal activities. Many urban dwellers are migrants from the cocoa-producing areas. Given the dislocation between local and world prices of cocoa, young people no longer wish to follow their fathers into cocoa-farming; in fact, the 'aging of the working cocoa farmers'[24] is becoming a severe problem. Nevertheless, in 1970 some 57 per cent of the work force in Ghana was still agricultural; another 27 per cent was engaged in commerce, services, and transport and communications (reflecting the typical overdevelopment of the tertiary sector in Third World societies), while only 12 per cent was engaged in 'manufacture',[25] of which it can be assumed a significant proportion was handicrafts or petty commodity production. The class configuration of contemporary Ghana is, like its economy, skewed; there is a large petty bourgeoisie, a large lumpenproletariat, and a large pre-capitalist sector, but there is no class basis for development towards either full-fledged capitalism or towards socialism.

The role of the interventionist state in directing the Ghanaian economy is crucial to approaching the theoretical problem of which mode of production and political system will eventually dominate. If, because of multinational investments, the development of the indigenous bourgeoisie continues to be limited to essentially comprador activities, then state capitalism, in which the state extracts surplus from both the peasantry and the small proletariat, will become entrenched. There is no indication that any of the post-independence regimes has made any significant attempts to mobilise either of these two latter classes as a base for long-term structural change; the regimes have rather contented themselves with extraction. Judith Marshall claims that, from 1961 to 1966, the Nkrumah regime was genuinely attempting to follow a socialist option of development. But both

Postscript: The Colonial Heritage of Contemporary Ghana

Marshall and Callaway and Card note that this socialism was more ideological than practical, and that in fact the state's move toward the left did not preclude continued reliance on, and indeed favouring of, expatriate multinationals.[26] This is not to deny that Nkrumah's regime was *perceived* as left-wing by the world capitalist powers, especially the United States and Britain, which were instrumental in ensuring that international aid and credit to Ghana were cut off in 1965;[27] it is merely to observe that the rhetoric obscured the reality.

Both civilian and military regimes are motivated by the necessity to keep themselves in power. In this context their financial base is of some importance. In 1973, 45 per cent of the Ghanaian government's revenues were derived from import and export taxes, and 29 per cent were derived directly from cocoa.[28] In attempting to 'modernise' the economy, the state must be careful not to undermine its own economic base; structural reforms in the patterns of production will be limited by this consideration.

Since independence, therefore, none of the political regimes in control of Ghana has been both willing and able to effect a withdrawal from the world economic system which is the basis of support both for the state apparatus and for the social class on which the state is based. In 1967 Roger Murray, reviewing Fitch and Oppenheimer, argued that the petty bourgeoisie (which formed the basis not only of the Nkrumah regime of which Murray writes, but also of subsequent regimes), had no specific role in the relations of production in Sub-Saharan Africa; therefore its political ideology was unpredictable.[29] But such an argument overlooks the objective influence of peripheral capitalism over the structure of social class and political relations. Whatever the social class which obtains state power in Ghana, its options will remain the same; either to continue its role as a dependent producer for the world market, or to withdraw from the world capitalist system. Nkrumah's failure, during his 'left' period, was not to make this withdrawal complete. Any social class which, having attained power, does not effect such withdrawal in the future, will be obliged to compromise with the core capitalist powers and will eventually opt for continuing compromises which will support its own position of class rule.

The only means by which a real withdrawal from the world capitalist system can be effected is by a massive mobilisation of the population to make the effort of redirecting productive activities and investments; in effect, the state must change its class base. The question for Ghana, therefore, is whether it is possible to politicise the so-called 'masses' to the point at which they adopt a socialist ideology which will spur them to work in the interests of such a reorganisation. One response to this question is to maintain that until the economy is in fact capitalised, and until there is a large proletariat, socialist class consciousness in Ghana is impossible. Another response is to note that there have been instances in Sub-Saharan Africa of mobilisation of both the peasantry and the proletariat around a socialist party, but only in times of anti-colonial warfare. Without a militant anti-colonial past, militant anti-neo-colonial struggle for Ghana in the present is unlikely.

Contemporary Ghana's colonial heritage is, in brief, its dependent political economy, the underdevelopment of its productive forces, its truncated class structure, and finally a pessimistic prognosis for progressive political policies in such a context. Nevertheless, as the past affects the present, so the future can render the past irrelevant; it is to be hoped that ongoing change in the world economic system, combined with continued analysis and internal change in Ghana, will remove its colonial heritage and re-orient it on the path to integrated economic, social and political development.

Notes

1. Not only Ghana's military regimes but also the Nkrumah regime, reputed at one time to be 'socialist', have taken repressive actions, including banning strikes, against the workers. See Eboe Hutchful, 'The Political Economy of Military Intervention in Ghana', paper presented to the Canadian Association of African Studies, Sherbrooke, Quebec (4 May 1977), p. 33.
2. Figures on imports, exports and Gross Domestic Product are taken from Ministry of Planning, *Ghana: Five-Year Development Plan* (Accra, January 1977), Part II, pp. 57, 270, 248, 11, 12 and Part I, p. 7.
3. Ibid., Part II, p. 11.
4. Ibid.
5. Ghana Association of University Teachers, *Statement: The Case Against the S.M.C.* (Legon, Ghana, 1 July 1977), p. 5.
6. Ibid., p. 1.
7. Ibid., p. 4.
8. *Five-Year Development Plan*, Part II, p. 243.
9. Ibid., Part III, p. 30 and Part II, p. 244.
10. Judith Marshall, 'The State of Ambivalence: Right and Left Options in Ghana,' *Review of African Political Economy*, No. 5 (January–April 1976), p. 61.
11. *West Africa*, 23 May 1977, p. 984.
12. Reginald H. Green and Ann Seidman, *Unity or Poverty? The Economics of Pan-Africanism* (Penguin Books, Middlesex, 1968), p. 176.
13. Marshall, 'The State of Ambivalence', pp. 52–5.
14. Barbara Callaway and Emily Card, 'Political Constraints on Economic Development in Ghana', in Michael F. Lofchie (ed.), *The State of the Nations: Constraints on Development in Independent Africa* (University of California

Press, Berkeley, 1971), p. 66.
15. Eboe Hutchful, 'The Ideological Basis of the Charter', speech delivered at the Arts Centre, Accra (24 February 1975), p. 11.
16. For an interpretation of the 'tribal' opposition of Ashanti cocoa-farmers to the regime of Kwame Nkrumah, see Bob Fitch and Mary Oppenheimer, *Ghana: End of an Illusion* (Monthly Review Press, New York, 1966), ch. 4.
17. Callaway and Card, 'Political Constraints', p. 86.
18. Hutchful, 'Political Economy', p. 38.
19. *Five-Year Development Plan*, Part II, p. 231.
20. Callaway and Card, 'Political Constraints', p. 80.
21. Green and Seidman, *Unity or Poverty?*, p. 176.
22. Akilagpa Sayerr, 'Multinational Corporations and Economic Development in Underdeveloped Countries: the Case of the Rubber Industry in Ghana',(Faculty of Law, University of Ghana, Legon), quoted in Hutchful, 'Political Economy', p. 26.
23. *Five-Year Development Plan*, Part II, p. 333.
24. *West Africa*, 11 April 1977, p. 704.
25. *Five-Year Development Plan*, Part II, p. 333.
26. Marshall, 'The State of Ambivalence', p. 53, and Callaway and Card, 'Political Constraints', p. 66.
27. Ruth First, *The Barrel of a Gun: Political Power in Africa and the Coup d'Etat* (Penguin Books, Middlesex, 1970), pp. 380–3.
28. *Five-Year Development Plan*, Part I, p. 13. Figures calculated from table on 'Actual Government Revenue, 1968/69–1973/74'. Figures in table 2, Part II, p. 58, give cocoa's contribution to government tax revenue as 26%; but re-calculation of the figures indicates 42%.
29. Roger Murray, 'Second Thoughts on Ghana', *New Left Review*, No. 42 (March–April 1967). Murray argued that the petty bourgeoisie was the politically dominant class in Ghana, but that because it had no real role in the productive process, Ghana was experiencing 'an uncertain historical movement whose social direction and meaning will be defined and re-defined through practice', p. 31.

BIBLIOGRAPHY

A. Primary Sources

National Archives of Ghana (Accra and Cape Coast)
British Government Sources, especially Command Papers and Colonial Office Documents
Incorporated Chamber of Commerce of Liverpool, *Annual Reports*, 1886–1901 and African Trade Section, *Minutes*, 1902–25
London Chamber of Commerce Incorporated, *Annual Reports*, 1882–1903 and West Africa Section, *Minutes*, 1904–38
Manchester Chamber of Commerce, African Sectional Committee, *Minutes*, 1892–1938
Cadbury Archives
John Holt Papers
United Africa Company Archives
Colonial Bank, *Reports*, 1917–39
Gold Coast Chamber of Mines, *Annual Reports*, 1931–39
Directory of Directors, 1885, 1895, 1905, 1915, 1925, 1935, 1939
Stock Exchange Yearbook, 1885, 1895, 1905, 1915, 1925, 1935, 1939

B. Selected Secondary Sources

Agbodeka, Francis, *Ghana in the Twentieth Century* (Ghana Universities Press, Accra, 1972)
Amin, Samir, *Accumulation on a World Scale* (Monthly Review Press, New York, 1974)
—— 'Underdevelopment and Dependence in Black Africa: Historical Origin', *Journal of Peace Research*, No. 2 (1972)
Bauer, P.T., *West African Trade: A Study of Competition, Oligopoly and Monopoly in a Changing Economy* (Routledge and Kegan Paul, London, 1963)
Benneh, G., 'The Impact of Cocoa Cultivation on the Traditional Land Tenure System of the Akan of Ghana', *Ghana Journal of Sociology*, Vol. 6, No. 1 (February 1970)
Betts, Raymond F. (ed.), *The 'Scramble' for Africa: Causes and Dimensions of Empire* (D.C. Heath, Lexington, 1966)
Bevin, H.J., 'The Gold Coast Economy about 1880', *Transactions of the Gold Coast and Togoland Historical Society*, Vol. 2, part 2 (1956)

Bevin, H.J., 'M.J. Bonnat: Trader and Mining Promoter', *Economic Bulletin of Ghana*, Vol. 4, No. 7 (1960)
—— 'Some Notes on Gold Coast Exports, 1886–1913', *Economic Bulletin of Ghana*, Vol. 4, No. 1 (1960)
Bonne, Nii Kwabena III, *Milestones in the History of the Gold Coast* (Wodderspoon, Middlesex, 1953)
Bourrett, F.M., *Ghana, the Road to Independence* (Oxford University Press, London, 1960)
Burton, Sir Richard, and Verney Lovett Cameron, *To the Gold Coast for Gold* (Chatto and Windus, London, 1883)
Callaway, Barbara, and Emily Card, 'Political Constraints on Economic Development in Ghana', in Michael F. Lofchie (ed.), *The State of the Nations: Constraints on Development in Independent Africa* (University of California Press, Berkeley, 1971)
Casely Hayford, J.E., *Gold Coast Native Institutions* (Frank Cass, London 1970, 1st edn. 1903)
—— *The Truth about the West African Land Question* (Frank Cass, London, 1971, 1st edn. 1913)
Davies, P.N., *The Trade Makers: Elder Dempster in West Africa, 1852–1972* (Allen and Unwin, London, 1973)
—— (ed.), *Trading in West Africa* (Croom Helm, London, 1976)
de Graft-Johnson, J.C., *African Experiment: Co-operative Agriculture and Banking in British West Africa* (C.A. Watts, London, 1958)
Dickson, Kwabina B., 'The Development of Road Transport in Southern Ghana and Ashanti since about 1850', *Transactions of the Historical Society of Ghana*, Vol. 5 (1961)
Dobb, Maurice, *Studies in the Development of Capitalism* (International Publishers, New York, 1963)
Dumett, R.E., 'British Official Attitudes in Relation to Economic Development in the Gold Coast, 1874–1905', (unpublished PhD thesis, University of London, 1966)
—— 'The Rubber Trade of the Gold Coast and Asante in the Nineteenth Century: African Innovation and Market Responsiveness', *Journal of African History*, Vol. 12, No. 1 (1971)
—— 'The Social Impact of the European Liquor Trade on the Akan of Ghana, 1875–1910', *Journal of Interdisciplinary History*, Vol. 5, No. 1 (summer 1974)
Emmanuel, Arghiri, *Unequal Exchange* (Monthly Review Press, New York, 1972)
Fage, J.D., *Ghana, A Historical Interpretation* (University of Wisconsin Press, Madison, 1961)

Fage, J.D., *A History of West Africa* (Cambridge University Press, Cambridge, 1969)

First, Ruth, *The Barrel of a Gun: Political Power in Africa and the Coup d'Etat* (Penguin Books, Middlesex, 1970)

Fitch, Bob, and Mary Oppenheimer, *Ghana: End of an Illusion* (Monthly Review Press, New York, 1966)

Frank, Andre Gunder, 'Destroy Capitalism, not Feudalism', in Andre Gunder Frank, *Latin America: Underdevelopment or Revolution* (Monthly Review Press, New York, 1974)

Frankel, S. Herbert, *Capital Investment in Africa* (Howard Fertig, New York, 1969, 1st. edn. 1938)

Fry, Richard, *Bankers in West Africa: The Story of the Bank of British West Africa Limited* (Hutchinson Benham, London, 1976)

Fyfe, Christopher, *Africanus Horton, West African Scientist and Patriot* (Oxford University Press, New York, 1972)

Gallagher, John, and Ronald Robinson, 'The Imperialism of Free Trade', *Economic History Review*, second series, Vol. 6, No. 1 (December 1953)

Ghana Association of University Teachers, 'Statement: the Case against the S.M.C.' (Legon, Ghana, 1 July 1977)

Ghana: Five-Year Development Plan (Ministry of Planning, Accra, 1977)

Gould, Peter R., *The Development of the Transportation Pattern in Ghana* (Northwestern University Press, Evanston, 1960)

Green, Reginald H., and Anne Seidman, *Unity or Poverty? The Economics of Pan-Africanism* (Penguin Books, Middlesex, 1968)

Greenstreet, D.K.,'The Transport Department: the First Two Decades (1901–1920)', *Economic Bulletin of Ghana*, Vol. 10, No. 3 (1966)

Hallett, Robin, 'The European Approach to the Interior of Africa in the Eighteenth Century', *Journal of African History*, Vol. 4, No. 2 (1963)

Harrop, Sylvia, 'The Economy of the West African Coast in the Sixteenth Century', *Economic Bulletin of Ghana*, Vol. 8, Nos. 3 and 4 (1964)

Hill, Polly, 'Some Characteristics of Indigenous West African Economic Enterprise', Nigerian Institute of Social and Economic Research, *Conference Proceedings* (1962)

Hindess, Barry, and Paul Q. Hirst, *Pre-Capitalist Modes of Production* (Routledge and Kegan Paul, London, 1975)

Holmes, Alexander Baron IV, 'Economic and Political Organization in the Gold Coast, 1920–45', unpublished PhD thesis, University of Chicago, 1972

Hopkins, A.G., 'The Creation of a Colonial Monetary System: the Origins of the West African Currency Board', *African Historical Studies*, Vol. 3, No. 1 (1970)
—— 'Economic Aspects of Political Movements in the Gold Coast and Nigeria 1918–39', *Journal of African History*, Vol. 7, No. 1 (1965/66)
Hutchful, Eboe, 'The Ideological Basis of the Charter', speech delivered at the Arts Centre, Accra (24 February 1975)
—— 'The Political Economy of Military Intervention in Ghana', paper presented to the Canadian Association of African Studies, Sherbrooke, Quebec (4 May 1977)
Ilegbune, Charles U., 'Concessions Scramble and Land Alienation in British Southern Ghana, 1885–1916', *African Studies Review*, Vol. 29, No. 3 (December 1976)
Kaplow, Susan Beth, 'African Merchants of the Nineteenth Century Gold Coast', unpublished PhD thesis, Columbia University, 1971
Kay, G.B., *The Political Economy of Colonialism in Ghana* (Cambridge University Press, Cambridge, 1972)
Kimble, David, *A Political History of Ghana, 1850–1928* (The Clarendon Press, Oxford, 1963)
Laclau, Ernesto, 'Feudalism and Capitalism in Latin America', *New Left Review*, No. 67 (May–June 1971)
Lenin, V.I., *Imperialism, the Highest Stage of Capitalism* (Foreign Language Press, Peking, 1969)
Leubuscher, Charlotte, *The West African Shipping Trade, 1909–1959* (A.W. Sythoff, Leyden, 1963)
McPhee, Allan, *The Economic Revolution in British West Africa* (Frank Cass, London, 1971, 1st edn. 1926)
Marshall, Judith, 'The State of Ambivalence: Right and Left Options in Ghana', *Review of African Political Economy*, No. 5 (January–April 1976)
Marx, Daniel, Jr., *International Shipping Cartels* (Princeton University Press, Princeton, 1953)
Marx, Karl, *Pre-Capitalist Economic Formations* (International Publishers, New York, 1965)
Metcalfe, G.E., *Great Britain and Ghana: Documents of Ghana History, 1807–1957* (Thomas Nelson, London, 1964)
Murray, Roger, 'Second Thoughts on Ghana', *New Left Review*, No. 42 (March–April 1967)
Newbury, C.W., 'Credit in Nineteenth Century West African Trade', *Journal of African History*, Vol. 13, No. 1 (1972)

Newlyn, W.T., and D.C. Rowan, *Money and Banking in British Colonial Africa* (The Clarendon Press, Oxford, 1954)

Omosini, Olufemi, 'The Gold Coast Land Question, 1894–1900: Some Issues raised on West Africa's Economic Development', *International Journal of African Historical Studies*, Vol. 5, No. 3 (1972)

Pedler, Frederick, *The Lion and the Unicorn in Africa: The United Africa Company 1787–1931* (Heinemann, London, 1974)

Poulantzas, Nicos, 'The Problem of the Capitalist State', in Robin Blackburn (ed.), *Ideology in Social Science* (Fontana/Collins, Glasgow, 1972)

Priestley, Margaret, *West African Trade and Coast Society* (Oxford University Press, London, 1969)

Reynolds, Edward, 'Trade and Economic Change on the Gold Coast, 1807–74', unpublished PhD thesis, University of London, 1971

Rhodie, Sam, 'The Gold Coast Cocoa Hold-up of 1930–31', *Transactions of the Historical Society of Ghana*, Vol. 9 (1968)

Robinson, Kenneth, *The Dilemmas of Trusteeship: Aspects of British Colonial Policy Between the Wars* (Oxford University Press, London, 1965)

Rodney, Walter, 'Gold and Slaves on the Gold Coast', *Transactions of the Historical Society of Ghana*, Vol. 10 (1969)

—— *How Europe Underdeveloped Africa* (Tanzania Publishing House, Dar es Salaam, 1972)

Sampson, M.J., *Gold Coast Men of Affairs* (Dawsons of Pall Mall, London, 1969, 1st edn. 1937)

Sederberg, Peter C., 'The Gold Coast under Colonial Rule; an Expenditure Analaysis', *African Studies Review*, Vol. 14 (1971)

Southall, Roger, 'Cadbury on the Gold Coast; 1907–38: the Dilemma of the Model Firm in a Colonial Economy', unpublished PhD thesis, University of Birmingham, 1975

Stavenhagen, Rodolfo, *Social Classes in Agrarian Societies* (Anchor Press, Garden City, 1975)

Szereszewski, Robert, *Structural Changes in the Economy of Ghana, 1891–1911* (Weidenfeld and Nicolson, London, 1965)

Thomas, Roger T., 'Forced Labour in British West Africa; the Case of the Northern Territories of the Gold Coast 1906–1927', *Journal of African History*, Vol. 14, No. 3 (1973)

Wallerstein, Immanuel, *The Modern World-System: Capitalist Agriculture and the Origins of the European World-Economy in the Sixteenth Century* (Academic Press, New York, 1974)

Webster, J.B., and A.A. Boahen, *The Revolutionary Years, West Africa*

since 1800 (Longmans, Green and Company, London, 1967)
Williams, Eric, *Capitalism and Slavery* (Capricorn Books, New York, 1966)
Williams, Gavin, 'There is No Theory of Petty-Bourgeois Politics', *Review of African Political Economy*, No. 6 (May–August 1976)
Wolfson, Freda, 'British Relations with the Gold Coast, 1843–80', unpublished PhD thesis, University of London, 1950

INDEX

Abontiakoon 65, 203
Aborigines Rights Protection Society (ARPS) 41, 42, 43, 46, 47, 77
Aburi 196
'abusa' system 38
Accra 23, 76, 82, 84, 100, 113, 133, 147, 152, 161, 166, 171, 174, 175, 191, 202, 212, 214, 225
Accra Chamber of Commerce 151
accumulation, primitive 37
Ada 84
Africa Steamship Company 116
African and Eastern Trade Corporation (A&ETC) 65, 66, 67, 96, 97, 98, 105, 106, 107, 109, 111, 114, 120, 136, 164
African Association 66, 95, 96, 97, 99, 100, 107, 115, 117
African Gold Coast Company 63
African Manganese Company 67
Aggrey, Prince Edward 192
Agona 175
agricultural exports 69–79
agriculture, diversification of 23, 75
Ahanta Company 52
Akim Abuakwa 68, 199
Akwapim 196
Alexander Miller 95, 107, 190
Alluvial Diamonds Ltd 147
Amin, Samir 16, 59, 132, 133, 193
Anyinam 175
Apatim 60, 63
Asamankese 217
Ashanti 17, 23, 30, 31, 33, 34, 35, 36, 42, 43, 48, 64, 74, 81, 82, 113, 148, 152, 166, 168, 198, 200, 202, 207, 209, 217, 224, 226
Ashanti goldfields 40, 48, 51, 62, 64, 65, 66, 67, 136, 166, 168, 169, 226
Ashanti-Obuasi Trading Company 66, 67
Association of West African Merchants (AWAM) 106, 109, 124, 142
Axim 72, 133

bank notes 130, 131, 132
Bank of British West Africa (BBWA) 116, 133, 134, 135, 137, 140, 149, 156
Bank of Ghana 226
banking 22, 23, 115, 131, 132, 133, 134, 139, 140, 150, 184, 187
Bannerman, James 183
Barber Line 122
Barclays Bank 135
Basel Mission 73, 204
Basel Mission Trading Company 96, 101, 107
Batty, J.H. 65, 164
bauxite 68, 224, 225
Beaverbrook, Lord 135
Bekwai 135
Belfield Commission 45, 47, 49, 51, 52, 150, 151
Bengbi 201
Benin 29
Berlin Conference 34, 165
Bikhazi Brothers 113
Black Star Line 227
Bonnat, M.J. 62
Bonne, Nii 191, 192
boundary disputes 38, 49
bourgeoisie 16, 18, 22–4, 59, 146, 147, 181, 182, 223, 226, 227, 228
Brandenburg 29
Brazil 28, 71, 74
Brew, James H. 41
Bristol 121
British and African Steam Navigation Company 116
Brofoyedru 175
brokers 191, 195, 197, 208, 209, 212, 213, 214, 218
Bromport Shipping Line 124
Brown, E.J.P. 44, 46
Bull Line 122
Burham Cement Company 122
Burton, Sir Richard 60, 62
Busi and Stephenson 99, 100
Busia 223

Cadbury 74, 98, 99, 111, 160, 226
Callaway and Card 229
Canalizo 210
Canary Islands 123

238

Index

Cape Coast 133, 158, 161, 175, 192
Cape Coast Chamber of Commerce 151, 152
capitalism 17, 29, 37, 206, 226; antile 29, 31; peripheral 15, 16, 19, 20, 22, 23, 24, 27, 31, 59, 133
cartels 19, 22
cash-crops 18, 23, 31, 32, 33, 34, 38, 39, 43, 45, 46, 55, 59, 74, 113, 127, 133, 181, 193, 194, 195, 197, 199, 200
cement 122, 123
Central Provinces 74, 75, 114, 207
Ceylon 74
Chamber of Commerce: Accra 151; Cape Coast 151, 152; Glasgow 35; Liverpool 35, 102, 123, 147, 155, 192; London 35, 82, 103, 123, 131, 147, 148; Manchester 35, 123, 147, 156; Sekondi 151, 164; Sheffield 102; Tarkwa 151; Winneba 152
Chamberlain, Joseph 41, 42
Chief Esselkojo of Apinto 49, 51
Chief Kobina Foli of Adansi 49
chiefs 36, 37, 40, 42, 43, 44, 46, 47, 49, 50, 64, 73, 77, 113, 114, 115, 146, 149, 150, 151, 161, 168, 181, 185, 194, 195, 200, 201, 202, 205, 206, 209, 210, 211, 212, 213, 214, 217, 218; Provincial Council of 114
Chinese 203
coal 122
cocoa 19, 20, 21, 22, 32, 33, 34, 39, 44, 45, 46, 52, 59, 66, 69, 71, 72, 73, 74, 75, 76, 78, 83, 86, 87, 97, 98, 99, 100, 106, 108, 109, 111, 112, 115, 119, 120, 130, 131, 135, 136, 149, 155, 160, 162, 164, 168, 170, 172, 173, 181, 191, 193, 194, 195, 196, 197, 198, 199, 203, 206, 223, 226, 227, 228, 229
Cocoa Boycott, 1937–38 24, 181, 206–19
Cocoa Marketing Board 208, 218, 226
'Cocoa Pool' 208, 209
coffee 71
coin 132, 133
Coker 190
Colonial Bank 135, 136, 137
Colonial Development Act 157

Colonial Development Advisory Committee 157
Colonial Office 67, 82, 96, 129, 148, 150, 151, 156, 163, 168
combine firms 105, 111, 114, 124, 130, 188
Committee on Trade and Taxation, 1921 150, 164
Compagnie Française de l'Afrique Occidentale (CFAO) 101, 148, 149, 150, 151, 156, 163, 173, 183, 185, 204, 226
Company of African Merchants 96
concessions 36, 40, 41, 43, 45, 48, 49, 50, 51, 52, 60, 63, 66, 67, 68, 73, 78, 159, 167, 171, 194
Concessions Ordinance, 1900 48, 49, 73
Congo 204
conservation 44, 46, 47
Consolidated African Selection Trust 67, 68
construction goods 79
consumer goods, 20, 29, 31, 79–83, 112, 113, 149
co-operatives 198
credit 73, 80, 133, 134, 137, 138, 139, 140, 183, 184, 187, 189, 191, 198, 214, 215
Crombie Steedman 109
crop-sharing agreements 115
crown agents 122
Crown Lands Bill 40
currency 127, 128, 129, 130, 131, 132, 135
custom duties 147, 158, 162–4, 165, 174, 184, 192

Denmark 29
depression, economic 100, 101, 109, 173, 174, 196
diamonds 60, 68, 87, 191, 224
Digby Commission 78
discounting 131
diversification of agriculture 23, 75, 76, 78, 79, 84, 191, 192, 195, 226
Dodowa 192
Dumett, R.E. 71
Dunkwa 135, 187, 188, 207
dyes 109, 192

Eastern region 74, 171, 207
Effentua Company 63
Elder, Dempster 76, 101, 116–26,

133, 134, 135, 149, 156, 173
Elders and Fyffes 76
Elmina 27

Fage, J.D. 28
Fanti 31, 33
farmers 24, 111, 163, 197, 211, 212, 213, 214, 217, 218
Fernando Po 74
feudalism 25
finance 115, 146, 156–65, 226
Finsbury Pavement House Group 65
firestone 227
fish 109, 187, 188, 189, 225
Fitch and Oppenheimer 229
Fitzgerald 63
Folded Woven Goods Ordinance 82
Fomena 175
food shortage 225
foodstuffs and provisions 79, 80, 83
forced labour 42
Forest Ordinance 44, 45, 46, 48
forest reserves 43, 44, 47
Forestry Bill 44
Forestry Ordinance, 1927: legislation 47
Forster and Smith 95, 184
France 29, 87, 102, 156
Frankel, S. Herbert 160
Freetown 100
Fry, Richard 135, 136
fuel 79

G.B. Ollivant 99, 100
Gallagher and Robinson 30, 35, 36
Gambia 134
German West Africa Trading Company 96
Germany 87, 102, 104, 123, 156
Ghana Commercial Bank 226
Ghana National Trading Corporation 226
gold 17, 27, 28, 33, 35, 36, 39, 40, 48, 50, 60, 62, 64, 65, 66, 68, 87, 127, 160, 191, 224
Gold Coast Chamber of Mines 149
Gold Coast Executive Council 150
Gold Coast Legislative Council 127, 148, 152, 153, 181, 185
Gold Coast Machinery and Trading Company 109
Gold Coast Merchants Association 152
Gold Coast Mining Company 63

Gold Coast Selection Trust Limited 64
gold mining 60–4, 157, 160, 176
gold rush 39, 50, 51, 65, 166
Grant, Pa 73
Grey, William Henry 111
Griffith, Sir William Brandford 154
Guggisberg 47, 53, 149, 202
gum copal 69, 95
Gwira, W. Essuman 77

Hamburg-America Line 118
Hamburg-West Africa Line 117
Harrop, Sylvia 28
Hayford, J.E. Casely 39, 147, 153, 183
Hershey 210, 211
Heussler, Robert 154
Hill, Polly 195
Holmes 205
Hopkins, Anthony 211
Horton, J. Africanus 63, 68
Hutton-Mills, T. 114

immigration 103, 104, 203
imperialism 19, 20
import-export trade 157, 159, 162, 165, 176, 191
imported goods 20, 79–85, 108, 130, 172, 175, 207, 224
India 29
industry 20, 84, 157, 159, 224, 225
infrastructure 17, 23, 73, 79, 162, 165, 176
investment 36, 42, 51, 52, 79, 80, 84, 85, 87, 137, 157, 160, 165, 224
investment goods 79, 80
iron 225
iron sheeting 82, 113
Italians, immigrants 103
ivory 69
Ivory Coast 29, 30, 31, 160, 204

J.J. Fischer and Company 96, 107
J.J. Horsfield and Company 67
J. Lyons and Company 98, 109
J.S. Fry 98, 160
Japan 102, 104, 191
Java 74
John Holt 99, 100, 118, 120, 122, 124, 125, 190, 214
John Holt Bartholemew 226
Joint West Africa Committee (JWAC) 147, 148, 150

Index

Jurgens 97

Kaplow, Susan 184
Kenya 27
Keta 68, 83, 100
Koforidua 135, 175
kola nuts 69
Komenda 33
Krobo 74, 78, 199
Kru 203
Krupp 225
'Kulakisation' 193
Kumasi 30, 31, 101, 133, 135, 152, 168, 171, 175, 225
Kylsant, Lord 124

labour 18, 23, 24, 29, 50, 75, 165, 170, 171, 193, 194, 198, 199, 201–6, 228; agricultural 33, 37; Chinese 39; forced 42, 205; migrant 24, 181, 194, 198, 199, 200, 206, 209, 214, 217; wage 37
Labour Theory of Value 20
Lagos 71, 134
Lancashire 215, 216
land 97, 138, 167, 193, 200; alienation of 38, 56; Crown 18; overalienation 50; ownership 37–55, 97; private property 18, 39; tenure 17, 37, 41, 43, 45, 46, 53, 224; waste 39, 40
Land and Native Rights Ordinance 43
Lands Bill, 1897 40, 41, 42, 43, 48
Latilla, H.G. 65
Lebanese 100, 103, 104
Lenin, V.I. 19, 20
Leubuscher, Charlotte 120
Lever Brothers/Unilever 76, 77, 78, 96, 97, 98, 106, 109, 124, 125, 204, 225, 226
Liberia 203
lighterage 120, 121, 125
liquor 79, 80, 81
Liverpool 99, 121, 123, 124, 147, 170
Liverpool Chamber of Commerce 35, 102, 123, 147, 155, 192
loans 158, 166, 195, 197
Lomé 111
London 112, 123, 132, 133, 137, 147, 150, 208, 212
London Advisory Committee 65
London Chamber of Commerce 35, 82, 103, 123, 131, 147, 148

Lonrho 226
lorry drivers 207, 216
Lorry Transport 172, 173, 175
lumber 95
Lumpenproletariat 228

machinery 79
McLaren Brothers 109
Maghreb 28
mahogany 72
maize 75
Mampong 73
Manchester 82, 102, 121, 122, 124, 147, 170
Manchester Association of Importers and Exporters 124
Manchester Chamber of Commerce 35, 123, 147, 156
manganese 60, 67, 68, 87, 172, 224
Mangoase 166
manufacturing 224, 228
market mammies 207, 215, 216
Marshall, Judith 225, 228, 229
Marx, Daniel 120
Mauritania 29
Maypole Dairy 98
medicines 95
Mende 203
Mengel Mahogany Logging Company 72
mercantile capitalism 29, 31, 226
Merchandise Marks Act 82
migrant labour 24, 181, 194, 198, 199, 200, 206, 209, 214, 217
military 224, 227
Miller Brothers of Liverpool Ltd 95
Millers Ltd 66, 95, 96, 97, 99, 105, 115, 133, 156, 160; *see also* Alexander Miller 332
minerals 19, 47, 52, 59
mines 18, 20, 36, 45, 48, 49, 51, 59, 60, 64, 73, 98, 127, 135, 136, 149, 150, 159, 162, 166, 167, 168, 169, 171, 181, 198, 199–205, 226
mining, gold 157, 160, 176
mode of production 15, 16, 25, 59; peripheral 23, 59, 86, 89, 125; pre-capitalist 15, 17, 18, 19, 20, 24, 206, 228
monetisation 17
money lending 18, 195, 196, 197, 198, 209
monkey skins 69

monoculture 59, 67, 75, 87, 218
monopoly 21, 22, 67, 76–8, 115, 125, 134
Morocco 29
Murphy, W.H. 166
Murray, Roger 229

National Liberation Council 223, 227
National Redemption Council/Supreme Military Council 223, 224
Netherlands 29, 87, 97
New York 99, 122, 208
Newlyn and Rowan 136, 137, 138, 139
Nigeria 65, 69, 87, 95, 100, 106, 135, 190
Nkawkaw 175
Nkrumah 223, 226, 228, 229
Northern Territories 23, 33, 34, 35, 36, 43, 48, 74, 148, 152, 161, 168, 194, 198, 200, 201, 224
Norway 102
Nowell Commission 74, 105, 207, 209, 210, 213, 218
Nsawam 113, 135, 173, 174, 196
Nsuta 172

Obomen 171
Obuasi 66, 166, 168, 169
Oda 135
Ofori Atta, Nana 111, 113, 114, 164, 210
oligopoly 89, 94, 126
Overseas Breweries 84
Overseas Trade Development Council 150, 151

palm kernels 19, 33, 69, 70, 78, 87, 118, 119, 189
palm oil 19, 32, 33, 34, 52, 69, 70, 71, 87, 95, 96, 98, 102, 118, 119, 125, 168, 189, 216, 225
Palm Oil Ordinance 1912 77, 78
palm processing 77, 78
palm products 39, 109
palm wine 71
Paterson Zochonis 99, 100, 226
peasants 18, 20, 24, 32, 37, 51, 55, 71, 74, 75, 182, 193, 196, 197, 198, 209, 210, 214, 217, 223, 224, 225, 226, 228, 230
peripheral capitalism 15, 16, 19, 20, 22, 23, 24, 27, 31, 59, 133; mode of production 23, 59, 86, 89, 125
petty-bourgeoisie 18, 22, 23, 24, 41, 54, 113, 114, 146, 181, 192, 193, 197, 198, 199, 208, 209, 226, 227, 228, 229
plunder 29
Portuguese 27, 28, 29, 62
pottery 83
pre-capitalist mode of production 15, 17, 18, 19, 20, 24, 206, 228
Prempeh, King of Ashanti 36, 64
Prestea Railway Ltd 166, 167
price agreements, price-fixing 95, 96, 100, 105, 106, 109, 111, 112, 113, 114, 115, 136, 137, 208
prices 108, 163, 164, 184, 186, 190, 195, 207, 212
Priestly, Margaret 182
primitive accumulation 37
Private Enterprise Committee, 1924 150, 167
Private Enterprise Railways Construction Bill 167
private property, land 18, 37, 38
professionals 113, 114, 182, 185, 227
proletariat 24, 46, 181, 182, 199–206, 223, 228, 230
Prussia 29
public lands 52, 53
Public Lands Act 1876, 41, 52, 53
Public Lands Ordinance 167

quality control 71, 82
Quarshie, Tetteh 74

railways 149, 157, 158, 165–74; revenues 157, 169, 170, 173
real estate 54, 80, 138
rebate system 117, 118, 119, 120, 124
reforestation 45, 46
rents 48, 51, 159, 171
reserves 45, 47, 130, 131
revenues, state 78, 84, 101, 130, 131, 229
Reynolds, Edward 183, 184
Rhodesia 65, 201
rice 82, 84
road gap policy 174, 175, 176
roads 165, 168, 170–6, 192, 202
Rowntree 98, 160
Royal Commission on Shipping Rings, 1909 and 1923 118, 119, 121, 122, 123, 124, 134

Index

Royal Mint 128, 129, 130
Royal Niger Company 95–7, 109
royalties 40, 42, 51, 52, 159
rubber 33, 34, 45, 48, 52, 69, 70, 71, 72, 87, 95, 109, 227
rum 80, 95
Russia 102

salt 20, 84, 109
Saltpond 111, 112, 113
Sao Thome 74
scramble for Africa 34, 36
Sederburg, Peter 158
seignorage 129
Sekondi 133, 161, 166, 168, 169, 171
Sekondi Chamber of Commerce 151, 164
Senegambia 29
Sese 216
share-distributing agreements 111
Sheffield Chamber of Commerce 102
Shephard, C.T. 196, 197
shipping 22, 23, 73, 76, 115, 134, 136, 150, 172, 183, 210, 211, 227
Sierra Leone 30, 42, 134, 161, 190, 203, 204
silver 129, 130, 131
Simpa 175
sisal 76
slave trade 17, 27, 28, 29, 31, 34, 60, 127, 182
slavery, abolition of 29, 32, 69; domestic 33
Smith, Joseph 184
socialism 229
Société Commerciale de l'Ouest Africain (SCOA) 101, 111, 204, 226
Society of Arts 63
South Africa 42, 64, 65, 201, 205
Southampton 124
Southeast Asia 72
Southwest Africa 204
state 16, 22, 23, 26, 47, 53, 75, 76, 78, 81, 82, 84, 101, 104, 115, 117, 122, 127, 139, 146–76, 198, 200, 223, 226, 227, 228, 229
Stavenhagen, Rodolfo 32, 206
steel 225
stratification 18, 24
sugar 20, 84, 109, 113
Suhum 217

super-profits 20
Supreme Military Council 227
surf-boat men 207, 216
Swanzy, Andrew 184
Swanzy, F. & A. 81, 95, 96, 97, 99, 107, 115, 121, 156, 160, 163, 184
Sweden 29
Swedru 113
Swiss African Trading Company 101
Switzerland 87
Syrians 103, 104, 113
Szereszewski, Robert 32

Takoradi 135, 171, 175, 216
Tamale 158
Tarkwa 49, 51, 62, 65, 133, 135, 166, 168, 169, 175, 226
Tarkwa Chamber of Commerce 151
Tarquah Trading Company 109
Tate and Lyle 113
taxation 84, 146, 160, 164, 217
technology 68, 69, 77, 78
Tema 225
Tete-Ansa, Winifried 211
textiles 79, 80, 81, 82, 83, 104
Textiles Quotas Ordinance, 1934 103
Thomas, Roger 202
Thompson, A. W. Kojo 54
timber 19, 45, 47, 48, 66, 69, 72, 73, 87, 98, 109, 159, 223
Timber Protection Ordinance 46
Togoland 100, 152, 207
tolls 35
Trade and Taxation, Committee on, 1921 150, 164
transport 17, 23, 31, 34, 50, 71, 72, 73, 74, 79, 83, 84, 115, 132, 136, 146, 160, 162, 165–76, 184, 225
treasury 129, 158
Turner, G.W.E. 62

underdevelopment 15, 16, 18, 22, 23, 24, 230
unequal exchange 21, 22
Union Trading Company 101
United Africa Company 66, 78, 82, 85, 94, 97, 98, 99, 100, 105, 106, 109, 110, 111, 112, 113, 114, 115, 116, 122, 124, 125, 126, 128, 137, 140, 154, 156, 160, 173, 186, 187, 188, 190, 208, 210, 216, 226
United Fruit Company 76

United Provinces 29
United States 17, 28, 87, 88, 102, 115, 121, 156, 211, 227, 229
usufruct 18, 24, 37, 38, 48, 193, 194, 195, 198

Valco aluminum project 225, 227
value, labour theory of 20; surplus 21
Van den Berghe 97
Volta Lake 225

W. Bartholemew 99, 100
West African Currency Board 129, 130, 135, 150
West African Lands Committee 150, 151
West African Merchants Freight Association 124
West African Shipping Conference 116–26
West Indies 17, 28, 29, 30, 74
Western Province 64, 74, 152, 197
whale oil 102
Williams, Eric 28
Winneba 100, 133, 135
Winneba Chamber of Commerce 152
Wiresei 175
Woermann 73, 101, 116, 117, 118, 121
women fish sellers 187, 188, 189
working conditions 205
world economic system 15–17, 35, 79, 85, 215, 229
World War I 123, 162
Wray, Major-General 62, 63

Yorubaland 29
Youngman 111

Zabarima 217

For Product Safety Concerns and Information please contact our EU representative GPSR@taylorandfrancis.com
Taylor & Francis Verlag GmbH, Kaufingerstraße 24, 80331 München, Germany

www.ingramcontent.com/pod-product-compliance
Lightning Source LLC
Chambersburg PA
CBHW061441300426
44114CB00014B/1782